Sonic Spaces of the Karoo

In the series **African Soundscapes,**
edited by Gregory Barz

ALSO IN THE SERIES

Julie Huntington, *Sounding Off: Rhythm, Music, and Identity in West African and Caribbean Francophone Novels*

Lisa Gilman, *The Dance of Politics: Gender, Performance, and Democratization in Malawi*

Patricia Tang, *Masters of the Sabar: Wolof Griot Percussionists of Senegal*

Marie Jorritsma

Sonic Spaces of the Karoo

The Sacred Music of a South African
Coloured Community

TEMPLE UNIVERSITY PRESS
Philadelphia

TEMPLE UNIVERSITY PRESS
Philadelphia, Pennsylvania 19122
www.temple.edu/tempress

Library of Congress Cataloging-in-Publication Data

Jorritsma, Marie R.
  Sonic spaces of the Karoo : the sacred music of a South African coloured community / Marie
Jorritsma.
    p.   cm. — (African soundscapes)
  Includes bibliographical references and index.
  ISBN 978-1-4399-0237-0 (cloth : alk. paper)
  ISBN 978-1-4399-0239-4 (e-book)
  1. Church music—South Africa—Graaff-Reinet.   2. Church music—Protestant churches.
3. Colored people (South Africa)—South Africa—Graaff-Reinet—Music—History and
criticism.   4. Graaff-Reinet (South Africa)—Social life and customs.   I. Title.
ML3151.S687G73   2011
782.27'08905960068754—dc22

                                                                            2010045082

This title has been subject to academic peer review.

Title page image: Last service at the Graaff-Reinet Dutch Reformed Mission Church building
before the congregation moved to Kroonvale, c. 1966. Photographer unknown. Courtesy of Gawie
Basson, Uniting Reformed Church archive.

♾ The paper used in this publication meets the requirements of the American National
Standard for Information Sciences—Permanence of Paper for Printed Library Materials,
ANSI Z39.48-1992

Printed in the United States of America

2 4 6 8 9 7 5 3 1

Ethnomusicology Multimedia (EM) is an innovative, entrepreneurial, and cooperative effort to
expand opportunities for emerging scholars in ethnomusicology by publishing first books accompanied by supplemental audiovisual materials online. Developed with funding from the Andrew
W. Mellon Foundation, EM is a collaboration of the presses at Indiana, Kent State, and Temple
universities. These presses gratefully acknowledge the help of Indiana University's Institute for
Digital Arts and Humanities, Digital Library Program, and Archives of Traditional Music for
their contributions to EM's web-based components and archiving features. For more information
and to view EM materials, please visit www.ethnomultimedia.org.

For My Parents, Joan and Hylke

Contents

Multimedia Examples

A selection of enhanced media examples (still images, audio, or video recordings) associated with this book can be accessed on the Ethnomusicology Multimedia website, www.ethnomultimedia.org. Keyed to specific passages, each example listed below has a unique persistent uniform resource identifier, or PURL. Within the text of the book, a PURL number in parentheses functions as a citation and immediately follows the text to which it refers, for example, (PURL 3.1). The numbers following the word "PURL" indicate the chapter in which the media example is found and the order in which the PURL first appears in that chapter.

There are' two ways for readers of the print edition of this book to access and play back a specific media example. The first is to type in a web browser the full address of the PURL associated with a specific media example. Readers will be taken to a web page displaying that media example as well as a playlist of all of the media examples related to this book. Once readers have navigated to the Ethnomusicology Multimedia website, the second way to access media examples is by typing into the search field the unique six-digit PURL identifier located at the end of the full PURL address. Readers of the electronic edition of this book will simply click on the PURL address for each media example; this live link will take them directly to the media example on the Ethnomusicology Multimedia website. Readers will be required to electronically sign an end-users license agreement (EULA) the first time they attempt to access a media example.

The list below, organized by chapter, includes the PURL number, the title of the media segment, and the full PURL with the six-digit unique identifier.

Illustrations

Preface

As a child, the Karoo always symbolized an escape for me. It was a refuge from the routine of school attendance and extramural activities, and from the restlessly windy, unpredictable weather of the coastal city of Port Elizabeth. The family farm lay only three and a half hours' drive away from the city, where huge breakfasts of porridge, toast, and tea fortified me for seemingly endless sunny and windless days spent walking in the surrounding veld, participating in (and most likely, hindering) the usual farming activities and playing in the water furrows. A typical Karoo child displays an endless fascination with the precious commodity of water, and diverting the small rivulets in the furrow to flow smoothly over the muddy gravel guaranteed countless hours of captivation.

When I was a child, my grandmother used to tell me to look for San tools such as grinding stones or arrowheads when walking in the Karoo veld. A collection of these artifacts was displayed in the farmhouse. It never occurred to me then that the San people, the forebears of many present-day coloured people, suffered merciless persecution on the part of my ancestors, the colonial settlers.

When I returned to the Karoo for fieldwork on the music of coloured people, this memory of looking for San "treasure" and proof of their existence in this area contrasted very strangely with the historical accounts I read about the violent treatment of the San people by the settlers. Immersed in my research, I seldom visited the veld and instead explored my childhood memories in new contexts of colonial history and apartheid. As much as this project was originally driven by a deep appreciation of and interest in this music and then an ongoing desire that it not be ignored, my own background as the granddaughter of a Karoo farmer had to be revisited and recontextual-ized as the project continued.

I remember sitting in June Bosch's home one day when for once my childhood memories did not clash with the historical and contemporary stories of coloured people's oppression and marginalization. June Bosch and her cousin, Loretta Fortune, told me a story from their childhood days on Caroline Street, Graaff-Reinet. On Tuesdays and Thursdays, water from the Van Ryneveld's Pass Dam outside the town would be led into the cement furrows lining the streets for the townspeople to use. As the neighborhood children saw the water, they would shout up the street to announce its presence and run for any and every available container. June was under strict instructions from her grandmother to water the garden roses first and then to spray the unpaved street in order to settle the dust. After fulfilling these duties, the children would play in the furrows until the water flow ceased. Recognizing the similarity in our childhood games and activities with their focus on water made it poignantly apparent to me that we were all once children of the Karoo.

This research project thus stems from my own connection to Graaff-Reinet and its surrounding area. Combined with a strong scholarly fascination with this music, my reasons for undertaking the project also included the opportunity to revisit and perhaps, in some small way, to recapture the past. While the Karoo is no longer a childhood escape for me, the spaces and sounds of this community have offered me a new perspective on my relationship to this place and its people.

Acknowledgments

So many people have given generously of their time and expertise in assisting with the preparation of this book. First and foremost, I never cease to feel humbled by the great kindness and generosity shown to me by members of the Kroonvale community. Dominee (Reverend) Gawie Basson of the Uniting Reformed Church allowed me to access and read the church record books while providing excellent background information to church traditions and Graaff-Reinet history in general. Rev. Jacobus Bezuidenhoudt of the Parsonage Street Congregational Church and Rev. Leon Barendse of the East Street Congregational Church generously gave of their time to meet with me and share their knowledge on church music in their congregations. All three ministers graciously allowed me to attend church services at their respective churches. I also wish to thank the members of the interdenominational women's choir, especially June Bosch and Aunt Marge Visagie for many Tuesday afternoons spent in singing and conversation. I have very fond memories of warm friendship and numerous cups of tea. Anziske Kayster, Jessie de Gama, and Denise van Wyk of the Reinet House Museum patiently guided me through the archival research process and were always available for conversation. Hermi Baartman, then head of the museum, also provided assistance. Many other community members spoke to me at church services, and I am grateful to them and also to those people who gave of their time in interview appointments, especially Willem Kayster, Villa Louther, Sabina van Jaarsveld, Joyce Grootboom, Marlene Jasson, Virginia Christoffels, and Dominee Esterhuysen.

For allowing me to stay at the family farm during my research trips, I would like to thank my aunt, Judy Dugmore, who always gave generously of her time despite her busy farming schedule.

As my writing progressed, I received helpful suggestions from the two

anonymous reviewers appointed by Temple University Press. Their construc-
tive feedback, together with comments by Greg Barz, the *African Soundscapes*
series editor, constituted invaluable advice on the book's structure and focus.
Gavin Steingo and Stephanus Muller read through the draft manuscript and
provided insightful comments. Carol Muller at the University of Pennsylvania continues to be an excellent mentor for all my academic endeavors.
I, however, remain solely responsible for any weaknesses in the work. Janet
Francendese and Amanda Steele of Temple University Press were always
available with guidance and expert advice as the publication progressed;
Temple University Press also secured additional funding for the book from
the Mellon Foundation's *Ethnomusicology Multimedia* series. I would also
like to thank Erik Albertyn of the Nelson Mandela Metropolitan University,
Marcia J. Citron at Rice University, and the University of Pennsylvania
music faculty for their intellectual guidance during my undergraduate and
postgraduate training.

I am grateful to Diane Thram (International Library of African Music)
and Zelda Potgieter (South African Society for Research in Music) for their
permission to use some material from articles published in the *African Music*
and *SAMUS* journals, respectively. Teddy Whitlock and the Graaff-Reinet
Tourism Office generously permitted me to use the map of Kroonvale in this
work. Wendy Job from the Cartography Unit, School of Geography, Archae-
ology and Environmental Studies at the University of the Witwatersrand
provided the map of South Africa in Chapter 2. Dominee Gawie Basson
generously made the cover photograph from the Uniting Reformed Church
archive available.

Finally, for their ongoing support, I would like to thank my parents, Joan
and Hylke Jorritsma, and my sisters, Cara and Anita. I am especially grateful
to my husband, Cameron Harris, who continues to offer constant personal
and intellectual encouragement for all my endeavors. In addition to providing
unwavering support throughout the process, Cameron also offered comments
on the manuscript and supplied the computer-notated versions of the music
transcriptions in the text.

Without the combined efforts of these generous people, this book would
not have been possible. My sincere appreciation goes to you all.

Author's Note

For the sake of consistency only, I use the term "coloured" throughout this book. I remain aware of the painful apartheid associations many attach to this term, and thus, I know that not all members of the community in Kroonvale and various communities beyond Graaff-Reinet would agree with this designation. I understand the term only as a social and historical construction, which belies a uniquely South African identity.

I

Introduction

The Challenges of Inscribing Coloured Voices

O ne of my earliest memories of coloured farmworkers is the sound of their hymn singing at Sunday morning church services. In my mind, these sounds became intimately connected with my visits to the Karoo, the name for the semidesert region in which the farming town of Graaff-Reinet is located.[1] These childhood associations resurfaced when, early one Sunday morning in August 2004, I traveled into Kroonvale (the residential area for coloured people on the edge of Graaff-Reinet) to attend the morning service of the Uniting Reformed Church. Brown-red dust, typical of the Karoo, hung in the air as I drove. As I stepped over the church threshold, I collided with a powerful wall of sound. While the congregation sang "Juig aarde, juig" (Rejoice Earth, Rejoice) at full volume, I reflected on the anomaly of the utter silence about this music in the Reinet House Museum archive, where I had spent the past month searching for historical evidence. As the service began, I looked around at the congregation from my position at the back of the church and realized that these distinct sounds, so thoroughly a part of this Karoo coloured community, survived only through their creation and possession by the many people sitting in front of me.

The South African apartheid regime held a deeply ambivalent position toward those it categorized as "coloured," the racial category it defined as "not a white person or a native" (Statutes 1950, 277).[2] Nurtured and sustained by a policy of racial purity, a common stereotype of those classified

as "coloured" in apartheid South Africa was that they had no authentic ethnic identity because of their mixed racial heritage. Oral and written sources
typically convey coloured people's cultural history and musical heritage as
similarly lacking. Coloured people also experienced ambivalence about their
position, which led to their subscription to both ideals of white Western culture and black power at different periods. However, music has been (and continues to be) an integral part of the religious practices of these communities,
although its performance has survived practically unnoticed by those outside.
This book therefore counters the lingering stereotype of coloured people's
ethnicity by examining how sacred musical performance enabled coloured
community members around the town of Graaff-Reinet to claim a place for
themselves collectively under apartheid and in post-apartheid South Africa.

   This project provides a narrative of the social history of coloured people
in the Graaff-Reinet region that is drawn from regional archives and empirical research in the form of fieldwork, specifically participant observation. I
concentrate on religious musical practice, namely, hymns, *koortjies* (choruses), choir performance, and the singing at women's society meetings. Studying song performance examines the complex nexus of music, race, religion,
politics, class, and gender identities within this community and constitutes
a vital way of retrieving history and oral repertories. This music thereby provides one vehicle for groups and individuals in this community to articulate
a more "legitimate" place for themselves in the contemporary landscape of
South African history and culture.

   By placing the voices of coloured people at the center of this study, I
move beyond the myopic apartheid view that saw coloured people purely
in terms of their ethnic origins and capacity for labor. Instead, I approach
coloured people's music and history in terms of the sounds and spaces of its
religious performance culture. The reference to "sonic spaces" in this book's
title has a threefold connotation. First, it refers to my emphasis on listening
to the sound of this religious community as the primary vehicle for interpretation and the awareness of how the unique geographic location of the Kroonvale community shaped this repertoire. Second, it recognizes the presence of
sacred song in this community as a testament to the survival of this musical
tradition despite the marginality, violence, and oppression coloured people
experienced in the actual localities where they lived. Finally, the reference to
"sonic spaces" wishes to acknowledge the sound of coloured people's voices
raised in song as an integral part of that very diverse and varied entity known
collectively as "South African music." This work thus claims a (scholarly)
space for the research of music within rural Karoo coloured communities.[3]

Frontier History

In the precolonial era, the oldest indigenous peoples of South Africa, the San hunter-gatherers and the Khoekhoe (or Khoikhoi) pastoralists,[4] lived mostly undisturbed in the Karoo region of what is now the town of Graaff-Reinet and its surrounding area in the Eastern Cape Province of the country (Newton-King 1999, 29).[5] Although the Khoekhoe and the San (also Sonqua or Soaqua) had contact with some European travelers and the Xhosa-speaking peoples to the west, the latter only settled permanently on the edges of the area (known as the Zuurveld) in the last third of the eighteenth century. European *trekboers* (Dutch-speaking farmers in search of grazing for their livestock) arrived in the late 1760s.

Europeans regarded the San and Khoekhoe peoples as not "African," since they had different physical features and languages from Bantu-speaking peoples such as the Xhosa and Zulu groups.[6] They referred to the Khoekhoe people as "Hottentots," due to the clicking sounds of their languages, and the San as "Bushmen," due to their nomadic existence. Today, in addition to being extremely derogatory and especially insulting, these terms also imply separate ethnic groups when, in reality, the interaction between groups on the frontier was far more complex. For example, not all Khoekhoe people herded livestock and not all San people were hunter-gatherers (this is why many contemporary historians refer to these groups collectively as "Khoisan" or, more recently, "Khoesan").[7] Another false distinction made by Europeans between "Hottentots" as servants and "Bushmen" as rebels against colonial rule is also problematic. For instance, when a group of people sided with the Xhosa people in a Xhosa-settler war (1850–53), they referred to themselves as "Hottentots," and thus assumed a rebel rather than a servant identity under that name (Elbourne 2002, 74, 362). In addition, interracial relationships between the Khoekhoe, San, Xhosa, European settlers, and slaves further complicated these imposed ethnic distinctions.

As more people moved into this eastern area of the Cape colony, the fluidity between groups and their cultural practices increased, but so did the probability of violent encounters.[8] The violent context of the eighteenth- and nineteenth-century eastern Cape frontier meant that the Khoisan could, and often did, attack white settlers (and vice versa) either unprovoked or in return for previous wrongs. According to Elizabeth Elbourne, "the institution of the commando . . . became a critical tool in white control of the frontier" (2002, 81). This term referred to a group of white settlers and their Khoisan servants formed to murder San people and to capture the remaining children to be brought up as farm laborers.

Established by British officials as a frontier administrative outpost in

1786 in order to better control these ongoing violent attacks, Graaff-Reinet is the fourth-oldest settlement in South Africa.[9] The results of the 2001 population census indicate a total population of 24,229 (Statistics South Africa 2001). Although coloured people form the majority of Graaff-Reinet's population, historical information about the coloured community in this town is relatively rare. The smallpox epidemic of 1713 and trekboer commandos mostly decimated the existing Khoekhoe and San populations (Dooling 1989; Newton-King 1999). Only a few trekboers brought slaves with them on their journey into the interior, and thus they mainly relied on the remaining Khoekhoe and San people for labor supplies in the initial days of the Graaff-Reinet settlement. Colonists in the early nineteenth century estimated that the region's population comprised 4,000 white farmers, with approximately 1,000 slaves and anywhere from 9,000 to 25,000 "Hottentots" (Elbourne 2002, 83–84). The slaves and Khoisan people worked mainly for white farmers, and their descendants form part of the contemporary Graaff-Reinet coloured community. Although many coloured people work on the farms in the surrounding area, within the town they are mainly employed as teachers, government officials, and professionals in the service and healthcare industries. Itinerant sheepshearers and "day men" (those hired for short periods of farmwork) also make the town their home base.

In Graaff-Reinet, as elsewhere in apartheid South Africa, the four official racial groups were "White," "African," "Coloured," and "Indian."[10] The state considered white people to be civilized and European, while the African group, in direct contrast, was regarded as the least civilized and most un-European. The presence of coloured people in South Africa thus continuously exposed the reality of racial crossing in a historical moment that privileged racial purity and difference. Coloured and Indian people therefore occupied the ambiguous in-between position of being neither white nor African. This hierarchy of white superiority dominating black inferiority also dictated education and job opportunities, housing, area of residence, and voting rights (Beck 2000, 126).[11] For example, originally, coloured people lived both in the main town of Graaff-Reinet (known locally as the "horseshoe") and in the Location (a South African term used to refer to residential areas for black people) (Oxford 2002b, 1242). The majority of Graaff-Reinet's black community still lives in this area, known as Umasizakhe (a Xhosa word meaning, "We built it ourselves").[12] When the apartheid government began implementing the Group Areas Act (1950), it forced coloured people to move from the town and Umasizakhe to the newly built coloured residential area of Kroonvale. The photograph in Figure 1.1 clearly shows these three Graaff-Reinet areas: the white part of town in the center, with Umasizakhe to the left and Kroonvale on the right. Even after sixteen years of democratic gov-

Figure 1.1   View of Umasizakhe, Graaff-Reinet, and Kroonvale. Photograph by author.

ernment in South Africa, the realities of apartheid's "separate development" policy remain physically inscribed on the town's layout.

This book attempts to write against these apartheid categories, despite these scars of segregation, and remains focused on the politically and socially constructed nature of ethnic groups. As Zimitri Erasmus states, "There is no such thing as the Black 'race.' Blackness, whiteness and colouredness exist, but they are cultural, historical and political identities" (2001, editor's note). My focus on three church congregations in Kroonvale assumes that residents of this area form a heterogeneous group that faces many of the social problems encountered by South Africans anywhere and utilizes varying strategies to deal with these challenges. When I speak of the "Kroonvale community," therefore, I am specifically referring to a selective community of churchgoers with whom I interacted during my fieldwork. My ideas and interpretations remain inspired by these personal encounters, but do not assume that all congregation members, Kroonvale residents, or those who live in the wider Graaff-Reinet area would offer the same or similar opinions.

The Burden of Race

The brief historical information presented above about Graaff-Reinet and its coloured population is only a glimpse into the deeply ambivalent world of what it means to be coloured in South Africa.[13] According to Ian Goldin, the first documented use of the term "coloured" in the South African context to refer to people of mixed racial heritage occurred for the purposes of the Cape population census in 1904 (1987, 12–13).[14] Before that, the word had a similar meaning to uses in the United Kingdom and United States, namely, to refer to black people. This particular usage, then, together with the apartheid government's policy on racial purity, meant that in order to survive, many coloured people sought to imitate white culture and worked toward cultivating respectability for themselves and their families through cultural absorption. This is powerfully demonstrated by a look at voting patterns in the Western Cape Province, one of the few parts of South Africa where black people constitute the minority population. Most coloured people in this region voted for the National Party rather than the African National Congress (ANC) in the first democratic elections held in 1994. In 1999, both the New National Party and the Democratic Party governed the province; only in 2004 did the ANC obtain a governing majority in this region, and the Democratic Alliance won the majority vote in the most recent election (April 2009).[15] This seems to show that coloured people have drawn a distinction between being identified as black/African and coloured/European. To be identified as European carried greater currency in apartheid South Africa, and this symptom of the country's particular history of slavery and colonization contributed toward these complex strategies of racial self-definition.

The apartheid government treated coloured people as belonging to a race category that is in between black and white, and/or neither black nor white (Erasmus 2001, 15–16, 18). The complaint of some coloured people that "during apartheid, we were not white enough and now we are not black enough" shows the extent to which this view was internalized (James, Caliguire, and Cullinan 1996, 12). In the scholarly literature, writers often focus obsessively on miscegenation or on the politics of naming in order to clarify the threateningly indistinct category of coloured-ness. The differing population groups and relations that gave rise to coloured people (Patterson 1953; Marais 1957) and apartheid definitions of coloured according to various legislative acts are common subjects of this discourse. Terms such as "Hottentot," "Khoikhoi," "San," "Khoisan," "Boesman" (Bushman),[16] and "*bruinmens*" (brown person) are hotly debated and thoroughly scoured for their essential (and often, essentialized) meanings. Although not all of these works should be tarred with the same brush, those that focused on a racialized view of coloured people as products of miscegenation conform to a predominant theme of studies about coloured people during the twentieth century. According to Mohamed Adhikari, an academic based at the University of Cape Town, this type of writing is typical of the "essentialist school," the first of four general categories in his recent historiographical analysis of South African scholarship on coloured people. The essentialist writers assume "racial hybridity . . . [as] the essence of colouredness. For essentialists there is usually no need to explain the nature or making of coloured identity because it is part of an assumed reality that sees South African society as consisting of distinct races of which coloured people are one" (2009, 7).[17] The essentialist school approach greatly contributed to the notion of coloured people as an "in-between" racial category, thereby making it difficult to separate a distinct coloured identity, social history, and culture from the mixed-race stereotype.[18]

This essentialist approach also prevented serious study of coloured people's music as an integral component of their distinct culture and identity. In fact, I argue that it led to a perception of coloured people's music merely as a "mixture" of black and white musics, therefore mapping coloured people's music onto their apartheid racial classification (see Mugglestone 1984).[19] In comparison to writing about white and black people's music, far less twentieth-century work on coloured people's music exists, except for some research on the music of the (Muslim) Cape Malay population (Du Plessis 1935, 1972; Desai 1985, 1993).[20] Shamil Jeppie shows that "'Muslim-as-Malay' came to be constructed against the 'Christian-as-coloured' in official and dominant discourses in the nineteenth century" (2001, 83). The Malay population thus were constructed as a "pure," "authentic," exotic Other with unique cultural and musical practices stemming from their diasporic homeland in comparison to the (local) Christian coloured people whose music appeared to be an inferior, inauthentic version of white people's music and therefore not worth studying in its own right. As an exception to this view, studies of coloured people's secular folk songs and their distinctive use of Afrikaans do exist, but they only appeared much later in the twentieth century (Drury 1985; Burden 1991).[21]

During the 1980s, the influence of the Soweto uprising of 1976 and the Black Consciousness movement contributed to a sense of general black solidarity in defiance of apartheid's "divide and rule" approach (Adhikari 2009, 11).[22] As a result, writing about coloured people made a significant paradigm shift. This new school of thought, which Adhikari terms "instrumentalist," reacted strongly to the essentialist ideas of coloured people as a separate racial group and "regarded coloured identity as an artificial concept imposed by the white supremacist state and the ruling establishment upon an oppressed and vulnerable group of people as an instrument of social control" (2009, 11). Adhikari describes his own work during this time as drawing strong criticism; people from all quarters viewed his research as a divisive product of apartheid-era thinking and, at times, even accused its author of being a racist (2009, 4). The change in focus within writing of this era shows a radical switch fueled by the height of violent anti-apartheid resistance; accordingly, research topics tended to focus mainly on histories of coloured people's political movements and resistance to white rule (11). The corresponding period in South African musicological historiography saw the publication of seminal volumes on black South African urban performance (Coplan 1985, 2007; Erlmann 1991). This approach constituted an ideological split from earlier ethnomusicological work that focused on "authentic" indigenous (rural) musical traditions, but neither of these positions understood colouredness as part of an African identity. During this period, Andrew Tracey at the International Library of African Music formed the annual Ethnomusicological Symposium, an informal gathering of anyone interested in African music. Only a few presentations at these events covered the musical traditions of coloured people as the majority focused on the musical traditions of black South Africans.

Adhikari explains that neither the racially stereotyped premises of the essentialist school nor the denial of the instrumentalists that coloured peoples' identity was anything other than a construct of the apartheid state offered an adequate approach to writing about coloured people. He places his own work in a third category, that of social constructionism which advocates that

> coloured identity cannot be taken as given but is a product of human agency dependent on a complex interplay of historical, social, cultural, political and other contingencies. . . . The creation of coloured identity is also taken to be an ongoing, dynamic process in which groups and individuals make and remake their perceived realities and thus also their personal and social identities. (2009, 13)

This far more nuanced approach makes it possible to analyze the apartheid state's domination of coloured people, as well as their varied and complex historical and contemporary responses to this situation. In addition, it makes allowances for different reactions and strategies within various communities according to geographic location, among other factors. As implied earlier in the context of Western Cape Province voting patterns, coloured people also sided with their oppressors at times (2009, 15). The social constructionism approach therefore enables researchers to investigate coloured identity as an entity that incorporates an ongoing process of making and remaking, resistance and complicity.

The majority of the post-apartheid studies of coloured people's music can be viewed as adopting this more fluid approach, for example, work on the New Year's festival in Cape Town, known (and referred to by its participants) as the Coon Carnival (Jeppie 1990b; Martin 1999) and the Cape jazz tradition (Jeppie 1990a; Layne 1995; Muller 1996, 2001, 2004, 2008, forthcoming). Recent work reveals two lesser-known but equally important traditions among coloured people in the Western Cape, namely the *nagtroepe* (Malay choirs), and the Christmas bands (Bruinders 2005, 2006).[23] Most of these studies, however, center primarily in the city of Cape Town, where the majority of the country's coloured population lives.[24] The more than two centuries of Christian coloured voices raised in song in Graaff-Reinet has therefore remained under the (ethno)musicological radar. At the time of writing, I am not aware of any other ethnographic studies on coloured people's Christian religious music. I believe that this is due to the combination of the historiographical, political, and ideological factors mentioned above. What this study proposes instead is to apply the current debates on coloured identity to this music. I aim to write against the notion of musical "authenticity" (apparent in the focus on Cape Malay traditions and the essentialist notions of "in-betweenness"), which determined earlier choices of research on coloured people's music. My work thus adds to the growing body of post-apartheid scholarship on coloured people's music in South Africa but also broadens the scope of this work in two main directions. First, the project is located in the Eastern Cape Province of the country, where different historical, geographical, and musical factors were in effect, and second, it focuses particularly on the sacred repertory of a Christian coloured religious community.

Creolization, Entanglement, Music

The theory of creolization, originally developed in the field of Caribbean studies, draws on postmodern theory and looks beyond South Africa for ways of examining colouredness. Adhikari identifies this as the fourth approach to studies of South African coloured people and although cautious about the effects of importing a term originally used for different geographical and social contexts, he believes that it has much potential.[25] The first uses of the term "creolization" in the South African sense referred to South African culture in general. For example, in his account of slavery at the Cape, Robert Shell explains that "slavery brought different people together, not across the sights of a gun, as on the frontier, but in the setting of a home. Each slave was exposed to each owner and each settler to each slave on a very intimate footing. There was, in fact, a common reciprocal legacy . . . this legacy was the as yet unexamined creole culture of South Africa, with its new cuisine, its new architecture, its new music, its melodious, forthright and poetic language, Afrikaans" (1994, 415).[26] Sarah Nuttall and Cheryl-Ann Michael echo this idea and define creolization as "the process whereby individuals of different cultures, languages, and religions are thrown together and invent a new language, Creole, a new culture, and a new social organization" (2000, 6). They argue that creolization theory is useful as a framework for the South African context as a whole, especially in order to discover connections between people and to avoid the "emphasis on separation and segregation" present in many works on South African cultural studies (1).

Nuttall and Michael's insights provide a valid argument for thinking about connections forged between South Africans as part of their everyday lives, and their work takes important steps in moving beyond narratives of racial difference to stories of cultural encounter. The rather frosty reception of this idea by some authors resulted from a perception that it skirted the issues of racism, violence, domination, and resistance in South Africa (Jacobs 2002).[27] Nuttall defends these criticisms in her latest book by suggesting that the concept of creolization, with its particular origins in slavery and its associated cruelty and violence, is still an appropriate tool (among others) for researchers, especially because it retains a "vivid sense (compared to, say, notions of hybridity and syncretism) of the cruelty that processes of mixing have involved" (2009, 25). I adopt Nuttall's views here because I believe that both hybridity and syncretism imply an equal blending of disparate items, which does not take specific historical circumstances and the varied nature of oppression into account. In addition, the term "hybrid" can imply miscegenation, a term used in apartheid discourse about coloured people that entrenched an extremely negative racial stereotype of their origins (see Wicomb 1998). My understanding of creolization here rests on the idea that no culture exists without interactions with other people(s) and thus subscribes to Edouard Glissant's statement that all cultures are creolized, thereby moving away from the idea of creolization as "a halfway [category] between two 'pure' extremes" (1989, 140). Nuttall and Michael's views are similar to this, in their search for connections and acknowledgment of encounter between people(s). However, while not dismissing the idea of all cultures as creolized, Nuttall reminds us of the term's associations with slavery and reframes her previous definition to focus on slavery origins and their associated pain and violence as well as to retain a sense of cultural encounter. I conclude from this that the term's overlapping meanings are not mutually exclusive in the South African context and thus believe that this theory still has much to offer for South African cultural studies.[28]

Zimitri Erasmus first suggested applying the theory of creolization to coloured identity in her introduction to a volume of collected essays on coloured people in Cape Town. Here, she refers to creolization as "cultural formations historically shaped by conditions of slavery" (2001, 22). In her conceptualization of coloured identity as a process of *cultural* creolization (my emphasis) she continues to dislodge the essentialist notion of racial hybridity and miscegenation. She also suggests a way of thinking about the formation of South African coloured identity as a process containing both severe domination and also creative agency. She effectively summarizes this conceptualization in her assertion that "coloured identities were formed in the colonial encounter between colonists (Dutch and British), slaves from South and East India and from East Africa, and conquered indigenous peoples, the Khoi and San. . . . The result [of this encounter] has been a highly specific and instantly recognizable cultural formation—not just 'a mixture' but a very particular 'mixture' comprising elements of Dutch, British, Malaysian, Khoi and other forms of African culture appropriated, translated and articulated in complex and subtle ways" (2001, 21).

The idea of encounter, within the context of creolization theory, is also particularly pertinent to ways of approaching the study of coloured people's religious music in this book. Within the general field of South African music studies, this notion is not new. A selection of well-known works within the ethnomusicological literature suggests that many South African music genres contain a fusion of various influences (Coplan 1985, 2007; Erlmann 1991, 1996; Ballantine 1993; James 1999; Muller 1999). These include interactions with rural and urban lifeways, migrant worker experiences, European missionaries, African American performers, musical repertories from within and beyond the country, and indigenous and exotic instruments and recordings, just to mention a few examples. These works tend to focus mainly on black South African performance, however. While not always explicitly stated in the more recent studies on coloured people's music in Cape Town, I believe the notion of encounter played an important role in forming those repertories and traditions.

This book therefore examines the Kroonvale religious repertoire as a product of encounters between frontier groups such as European missionaries, British settlers, Dutch/Afrikaans farmers, Xhosa people, slaves, and Khoisan survivors. Adopting this approach reveals, significantly, that the particular process that formed this repertory is not unlike those already identified in the development of other South African music genres. Thus, this book situates the religious singing of the Kroonvale community firmly within the sonic landscape of South African music, not as a genre "in-between" but one that, due to instances of encounter and cultural creolization, developed in similar ways to many other South African music genres. Yet, it also features a distinct musical repertory and style of singing that can only be identified as that of a rural Karoo coloured community.[29] My work therefore reveals critical theoretical and cultural insights into both rural Karoo musical practices in particular and South African music studies in general.

Inevitably, experiences of deep pain and vulnerability, the unavoidable corollaries of coloured identity formation, also accompanied the creation of this musical repertory in Kroonvale. Erasmus explains that the process of making coloured identity is always a fragile one because it is "produced and re-produced in the place of the margin" (2001, 23).[30] Despite the process of creative agency and expression required to form this identity and culture, nonetheless, dominant powers designated coloured people throughout South African history as peripheral. Glissant characterizes this formation of a cultural identity in the face of domination and the violent crushing of preexisting cultural practices as an example of a "cornered community" (1989, 103). In addition, the creolization of colouredness in the special circumstances of South Africa meant a certain degree of complicity with the imposed racial hierarchy of white as superior and black as inferior, in other words, the acceptance of black people as subordinate to both coloured and white people. Therefore, the South African coloured "cornered community" had to contend with not only the historical contexts of slavery and cultural eradication but also complicity with certain apartheid political ideologies and policies.[31] In order to avoid denial of this uncomfortable situation, Erasmus suggests a return to the origin of creolized beginnings (more a psychological return than an historical one) despite the fact that this is a process fraught with pain and difficulty (2001, 24).[32] Glissant believes that the return to these origins, which he terms "the point of entanglement," should take place in order to oppose the force of diversion away from these origins. In other words, this return to the "point of entanglement" represents a confrontation and acceptance of a painful, often denied past, and requires an engagement with its (often fragmented) lived experiences. According to Glissant, the experience of these reconnections (or "reversion") should then be channeled into self-expression and creativity (1989, 26). Music, a constant aural backdrop to this incomplete and fragmentary process, also becomes an important site of (re)connection between the past and the more recent present. I argue therefore that musical practices not only form a way of reconnecting to that illusive "point of entanglement" and commenting on that experience, but also constitute a particularly promising vehicle for analyzing those instances of creative agency that surfaced throughout the history of this community.

While Glissant envisages the "point of entanglement" as located in the past and offering a liberation of consciousness and outlet for creative expression in the present, Nuttall characterizes the concept as a way of forging connections across spaces previously thought to be separate. She believes that this concept can therefore assist in understanding and conceptualizing post-apartheid society. Entanglement, for Nuttall, "offers a rubric in terms of which we can begin to meet the challenge of the 'after apartheid.' It is a means by which to draw into our analyses those sites in which what was once thought of as separate—identities, spaces, histories—come together or find points of intersection in unexpected ways. It is an idea that signals largely unexplored terrains of mutuality, wrought from a common, though often coercive and confrontational, experience" (2009, 11).[33]

While acknowledging the difficulty, pain, violence, and cruelty in the past (and remaining aware that these forces often persist in the present), I believe that the sound of sacred singing in the Kroonvale community constitutes one of these sites where connections between identities, spaces, and histories can be located. Both Glissant's and Nuttall's interpretations of the entanglement concept offer useful ways of examining the processes inherent in the formation of the Kroonvale coloured community's culture, identity, and, most importantly, music. In the chapters that follow, I investigate the various genres within this repertory, using lenses such as history, politics, class, and gender in order to examine what the musical sound reveals about these issues. My overall argument in this book emphasizes that careful listening to the sound of sacred song in the Kroonvale churches reveals additional theoretical, historical, and cultural insights about past and present in this community. While not always explicitly stated, ideas of creolization and entanglement and their effects remain central to my thinking within the chapters that follow.

Steven Feld's insights provide a strong theoretical foundation for my focus on sound in this book. In his work with the Kaluli people in Papua New Guinea, Feld first studied their sonic interactions with the forest sounds as a way of understanding the deeply expressive forms of Kaluli laments and their association with birds in their cosmology (2003, 225–26). After his "ethnography of sound" appeared in print (1982), he recently extended these ideas to incorporate the notion of "acoustemology." By this he suggested "a union of acoustics and epistemology" and a call "to investigate the primacy of sound as a modality of knowing and being in the world" (2003, 226). He adopted this approach partially as a way of continuing his investigation into the sound world of the Kaluli people, and also to write against the separation of "sonic environments from human invention" that occurs in acoustic ecology research (226). On the latter point, he explains that "soundscapes, no less than landscapes are not just physical exteriors, spatially surrounding or apart from human activity. Soundscapes are perceived and interpreted by human actors who attend to them as a way of making their place in and through the world" (226).

I believe that a similar separation of sonic environment and human activity has already taken place through the way in which the Karoo is marketed. Real estate agencies and travel magazines perpetuate a general sonic association of this landscape with relative (human) silence. This romanticized view is of a soundscape dominated mainly by the sounds of natural environment, for example, wind, rain, thunder, birds, monkeys, and antelope. What this does, however, is minimize the man-made sounds of the area, namely, the crack of rifles in game-hunting season, the sounds of diesel tractors and other farm vehicles, and at a most fundamental level, the voices of long-established Karoo residents occupied in conversation and song. In the case of the coloured people in Kroonvale, not only is their sonic contribution to the landscape overshadowed by the dominant rhetoric of an escape from city life to the quiet, natural Karoo, but also the centuries of their silence in the historical record resulted in a minimal regard for their particular contribution to the soundscape of this region. Perhaps due to the historical oppression that caused this silencing, Kroonvale residents seldom talked about themselves or their past experiences (see Field 2001; Denis 2003). Instead, I often heard traces of historical encounters and ideas about race, class, politics, and gender in the music first, and then during the research I conducted, I focused particularly on obtaining substantiation of this aural evidence. Following Feld, therefore, I argue that without the sacred singing of this particular coloured community, their narrative of being in this place would be more difficult to ascertain. This book and the ideas contained therein thus developed primarily as a result of my aural encounters with the sounds of Kroonvale church music. Of course, this close-listening approach also became further expanded and enriched as a result of my personal encounters with community members during the fieldwork process.

Fieldwork Beyond the Railway Line

Late one Friday afternoon in July 2004, I offered to go with my aunt into Kroonvale in order to take eleven coloured men home. These men worked on the family farm during the week as sheep shearers and had just finished a week of back-breaking work in order to relieve a flock of Merino sheep of its wool. In the usual farming style, my aunt and I climbed into the front of the rugged 4x4 Landcruiser. The men climbed onto the back, where they rolled cigarettes from newspaper and loose tobacco, and swapped stories among themselves to keep entertained for the half-hour drive into town. As we entered the town outskirts I thought I saw Jessie, one of the coloured women who worked at the Reinet House Museum archive and I cringed as we drove past. Until this moment I had managed to keep my farm life and my research project reasonably separate. I wondered how I could possibly reconcile the unequal power relationships between white farmers sitting in the front and coloured farmworkers standing on the back, with my recent attempts to learn about music as an equal participant within the community.[34]

During my first period of fieldwork in Graaff-Reinet, I realized that five years of full-time graduate study as a white South African in the United States had considerably changed many of my attitudes and approaches. The type of embarrassment and ambivalence I describe above is symptomatic of being both a South African living in her native country, and a South African viewing her own country from the outside.[35] These kinds of experiences made me aware of how important it was to adopt a critical stance to my own background as a white South African woman with farming connections.[36] I myself occupied an "in-between" position as both an outsider and an insider to this community. I could be characterized as an insider because I am a citizen, born in the Eastern Cape, and a frequent visitor to the area.[37] I have relatives in Graaff-Reinet and have spent much time at the family farm outside the town. This means that I was familiar with the farming routines and schedules and how these interacted with the running of the town. I also speak Afrikaans (the language of the coloured community), which is a distinct advantage to undertaking research in this particular area of South Africa. Thus, my insider status facilitated communication in many ways, and my familiarity with the area helped me to find research sites and establish research relationships quite quickly.

My outsider status, however, was also very clear: I am not a coloured person. Even in post-apartheid South Africa, there are power associations embedded in my whiteness, which made the research process additionally challenging. Despite my wish to downplay these aspects and be accepted as merely a student of coloured culture, I expected to be identified as a white employer (or at the very least, the relative of a white employer). This was aptly illustrated one day in November 2005 when I attended a church service in the farming area of Kendrew.[38] The dilapidated church building contained a row of wooden benches for the congregation, with a single chair next to the front row of benches. Much to my embarrassment, my hostess motioned that I should sit there. Although my initial discomfort at the idea of someone reserving the only chair for me, the white guest, lessened when I realized later that any visitor to a remote farm church would probably receive the same or similar treatment, I was always sensitive (and at times probably oversensitive) to this type of issue in my fieldwork. I regarded this sensitivity and awareness as necessary, however, as the ever-present apartheid legacy on the consciousness of all South Africans meant that "we all lived in separate worlds" and that apartheid created not only "physical boundaries between its peoples, but also . . . emotional, cultural, and economic divisions" (Muller 1999, 13). Thus, while I agree with certain writers on "insider" ethnography that point out the accelerated access and facilitation of research relationships in this position (Muller 1999; Halstead 2001; Chiener 2002; Labaree 2002), I realized quickly that "the color of your skin continues to mark you as insider or outsider with respect to the camp of the powerful and the oppressor" (Muller 1999, 8). Just as I had to cross the physical boundary (represented by the railway line that divided the white residential part of town from Kroonvale) and experience the emotions that accompanied this action, the community residents I spoke to had to cross boundaries of their own in their interactions with me. To overcome any apprehension about this, I often worked consciously to emphasize different, more neutral connections, such as gender or age. For example, as a young female researcher approaching this project in the role of a student willing to listen and learn, many community members who were retired teachers could identify with this teacher-student relationship, and this often assisted and facilitated conversations.[39]

As my fieldwork progressed, however, my initial oversensitivity to my whiteness eased, and I learned two things. First, I became aware that people found my research interest in their church music both surprising and flattering. As far as I know, researchers or academics have not approached people in this community before, and because of this, many people questioned me, often in much detail, about my musical interests and my background. This led to my second realization, namely, that without giving of myself and imparting my personal information, I would not be able to exchange information with people about music in this community. I soon became accustomed to answering questions about where I lived, what route I used to drive home, why I was interested in church music, and so on. People, sometimes immediately after I had spoken, then passed on this information to other people standing nearby, which often made me feel extremely vulnerable. Thus, in a similar way to my initial interactions with members of the Kroonvale community, I also experienced what it was like to be questioned by strangers; this reality complicated the traditional binary opposition between ethnographer and informant.

Mostly, people wanted to know about my Graaff-Reinet family connections. I remember having a brief conversation before a church service at the Parsonage Street Congregational Church with a church deacon who did not introduce himself, but who asked me similar questions to what I described above. After I answered one of his questions by stating my name and last name, he seemed visibly disappointed because "Jorritsma" did not seem familiar as a local Graaff-Reinet last name. When I added quickly that I also had relatives in the McNaughton and Rubidge families, I saw immediate relief on his face. He informed me that he knew of my grandfather and his brothers and inquired about their children and grandchildren. In that moment I discovered that the physical divisions between people's places of residence in Graaff-Reinet never completely separated white, coloured, black, farmer, town resident, and farmworker. Gossip and the knowledge of people's genealogical background, typical of a small town, transcended racial boundaries, and if I positioned myself within this system, no matter how vulnerable it made me feel, people seemed less suspicious of me and more likely to continue a conversation about music.

In total I made five separate research trips to Graaff-Reinet during 2004 and 2005, with a brief follow-up visit in July 2006.[40] I usually stayed for six to eight weeks at a time and then returned to Port Elizabeth (my hometown) or traveled to Philadelphia for feedback on my research process and writing. I chose three churches in Kroonvale to serve as the basis for my research, namely, the Uniting Reformed Church (which used to be the Dutch Reformed Mission Church), the Parsonage Street Congregational Church, and the East Street Congregational Church (hereafter referred to as the URC or DRMC, PSCC, and ESCC, respectively). I began my project by attending weekly Sunday services at the URC and then attended services at the PSCC, followed by the ESCC. I chose these particular churches because of their origins in missionary churches established for coloured people by the London Missionary Society and the Graaff-Reinetsche Zendelings Genoot-schap (Graaff-Reinet Missionary Organization, later affiliated to the Dutch Reformed Mission Organization of the Dutch Reformed Church of South Africa). As these churches are the oldest churches with coloured congregations in Graaff-Reinet, I decided that this would be the most beneficial to my research, given my interest in investigating both the historical and contemporary manifestations of coloured people's church music in this region (see Figure 1.2).

I began each phase of research at a new church by making an appointment for an interview with the church minister and asking for permission to attend and record the Sunday services. As I introduced myself and spoke to more people within the community, these connections expanded, enabling me to contact more people involved in music for interview appointments. Community members often recommended the names of other members and suggested that I spoke to them as well. This advice often governed the choice of whom I next contacted for an interview. In this way, I believe that the community members not only guided me toward those people they thought were knowledgeable, but, because they knew the people involved, they also had a measure of control of the type of information that people shared with me.

Aside from adjusting to the fieldwork process, I also had to adjust to

Figure 1.2   Map of Kroonvale. From left to right: the seven churches represented are New Apostolic Church, Uniting Reformed Church, Parsonage Street Congregational Church, Apostolic Faith Mission, East Street Congregational Church, Catholic Church, and Methodist Church. Map by Teddy Whitlock, courtesy of Teddy Whitlock and Graaff-Reinet Tourism Office.

the specific living circumstances of the region. I discovered anew that the Karoo is a place that requires patience. For example, the family farm where I lived during my fieldwork only went from obtaining electricity powered by a generator to being linked to the national power supply in 2000. I remember the first time I visited after the electricity had been changed. It was a minor miracle to switch on an electric light at any time during the day (instead of the limited period at night as in the past), but I also felt a particular nostalgia for the cold, dark winter mornings when I would walk up the long passage to the kitchen where family members would be enjoying their first cup of tea by candlelight, warming themselves next to the coal stove. Of course, this also meant that power cuts became part of our lives, especially when lightning struck the remote farm power lines. Similarly, the farm telephone was connected in what was known as a "party-line" system, in other words, several farms would be linked to one phone line. This meant that only one farmer could use the phone at a time, and trying to connect a computer via dial-up connection to the Internet was simply impossible. Aware of this, I invested in technology that would enable me to connect to the Internet using a Bluetooth-enabled cell phone and laptop. I found a specific position in the farmhouse where the cell phone could obtain the two bars of reception required to make a connection and this system usually worked. But, any cloudy or windy weather meant that there would be no Internet or email that day. Thus, I gradually learned to let go of the daily email-checking habits I acquired in the United States, and also to let go of the reliance on constant availability of electrical power and a phone line.

One is at the complete mercy of the weather in the Karoo. The weather dictates the next day's farmwork, whether livestock needs to be put in sheds for protection from the elements, or whether there will be enough grazing in the long term. The weather also changed the shape of the dirt road I drove on for half an hour (sometimes forty-five minutes) into the town every morning and evening. If it rained the night before, there was every chance that the road would be flooded and my fieldwork appointments would simply have to be canceled. After the water on the road dried up, I had to familiarize myself with the shape of the road again, as the water always wore new paths and grooves in the track, and one had to be aware of this if one wanted to avoid nasty bumps and damage to the vehicle. Instead of taking in the wonderful scenery around me, my drive into town was often spent with full concentration on the couple of yards of road immediately ahead of my vehicle's tires. During my drive back to the farm in the late afternoon or evening, however, I generally focused on the bush immediately around me, while I searched intently for the glowing of wildlife eyes in the headlights. The kudu antelope in particular, while beautiful to watch, can jump with ease over a farm fence and try to jump straight over a vehicle as well, often causing severe car accidents in South African rural areas.

Despite these characteristic elements of Karoo life, my fieldwork settled into a routine quite quickly. I read church records once a week on a Tuesday morning, visited the Reinet House Museum once or twice a week to read newspapers in its archive, attended a "ladies' choir" rehearsal every Tuesday afternoon, a women's society meeting every Thursday afternoon, and of course, a church service every Sunday morning. In between these fixed appointments, I met various community members for interviews, attended extra church services or events, or spent time typing field notes and annotating field recordings. Thus, I collected the two types of evidence for this project (archival and oral) on a weekly (sometimes daily) basis. This meant that I could report to the people I interviewed about what I had read that morning and ask their opinion, or I could ask them for help in understanding and providing further explanation for what I had read in the archives. This combination was difficult to balance at times, especially when I read prejudiced views about coloured people in newspaper articles and then met with contemporary members of the community shortly afterward, particularly aware of how hurtful this writing would be for them. Although the oral evidence gathered during my fieldwork constituted the main source of musical information for this project, the interaction between the written and oral records through my fieldwork research made the generating of an archive of coloured memory, history, and music all the more rich and complex.

Notes on Format and Chapter Summaries

Throughout this book, I often include narratives of my fieldwork experiences and place these in italics to differentiate them from the rest of the text. I have used Western staff notation for the transcription examples found in the text because European missionary and hymn traditions form one background of the music in these churches. As the community is mostly Afrikaans-speaking but conversed equally well in English (or switched to English when they heard my accent), a conversation often comprised both languages (this is characteristic of conversations in South Africa, but particularly typical of the Eastern Cape Province).[41] I have translated many of these terms and dialogues directly into English in the text, but at times have retained the original conversation in both languages and provided translations of the Afrikaans sentences. My reason for placing the mixed dialogue in the main text is to endeavor to retain some sense of the original vibrancy of the discussion. Too often, translating everything into English makes the original discussion seem flat and expressionless. It is well known that South African English is peppered with Afrikaans phrases, which are ironed out when South Africans emigrate and are therefore not heard overseas. By retaining these Afrikaans words and sentences I remind readers of a different English usage that is peculiar to South Africa. The Glossary at the end of the book provides explanations of many Afrikaans terms used in this community that pertain to South African history, religious denominations, and/or music. Translations from Dutch/Afrikaans to English throughout the book are mine unless otherwise noted.

The chapters that follow focus on particular ways of understanding religious music performance in this community. Although seemingly disparate, the themes used ensure that each chapter engages with the ways that colonialism and apartheid shaped this community and its musical repertory. It is impossible to conceptualize work in the South African context without recourse to such thematic connections because of apartheid's enduring leg-acy in the nation's consciousness. Chapter 2 provides historical information on Graaff-Reinet, Kroonvale, and the churches that formed the main sites of my research. I utilize theoretical concepts such as the frontier and the seam, from the fields of South African history and literature studies, respectively, to frame a counternarrative to the dominant tradition of writing about white people in this town. Chapter 3 examines the history of encounter embed-ded in the sound of the religious repertory and introduces the reader to the three main genres within this musical tradition. Here I draw on James Scott's theory of hidden transcripts to investigate the musical "point(s) of entangle-ment" in this community and argue that this community archived its oral his-tory within the sounds of its sacred song. Chapter 4 focuses on anti-apartheid gestures within the music and performance traditions as a way of providing commentary on the historiography of religious music in South Africa. The content of this chapter evokes Nuttall's idea of entanglement (mentioned above), with its examination of more contemporary connections between previously disparate entities (here the mission church and Independent African church traditions in particular). I argue here for the recognition of a more permeable boundary between the musical styles of churches with mis-sion origins and those within the Independent African church tradition. In Chapter 5, I study the church choirs and their repertories as a manifestation of middle-class status within this community. I assert that choir members make this statement musically, through performing a particular repertory (with its roots in South African colonial and missionary history) in a particu-lar way. Chapter 6 examines the tradition of women's society groups within this church context and their musical styles. Here I interpret the church as a space of independence for women's society members. This independence can be heard in the individual lines of their singing and is in contrast to the expected domestic (and often subordinate) roles of women in this commu-nity. In Chapter 7, I conclude with a commentary on recent media interest in the Karoo region and a (re)contextualization of the book's relationship to the post-apartheid moment.

There are several common concepts underlying this work. The first relies on the notions of creolization and entanglement in order to examine how music in Kroonvale reveals a particular formation of South African coloured-ness. These theories not only allow for acknowledgment of the unique origins and heritage of coloured people in this country, but also provide a useful way of moving beyond stereotypical apartheid categories and defini-tions. The second concept is that close attention to the sound and style of musical performance offers ways of gathering information on identity, his-tory, and culture in this community. In addition, sound offers a vehicle to express ideas about race, gender, politics, and class. The insertion of oral history and other statements about this community within its music provides important information that is preserved for posterity in the sound and style of sacred song. The third idea is the understanding of this music as a living archive of coloured congregational song. This living archive represents an embodied history, and the congregation members emphatically reclaim this history through their singing at regular church services. The existence of this repertory is a statement of survival, an expression of contemporary social and political features, as well as a purposeful imagining of and engagement with the past, present, and future.

2

Karoo People and Places

My visits to Reinet House (the Graaff-Reinet museum) began in mid-2004 and continued throughout (and after) my fieldwork research period. The prevailing post-apartheid political climate meant that the museum experienced a complex transitional phase at the time and needed to "transform" its exhibitions and their accompanying narratives to address the silences engineered by the previous regime.[1]

Two incidents that occurred during the period of my visits remain prominent in my memory. In June 2005, during the planning phase of a proposed exhibition on slavery in the Eastern Cape, I remember talking to Anziske Kayster about the challenges involved. "It's so difficult," she said, "because museums have traditionally relied on objects to display and for an exhibition like this, we don't have any objects." Nonetheless, the staff at Reinet House persisted in their endeavors and compiled a successful traveling exhibition, "Slavery and the long road to restitution," which featured little-known information on this chapter of South African history. The exhibition received national media attention and credit for its firm commitment to transformation in post-apartheid museum displays.

The second incident occurred one morning in December 2006 when I arrived at Reinet House to visit the staff. Jessie Gouws was at her usual place at the reception desk but I sensed a tension in her voice as she spoke in rapid Afrikaans to her colleague, Denise van Wyk. "Is everything all right?" I inquired. "You know the rhino horn that used to stand in the display case in this corner?" she asked. "Well, it was stolen last night. I just can't believe it," she continued, "such a valuable object being sold on the street for muti. . . ."[2]

Jessie's obvious distress at the loss of this item reveals her acknowledgment of the museum's existing (white people's) historical narrative. The material available for sale at Reinet House and other tourist sites overwhelmingly favors the founding of Graaff-Reinet as a frontier outpost, the various (white) leaders and magistrates, the Dutch-speaking farmers' defiant declaration of Graaff-Reinet as a republic independent from British rule (1795–96), and the strategic role played by Graaff-Reinet in the Anglo-Boer War (1899–1902).[3] This narrative faithfully follows Graaff-Reinet from its very humble beginnings more than two hundred years ago and survives in the present day to provide much of interest for local and international tourists alike.

Yet, the staff's successful completion of the slavery exhibition with its introduction of stories from previously marginalized groups also shows a commitment to balancing the historical record. The challenge I faced in the context of my research is similar to that experienced by Anziske, Jessie, and Denise, namely, how to best narrate the story of the coloured community in Graaff-Reinet despite the existence of well-entrenched historical biases and, often as a direct result, a lack of accessible information. Writing a history of Karoo people and places in this setting is thus a very difficult proposition and raises complex questions, for example, where in time should the narrative begin? In other words, does one start with the colonial encounter or with archaeological evidence and precolonial history? How is it possible to tell the story of people who rarely featured in historical records due to the complete lack of interest shown by colonial officials (Elphick 1985, 148)? How can twenty-first-century writers interpret the limited oral history of that period when its narrators are no longer alive and the written record most likely contains further distortions by those in power? Historians usually encounter such problems to a greater or lesser extent, and fortunately, South African historians have already grappled with many of these questions. I thus rely on the insights and richly detailed work of important writers in this field, particularly those focused on the Eastern Cape region and its historical actors. What follows, therefore, is an attempt to frame and deliver a counternarrative of the people and place of Graaff-Reinet that intends to provide sufficient historical background for the musical focus of this book.

Of Karoo Frontiers and Seams

In his work on the Xhosa people in the eastern Cape region, Noël Mostert states, "The wars and the moral struggle on the Cape frontier provided the main formative experience of South Africa" (1992, xvii–xviii). The nine wars that took place between 1778 and 1878 on the eastern Cape frontier suggest a

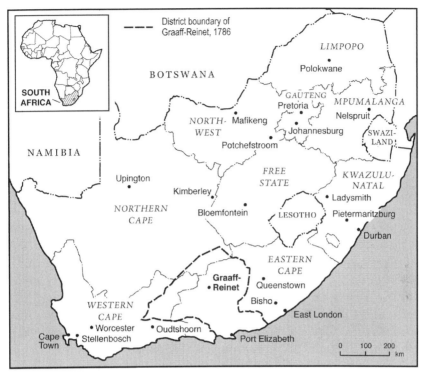

Figure 2.1   Map of South Africa, showing the colonial Graaff-Reinet municipal district (1786). Map by Wendy Job.

period of not only intense physical conflict but also severe suspicion, differing ideologies, and attempts of varying success to assert power over others. Historians recognize this phase as essential for an understanding of broader South African history.[4] For example, Rodney Davenport and Christopher Saunders state that "far more than any other frontier, it was one on which policies were thought out and deliberately applied. . . . [A]ll these [policies] were tried in various combinations, in a bid to maintain order and peaceful coexistence at the meeting point of two disparate but competing cultures" (2000, 132).[5] Graaff-Reinet's association with the endlessly shifting geographical, social, and even mythical location of the frontier thus offers one possible lens through which to view this rich history (see Figure 2.1). In order to present a history of Graaff-Reinet and its surrounding district, then, it is necessary to investigate the notion of the frontier as well as its related historiographical interpretations.

Martin Legassick is usually credited with suggesting an alternative way of viewing the South African frontier. His pioneering work fundamentally questions the previously entrenched and accepted 1930s-era notion that the "frontiersman regarded the non-white [person] only as a servant or enemy" and that the sustained and bitter conflict between races on the frontier formed the basis of future white racist attitudes and ideologies (1980, 45).[6] He argues that "enemies and friends were not divided into rigid, static categories; non-whites were not regarded implacably as enemies . . . [and] if there was a trend in class relationships, indeed, it was a trend away from master-slave towards chief-subject or patron-client" (65, 68). In the South African history field, Legassick's work thus paved the way for researchers to focus on the so-called nonconflictual aspects of the frontier.

Scholars subsequently applied these insights in their work; for example, Nigel Worden's research suggested a deeper level of domination in the arable farming areas of the southwestern Cape than on the predominantly pastoral frontier (1985) and Robert Ross presented evidence of the more free and fluid interactions between Khoekhoe and colonists in this area (Ross, Van Arkel, and Quispel 1993, 87–88). Hermann Giliomee's theory of the open and closed characteristics of the eastern Cape frontier, however, is particularly pertinent for my work on the Graaff-Reinet region. While Giliomee is careful to state that different areas of the frontier exhibited varying (and sometimes overlapping) traits of open and closed characteristics at different times, the eastern Cape frontier generally experienced the "open" phase from 1770–93 and the "closing" phase from 1793–1812. He identifies three important characteristics of the open frontier: first, no single group managed to claim the land, which resulted in more fluid ownership; second, a weak government provided little authority over illegal activities or conflict situations; and third, negotiation rather than violence more often marked interactions between peoples (1989, 427). Related to these observations, he adds that "Europeans were not all masters, non-Europeans were not all servants" (430). Although the probability of violent encounters always existed in this open phase, the low density of population numbers in the area generally allowed for more fluidity and freedom of movement as well as trade/bartering on more equal terms.[7] In contrast, the closing frontier featured a loss of liberty and independence on the part of all the people involved, a more densely populated land area, and finally, a far more severe deterioration of non-European laborers' status who found it increasingly difficult to exist beyond the world of the colonial farm (450).

Despite these interpretations that highlight the nonconflictual aspects of the frontier, Susan Newton-King argues that while this particular understanding remains significant, the continuum of relationships between master and servant in this area would be better understood "if they were viewed in the context of a coercive rather than a free labour system" (1999, 44). She reminds us of the overwhelming evidence that the European population, although "relatively weak and thinly spread," treated the indigenous peoples on whom they relied so heavily with "unrelenting and provocative harshness" (43). She refers to three aspects as a possible explanation for this historical reality. First, she believes that the unmitigated hatred felt by the trekboers (Dutch-speaking farmers) toward the groups of hunter-robbers who regularly raided their farms, permeated all the European colonists' interactions with indigenous peoples to some degree.[8] Second, she proves that the desperately poor financial state of many colonists made them unable to maintain regular labor forces on their farms without regular recourse to some kind of coercion. The final aspect is the attitudes and ideologies of the colonists themselves, which produced unyielding dualisms such as Christian/heathen or master/servant, for example (43–44, 207).[9] At the heart of the colonists' belief in their rights over the Khoisan rested a fundamental conviction of the Khoisan as completely other and "forever outside the moral community" (207).

Newton-King's interpretation never dismisses the nonconflictual viewpoints, but simultaneously asserts that the idea of irreconcilable difference (and its ever-present threat of corresponding physical violence) also remains a fundamental characteristic of the frontier zone.[10] Leon de Kock, in the context of South African literary studies, responds to this perception of difference by observing that the arrival of Europeans in South Africa and the accompanying arrival of writing brought a "crisis of inscription" and representation (2001, 274; see also de Kock 2004). Writers faced the immediate challenge of bringing order to a "place of profound difference"; as a result, narrative styles included "various mechanisms of homogenisation and erasure" (2001, 274). For example, writers used the first person as a way of presuming homogeneity or assumed the use of a collective "we" or "us" in their texts. De Kock's proposed solution, while acknowledging the difference contained in the "traditional" frontier metaphor, is to consider the notion of the seam as an integral part of the frontier. As a seam (in clothing) attempts to bring together two disparate halves by the act of stitching and yet retains the visible evidence of the original difference in the marks of suture, so the seam metaphor acknowledges the meeting of disparate items and yet retains a visible imprint of their difference. De Kock suggests that "the ubiquitous South African 'frontier,' as much cultural and psychological as territorial, has historically constituted one of the great meeting points: a place . . . of simultaneous convergence and divergence and where a representational seam is the paradox qualifying any attempt to imagine organicism or unity. . . . I propose that the seam is the place where difference and sameness are hitched together . . . " (277).[11] This idea of joining sameness and difference in a metaphoric seam contains useful interpretive possibilities for my purposes. First, the metaphor of the seam allows the existence of both the conflictual and nonconflictual representations of the frontier to survive in a jostling chaos; it is possible for the rough edges and contradictions of the historical narrative to remain clearly visible. Second, this approach also acknowledges that no matter how much we would like these stories to be told in their entirety, the maddeningly obscure mists of history and the dominant early tradition of (white) writing in South Africa furnish major stumbling blocks in this venture.[12] According to de Kock, this is symptomatic of the poetics of the seam, for the endeavors to present a unifying narrative always retain the marks of unsuccessful attempts to flatten out difference (2001, 277). Third, the ongoing paradox of the seam also pays its respects to those written out of (or never written into) history, as the absence of these voices from the margins and their perspectives means that the story can never be (and should never be) deemed complete. The inscription and representation of difference will constantly bear the visible marks of suture in this respect.

Applying these theoretical ideas to the Graaff-Reinet context, then, I interpret the constant formation and destruction of those fragile frontier connections, the changing continuum of master and servant relations, and the often inexplicable and horrific instances of violence perpetrated by all the groups involved as indicative of this particular historical seam. I argue that the seam of this frontier meeting point should remain visible and in constant relief for future analysis and interpretation, no matter how paradoxical the evidence and information appears to be.[13] In other words, I believe that a better story will be told if the narratives of various groups in the area remain in the same physical as well as metaphorical space within the Reinet House Museum. An approach that neglects certain aspects will only perpetuate colonialist and apartheid tendencies of keeping unwanted or politically incorrect histories out of sight and subjecting them to de Kock's identified negative strategies of erasure or homogenization. That said, I intend the more detailed description of the disparate groups on the eastern Cape frontier and their interactions in the Graaff-Reinet area offered below, to emphasize as much as possible the coloured people of the town and their ancestors. This is a counternarrative writing strategy toward correcting the existing imbalance in the record.

The People: An Introduction

Before the 1760s, the Khoekhoe group known as the Inqua (or Hamcumqua), under the leadership of Chief Hijkon and later Chief Hinsati, initially occupied what would become the Graaff-Reinet region (Newton-King 1999, 28, 30, 33).[14] Pastoralism and availability of seasonal grazing formed the basis of Khoekhoe society; smaller groups moved around with their stock and depended on land use rather than its possession. Sometimes a number of groups banded together under the leadership of a wealthier or more skilled individual, but these leaders did not assume a strong political power or demand undivided loyalty; thus, groups often split from these "chiefs" and moved elsewhere. The Khoekhoe's conception of wealth rested in ownership of livestock, which created a constant risk of a sudden change in status due to stock theft, disease, or the effects of drought. The common tactics Khoekhoe people pursued when they lost their stock included becoming herders for wealthier Khoekhoe and earning livestock in return to rebuild their herds; reverting to hunter-gathering; or stealing stock from neighboring Khoekhoe or other groups (Elphick and Malherbe 1989, 6).

The Khoekhoe leadership style and their strategies to overcome poverty provide important insights on interactions between them and other groups in this area, namely, the hunter-gatherers, Xhosa, and colonists.[15] It is impossible to describe relationships between Khoekhoe and hunter-gatherers without mentioning the accompanying terminology and its meanings. For example, the Khoekhoe used the term "San" to refer to hunter-gatherers, small-scale stock breeders, fellow Khoekhoe groups who had lost their cattle, and/or robbers; thus, it implied those of lower wealth or status. Richard Elphick argues that the " 'San' were not perceived as an ethnic group but as an undesirable social class, however vaguely demarcated" (1985, 28). The colonists and travel writers, however, perceived the Khoekhoe and the "San" as two separate ethnic groups; this view is no longer accepted. As Khoekhoe and San people had already interacted to varying degrees over the course of their history, a great degree of assimilation had already occurred by the time of the early colonial phase (Elphick 1985, 10, 41; Newton-King 1999, 90). Since the 1970s, then, historians generally applied the term "Khoisan" to the indigenous hunter-gatherer and pastoral peoples of the southern Cape (Newton-King 1999, 249 n. 25). I maintain this usage here especially in the colonial context, but continue to use the terms Khoekhoe and hunter-gatherer where applicable.

The integration between Khoekhoe and hunter-gatherers originated, according to Elphick, in a "downward phase" of the ecological cycle when pastoralists experienced a loss of cattle. The resultant poverty led to physical and cultural integration between the hunter-gatherers and the Khoekhoe (1985, 41). For example, the pastoralists adopted the hunting bow of the hunter-gatherers and the latter became skilled in cattle and sheep herding. The ultimate result was not an equal mixture, however, as "Khoikhoi [or Khoekhoe] culture displaced aboriginal culture rather than the reverse" (Elphick 1985, 37).[16] Thus, the cycle of pastoralism followed by hunter-gathering meant that interactions between Khoekhoe and hunter-gatherers led to a greater or lesser degree of cultural assimilation, depending on the particular phase of the ecological cycle and circumstances of the people involved. While acknowledging this interaction between the Khoekhoe and hunter-gatherers, Newton-King disagrees with the aspect of Elphick's interpretation that assumes the superiority of pastoralism over hunter-gathering and also believes that his herding-hunting-herding cycle "underestimates the tenacity of those hunter-gatherers who chose to preserve their mode of life in the face of pressures from immigrant pastoralists" (1999, 28). The bands of "mountain people" (her term) who constantly attacked the trekboers in the Graaff-Reinet area certainly appeared to be fighting strongly for a mode of existence different to pastoralism (90).[17] Thus, while historians agree on the matter of Khoekhoe and hunter-gatherer interactions, the exact nature of these interactions during the precolonial and colonial phases remains a subject for debate.

Associations between Khoekhoe and Xhosa occurred mainly on the fringes of Xhosa territory, a large distance away from what would become Graaff-Reinet. The inhabitants of the westernmost Xhosa tribes (imiDange, amaGwali, amaMbalu, and amaGqunukhwebe) only became permanently settled in the area west of the Fish River after the 1760s (Newton-King 1999, 29). Earlier, trade between Khoekhoe and Xhosa took place, mostly in metal, livestock, and *dagga* (marijuana), the latter cultivated by the Xhosa. As the colonists pushed the Khoekhoe further toward Xhosa territory, some groups sought the protection of the Xhosa chiefdoms and became herders in their service. This practice already existed within precolonial Khoekhoe culture, so it did not cause undue disruption, except that the Xhosa people often kept cattle belonging to the Khoekhoe when they wished to leave (Giliomee 1989, 430). Many Khoekhoe who sought Xhosa protection from the dangers of the environment (then chiefly perceived to be lions and raids by hunter-robbers) became assimilated as Xhosa people due to the openness of Xhosa society (430, 434). Some Xhosa became Khoekhoe as well; for example, the Gonaqua people physically resembled Xhosa people but maintained important characteristics of Khoekhoe culture and language (Newton-King 1999, 33). Ultimately, however, the Xhosa Gqunukhwebe people, themselves partially of Khoekhoe origin, assimilated the Gonaqua (Giliomee 1989, 425; Newton-King 1999, 35). As colonial expansion increased, Khoisan servants and slaves often escaped the colonists to live with the Xhosa, particularly the Gqunukhwebe people.[18] Their hosts usually protected them and refused to hand them back to their former masters (Armstrong and Worden 1989, 160; Giliomee 1989, 437).[19]

On the topic of interactions between the Khoekhoe and the colonists, Giliomee argues that the Khoekhoe did not necessarily find the approaching trekboers from the west a particular threat (1989, 430).[20] As a tradition of clientship existed already among the Khoekhoe, some of these individuals "voluntarily transferred their allegiance from one set of cattle-keeping patrons [the Xhosa] to another" (Newton-King 1999, 38). This relationship was initially open for negotiation, and the Khoisan often moved to the colonial farm with their entire families as well as herds of livestock. Khoisan servants soon became skilled in horsemanship and marksmanship as they often accompanied their masters or went alone as the farmer's representative on commando raids against the "Bushmen" (Giliomee 1989, 430, 437).[21] In exchange for looking after the colonist's stock and being involved in these raids, the Khoisan servant acquired "payment" in the form of additional livestock for his herd.

Increasingly severe coercion and threats of physical violence gradually replaced the independent Khoekhoe's ability to negotiate labor terms and contracts as the trekboers primarily desired forced rather than free Khoisan labor (Newton-King 1999, 182). Even though the majority of trekboers could not afford slaves (Mostert 1992, 175), the colonists nevertheless "brought to the interior the cultural tradition of slavery and were gradually able to transform free indigenous peoples into unfree laborers" (Giliomee 1981, 93).[22] They accomplished this by ignoring the colonial government's policy that the Khoisan should be regarded as free people and therefore that labor should be voluntary, and by devising various means of indentured labor. In addition to the free Khoisan servants and the presence of slaves brought from the Cape, a bewildering complexity of other subordinate categories developed for this purpose, often subsumed under the term *inboekselen*. The last-mentioned category could include war captives, or *krijgsgevangenen* (mainly women and children captured during commando raids on hunter-gatherer groups), *Bastaard Hottentotten* (children of slave and Khoisan parents), and *huisboorlingen* (children of Khoisan servants born on colonial farms), all of whom were indentured to work for the farmer until coming of age (Newton King 1999, 117).[23] As Andries Stockenström Junior (*Landdrost* of the Graaff-Reinet area) disapproved of the huisboorlingen system, the only Khoisan people to be apprenticed in this way during his governance period were "at the request of their parents, or if they were without effective guardians" (Smith 1976, 207).[24] Nevertheless, in stark contrast to the integration of the Xhosa and Khoisan, the colonists' societal structure and religious beliefs of their superiority over the indigenous peoples rarely allowed for relationships on an equal footing, so Khoisan servants gradually became fixed in an unfree, underclass status position (Elphick and Giliomee 1989, 547; Giliomee 1989, 431). By 1797, the explorer John Barrow observed that no independent groups of Khoekhoe remained in the Graaff-Reinet region and very few remained as free individuals (Elphick and Malherbe 1989, 28).

The early frontier history of the Graaff-Reinet area, then, is dominated by interactions between the Khoekhoe, hunter-gatherers, and colonists and the consequences of European and Khoisan interactions with the Xhosa people further to the east. A little later on, the Xhosa and British would feature more fully in the area's history, but in order to mention the arrival and circumstances of these two groups, we need to describe the history of the settlement itself in more detail. For, by 1850, Graaff-Reinet was no longer a town on the volatile eastern frontier (Giliomee 1981, 100); it was a settled community within what would be known as the Cape Midlands. The geographical frontier may have moved farther away, but the social and psychological frontier of this settlement in the midst of the Karoo remained.

The Place

In 1797, eleven years after Graaff-Reinet's establishment, Barrow rather disparagingly described the settlement as merely "an assemblage of mud huts placed at some distance from each other, in two lines, forming a kind of street" (1801, 249). The lawlessness and lack of authority in the early district of Graaff-Reinet obviously affected the town's development, and little existed to entice people to live there or to treat it as a central meeting place.[25] A few European immigrants lived in the town and practiced various trades such as saddling and carpentry, but their stock of items was limited. Inhabitants relied instead on obtaining items from Jewish peddlers (*smousen*) or undertaking the long trip to Cape Town to obtain essential goods.[26] Beyond the settlement, the trekboers lived with their families and servants. When Hinrich Lichtenstein accompanied the commissioner-general, J. A. de Mist, to the area in 1804, little had changed. At this time, 3,206 white people, 4,924 Khoekhoe, and 964 slaves were registered in the district (Minnaar 1987, 9). By 1811, however, the town boasted forty-eight houses and twenty-two tradesmen, and by 1823, George Thompson estimated the number of houses at three hundred (now made from sun-baked brick, mud plaster, and indigenous yellowwood tree beams) and a population of eighteen hundred. Many townspeople supplemented their incomes by harvesting fruit from their properties (or *erven*) (11). The town thus had become a place where farmers could bring goods to market, and by the 1830s, they no longer needed to make the long trip to Cape Town for essential items (Giliomee 1981, 99).

The European population fluctuated somewhat during this period. British settlers arrived in South Africa in 1820, and although they mainly settled in the Albany region (the area surrounding Grahamstown) in the southeast, by 1826 some had ventured to the Graaff-Reinet region. These settlers eventually introduced wool farming to the area, a trade that led to the town's commercial boom in the 1850s. From 1835, many Dutch-speaking farmers (the descendants of trekboer families) left the town to participate in the Great Trek into the interior; British settlers moving in from the Grahamstown district filled the vacuum left by the departing trekkers. Soon, an opposition between the west enders (those Dutch/Afrikaans conservatives who remained) and the east enders (the more liberal-minded English speakers) arose in the town (Minnaar 1987, 14–15). Arguments between these groups affected decisions for and against proposed "progress" in its many guises, and this political conflict over many municipal decisions characterized much of local government activity for years to come. The eventual construction of a railway linking Graaff-Reinet and Port Elizabeth in 1879 for better wool transport did not bring a return of the economic boom experienced earlier in the century. Other lines continued to be constructed to the north, and Graaff-Reinet soon became a dead-end station. The Anglo-Boer War inadvertently added to the town's population as many farmers (both of Afrikaans and English origin) as well as their workers fled to the town for protection. Officials also forced Afrikaans people to leave their farms due to fears of their loyalty to the Boer commandos (Westby-Nunn 2004, 42). Today, the town still serves as a supply and market point for the region's farmers; it currently also derives much income from tourists and travelers en route to and from the coastal cities.

Like those on the frontier, relationships between people in early Graaff-Reinet history appeared much more fluid than the strictly segregated apartheid structures that would follow in due course. This does not mean, however, that conservative townspeople did not state their disapproval of these interactions.[27] In 1823, traveler John Montgomery enjoyed an evening of dancing with attractive "brunettes" (Khoisan women) at a merchant's wedding, but received a scolding for this the following day by a Dutch woman, who "was herself far browner than any of the brunettes at the marriage festival" (Smith 1976, 50). Town officials tended to assign places of residence according to criteria of acceptable status and position rather than race; for example, the governor granted a certain amount of smaller erven on the west end of the town to "industrious poor Coloureds" from 1837 (219). Another example is the sale of a portion of the land behind the Drostdy building to Captain Charles Lennox Stretch in 1855.[28] According to C. G. Henning, Stretch most likely divided up this land and sold it to coloured laborers although townspeople maintain that he sold it to freed slaves (1975, 191). Evidence also exists of coloured businessmen in the town; for example, Allen J. Coping, who died in 1926, ran a shop in Somerset Street (*Graaff-Reinet Advertiser,* September 20, 1926). Kroonvale residents to whom I spoke on this subject also remember visiting the stores of coloured shopkeepers in their childhood days (Bosch communication, February 2010). Generally, coloured servants lived in hire rooms (*huurkamers*) at the back of the large erven owned by white Graaff-Reinetters, and this situation persisted until the early twentieth century (Smith 1976, 219). Many of the approximately three hundred Sotho-speaking refugees who arrived in the 1820s also lived in Graaff-Reinet's huurkamers; they had fled the effects of the *Lifaqane* (pronounced *difiqane*) wars. When Xhosa-speaking people fled the widespread starvation that followed the cattle killing of 1857, they followed suit. Those who could not secure place in the huurkamers lived as squatters on the town's outskirts, or, by the 1850s, in a "location" outside the town, at the foot of Magazine Hill.[29]

Fierce debate took place between the proponents of liberal and conservative views on the rights of servants and laborers. The early Graaff-Reinet colonists had a reputation both for exhibiting rebellious tendencies and also for treating those in their service harshly. Mostert argues that "[John] Barrow gave Graaff-Reinet and its surroundings a reputation in Europe similar in its cruelty to that of the Middle Passage. . . . The shabby and impoverished village of Graaff-Reinet thus became the first point of focus for international outrage and agitation over race relations in South Africa" (1992, 278–79). Yet, with the arrival of a more stable government and the growing awareness of the atrocities of the global slave trade, the townspeople developed more recognition of the rights of slaves. This culminated in a meeting of Graaff-Reinet slaveowners in 1826, which adopted the proposal that all female children born of slave mothers should be free and added a suggestion from "a simple slave-holding Boer" that this should apply to boys as well (Stockenström 1887, I:259 ; Thom 1965, 63). Although Governor Richard Bourke stated soon afterward that "it is possible that the foundation for the final extinction of Slavery in this Colony may be laid in Graaff Reinet," nothing came of these resolutions after they were submitted to the colonial government (Theal 1905, XXVIII: 272). When the emancipation of slaves occurred eight years later, slaves in the Graaff-Reinet area numbered 2,809 (Armstrong and Worden 1989, 135).[30]

Despite these liberal expressions on the matter of slavery, early papers are full of concerns of the unsanitary and overcrowded condition of the huurkamers, more often due to fears about diseases spreading to the European population than real anxiety about the unacceptable living conditions for the town's servants (Smith 1976, 222). In fact, the establishment of the first "location" in 1858 was as a direct result of news of a smallpox outbreak in Cape Town and the Graaff-Reinet local government attempting to prevent a similar situation in the town (Smith 1976). Debates at municipal meetings and reports in local newspapers suggest an ongoing discussion about whether black and coloured people should live in the town or in the location; factors that influenced these (inconclusive) arguments included control of squatters, sanitation and health issues, crime, rental income, and the easy availability of servants for night work if they lived in the town (Smith 1976, 224–25). Many black and coloured people frequently wrote to the local newspapers with objections about their portrayal by white writers or petitioned the municipality with requests for lower rental. Sadly, the town council ignored these pleas for recognition and thus missed an opportunity for their authors' possible participation in local decision-making (238–39).

The forced removal of all coloured people to Kroonvale took place in 1966, with the implementation of the Group Areas Act (Minnaar 1987, 115).[31] There is no doubt that forced removals from Graaff-Reinet to Kroonvale resulted in a deeply traumatic experience for these residents, matched by those of black, Indian, and coloured people all over the country. Although the brute force exhibited by the physical tearing down of buildings did not occur in Graaff-Reinet as it did in Sophiatown (Johannesburg) and District Six (Cape Town), coloured community members saw their church and school buildings as well as their former residences purchased and gradually changed into museums, a library, art galleries, a theater, and of course, homes for white townspeople.[32] As the amount paid to churches by the municipality in exchange for their buildings seldom matched the cost of building new churches in Kroonvale, congregations accrued massive debt and struggled for years to pay the outstanding mortgages. Community members with whom I spoke seldom talked openly about the trauma of this period, so I had to be very sensitive to the hints contained in passing remarks. "You know Caroline Street [in town]?" June Bosch asked me. "Well, I grew up there. You must look at the size of the streets there—the coloured people often lived in the more narrow ones" (interview, August 19, 2004).[33] Then she changed the subject. Virginia Christoffels told me of an incident she remembered from her childhood. Soon after her family moved to Kroonvale, her sister attended the Parsonage Street Congregational Church School in the town as usual one morning as she came from a family of Congregationalists (children usually attended the school attached to the respective church). All schoolchildren living in Kroonvale were requested to put up their hands and thereafter sent to the Dutch Reformed Mission Church School, which had already moved to Kroonvale. Virginia vividly recalled how upset her father was that day at the fact that Congregational Church children had been sent to the incorrect school with no regard for their parents' wishes or their chosen church denomination (interview, October 28, 2005).[34]

Since the repeal of the apartheid segregation laws, coloured people live in the main town once more, but many continue to live on its outskirts, remaining in the spaces that apartheid policies constructed as marginal.[35] More recently, however, tourist and local media attention has focused on Kroonvale, due to the Acacia Street tradition (which celebrated its ten-year anniversary in the 2009/2010 festive season). Each year the residents decorate their houses and street with hundreds of lights to create a Christmas/New Year spectacle. Volunteers in the street request visitors to donate a small amount to charity; the residents give the amount collected to the local cancer organization. At first, June Bosch told me, curious townspeople from Graaff-Reinet would drive to Kroonvale to see the lights, but keep their windows tightly closed as they drove from one end of the street to the other. This is clearly reminiscent of the fear and suspicion associated with apartheid "nonwhite" areas. For the past few years, however, this pattern has been changing, much to the satisfaction of those running the display. "Marie, this year," June Bosch said to me in January 2010, "they parked their cars at the bottom of the street, got out with their children and *walked*" (communication, January 4, 2010). In countries that have not experienced segregation, this may seem insignificant at best and, at worst, indicative of an ongoing prejudice in society long after apartheid. Yet, this also shows that people feel safe to walk in the neighborhood, safe to walk outside the "main" area of town, and ultimately, that residents have begun to recognize Kroonvale as a part of the town itself. The Acacia Street tradition indicates a collective reclaiming of space for communities and a refiguring of that space during the post-apartheid era.

The Music

Unfortunately, very little information exists on the music of coloured people in Graaff-Reinet during the colonial era. In his nineteenth-century travel journal, George Thompson recounts an evening spent at a farm with the entertainment of a San woman on an instrument he calls the "raamakie" (1827/1962, 219). His description corresponds to that of a *ramkie* (a long-necked lute), an instrument originally borrowed from the Portuguese by the slaves at the Cape settlement during the eighteenth and nineteenth centuries (Kirby 1934/1953, 246–59). The Khoekhoe, San, and Bantu-speaking peoples constructed their own ramkies from calabashes and animal skin. In the twentieth century, the calabash was replaced with a tin can or oil can (Rycroft 1977, 241–42). It is very likely that travelers to the eastern Cape area took the ramkie with them, and much later, this instrument was substituted with the Western guitar. There is also evidence of choirs formed by the *agterryers* (coloured servants of white soldiers) during the Anglo-Boer War to entertain both themselves and their masters (Labuschagne 1999, 76–77).

Newspapers during the colonial period offer at best only snippets of information about the music of coloured people in Graaff-Reinet. For example, this excerpt describes a New Year's parade: "A few extremely innocent bands parad[ed] . . . the streets, not so much for what they could get as for the pleasure of having flags, drums, concertinas, whistles, etc, to add to their mirth" (*Graaff-Reinet Herald,* January 5, 1884). Even though this rather patronizing report does not provide information on the sound of the music, it suggests that the New Year's parade tradition, originally related to the history of slavery in this country and today still very prominent in Cape Town, also appeared on the rural eastern frontier.[36] The existing writing on the music of white people in Graaff-Reinet is also helpful in terms of providing background and context, but it seldom engages in any musical discussion beyond the social dances, military music, and amateur musical and theatrical societies that flourished in the town during the nineteenth and early twentieth centuries (Henning 1975, 1979).[37] Read carefully, however, these studies provide a sense of what European-based music coloured people probably encountered during the town's earlier years. While I provide a more detailed description of musical practices at the frontier in the following chapter, I note here that an important similarity between Xhosa, colonist, San, and Khoekhoe musicking involved collective singing. Missionaries in South Africa generally made use of indigenous peoples' existing culture of singing together in order to introduce Western hymn melodies and ways of life to their converts.

Converting the Khoisan, Calming the Colonists: Early Mission Churches in Graaff-Reinet

At the monthly missionary prayer meeting on 1 June [1801 in Graaff-Reinet], Khoisan in attendance sang psalm 134, which proclaimed (in the King James version), "Lift up your hands in the sanctuary and bless the Lord." Colonists in the congregation responded by singing verses 4 to 10 of psalm 74, beginning "thine enemies roar in the midst of thy congregation," and concluding with "O God, how long shall the adversary reproach? Shall the enemy blaspheme thy name for ever?" (Elbourne 2002, 133)

This prayer meeting illustrates the tension between Dutch colonists and the Khoisan people of the area in a particular historical moment. Apart from settler disapproval of Khoisan worship at the same shared venue,[38] the reason for this state of affairs centered mostly on Khoekhoe labor issues. In the early nineteenth century, settlers wanted permission to form commandos so that they could hunt down Khoekhoe people who had fled from colonial territory in order to escape harsh working conditions on the white farms and the threat of further violence from the white settlers. Under the protection of the Landdrost, Honoratus Maynier, three hundred Khoisan families lived as refugees in the town, with a Dutch settler camp on the outskirts. Maynier's insistence that white farmers treat the Khoisan better and his refusal to allow commando formations to punish them did not win him any popularity with the settlers.

The missionary who presided over the June 1801 prayer meeting, Johannes Theodorus van der Kemp, made a significant impression on the minds and imaginations of colonial Graaff-Reinet residents. Van der Kemp (1747–1811), a Dutch missionary affiliated with the London Missionary Society (LMS), disembarked in Cape Town in March 1799, along with three other LMS representatives. He and the British missionary John Edmond arrived in Graaff-Reinet on May 14, 1801, during a short-lived period of respite in the middle of the Third Frontier War (1799–1803).[39] On arrival, van der Kemp shared the preaching duties at the Dutch Reformed Church with another Dutch missionary sent by the LMS, A. A. van der Lingen.[40]

Van der Kemp shared Maynier's very liberal attitude of the time, which is where he also lost favor with the settlers and, as the story goes, even dodged a few settler bullets when violence erupted in the town shortly after his arrival. The missionary made things worse when he explained the attacks on white settlers as a punishment from God because of their harsh treatment of the Khoisan people. To add insult to injury, he also refused the position of minister of the town's Dutch Reformed Church because it would draw him away from his work among the "heathen" Khoekhoe, and he would not baptize settler children because he believed they had not shown sufficient remorse for their sins.[41] His work with the Khoisan prospered, however, probably due to his connections with indigenous converts such as Cupido Kakkerlak, the slave woman Putwatier (known in Graaff-Reinet as Suzanna), and the Khoisan captain known as Stuurman.[42]

Even though van der Kemp moved his services for the Khoisan from the town church to his house shortly after the June 1801 "prayer" meeting, this did not change the colonists' dislike of his overall attitude toward the equal rights of Khoisan people and the baptism of colonists' children. On February 20, 1802, less than a year after his arrival, van der Kemp and James Read (a British missionary also affiliated with the LMS) left Graaff-Reinet with about 300 of the 463 Khoisan people living in the town at the time. After many further trials, tribulations, departures, and arrivals of the Khoisan traveling with them, van der Kemp established the Bethelsdorp mission station (Elbourne 2002, 130–39).

Although the historical record is somewhat sketchy about religious activities after van der Kemp's departure from Graaff-Reinet, it is fair to say that Christian services among the Khoisan were probably disrupted for a few years thereafter, due to the continuation and aftermath of the Third Frontier War. Town elders, concerned about a lack of religious stability, established the Graaff-Reinetsche Zendelings Genootschap (Graaff-Reinet Missionary Organization) on August 1, 1819. In 1821, the Landdrost at the time, Andries Stockenström Junior, donated the money for six windows for the newly built church known as the *Oefeningshuis*, specifically for coloured people.[43] The name Oefeningshuis (or, practicing house) referred to the practice of religion without using the word "church." Thus, it disguised the fact that this building (literally across the street from the main Dutch Reformed Church building in the town) was used for church services. This avoided overt violation of a colonial law of the time, which stated that church buildings had to be at least a three-day horse ride apart (Basson communication, July 4, 2006; Minnaar 1987, 92). The Oefeningshuis congregation became affiliated with the newly formed Dutch Reformed Mission Church (DRMC) in 1881, and it held services continually in this building until 1964, when the church moved to its new building in Du Plessis Street, Kroonvale. In 1994, this church became known as the Uniting Reformed Church (URC).

Herbert Daniel Liebenberg, who wrote a history of the Parsonage Street Congregational Church (PSCC) for the occasion of its 180th anniversary celebration, mentions the arrival and departure of various ministers in the first half of the nineteenth century (n.d.). He states that the PSCC only consecrated its first church building in 1850.[44] This church congregation, known as Groot Londen (Big London) from its London Missionary Society origins, also sustained a long period of services in the town and consecrated a new church building in Kroonvale in 1972.

The East Street Congregational Church (ESCC) is formed from a group of Klein Londen (Small London) or Middle Street Basotho Mission Church members who decided to break away and form a new congregation due to language issues (some members spoke only Afrikaans and others, only Sotho) (Minnaar 1987, 96).[45] The new congregation then briefly joined the PSCC, but a divisive barrier arose due to the implied superiority of the "number one" church (PSCC) versus the "number two" church (ESCC). In 1938, the ESCC began holding separate services in an old wool shed in East Street, Cypress Grove (a Graaff-Reinet suburb). In 1964, like the DRMC and PSCC, the ESCC also moved to Kroonvale. Rev. B. B. Botha, minister of the ESCC, made a specific request to the municipality that the street next to the newly built church building in Kroonvale also be named East Street (Barendse interview, November 11, 2004; West 1964).

These three churches, where my fieldwork took place, survived both the chaos and fusion of frontier encounters; the historical and contextual information described above forms the background to their origins in Graaff-

Reinet. Congregations continued to gather for services of worship throughout the changing economic fortunes of nineteenth-century Graaff-Reinet and, more recently, the trauma of apartheid segregation and its aftermath. Despite the severe prejudice endured by the coloured people of this town and their ancestors, a mostly unbroken tradition of religious worship exists in this community, spanning a period of two hundred years. Sacred song constituted a vital part of the official services and gatherings of the congregations throughout this period.

3

Hidden Transcripts

How Hymns Reveal History

In July 2004, I had been in the area to conduct fieldwork for less than a week and, very predictably, had made little progress. I would soon discover the stock response to my eager questions on church music in Kroonvale. "Don't you rather want to study music in Umasizakhe instead?" people asked. "They [the Xhosa people] sing so nicely there."[1] On July 14, I arrived for an interview with Dominee Gawie Basson, the minister of the Uniting Reformed Church. When I asked my first question about the church music, his response was that I should rather not ask this, as he did not know anything about it. After this initial statement, however, he went over to the huge bookshelf along one wall of the room, took down some old hymnbooks, and began talking very animatedly (and knowledgeably) about their history. He confirmed that the hymns sung in Kroonvale were based on European hymns and then said something that would become a significant influence in my future research. "When I first arrived in Graaff-Reinet, a few congregation members approached me to discuss a musical matter," he said. "They informed me that they did not sing Psalm 100 ("Rejoice Earth, Rejoice") to the official Dutch Reformed Church melody. Some congregation members can sing this hymn to six different tunes." Soon afterward, Dominee Basson kindly granted me permission to attend services at his church, and I heard one of these melody versions for myself. For the rest of my fieldwork period, I endeavored to record as many alternative melodies for hymn texts as possible.

The seemingly ordinary, European-influenced hymns performed in the three

Kroonvale churches clearly offered a wealth of interpretive possibilities. While the use of texts usually conformed very closely to the official Congregational or Uniting Reformed Church hymnbooks, the style and sound of the music contained subtle auditory clues to the history and tradition of sacred song in this community. My fieldwork research on the church hymns and koortjies (choruses) shows that this musical tradition dates back more than two centuries, formally beginning soon after the arrival of missionaries in the area, but also originating prior to this in the frontier meeting place between disparate cultures and the exposure of indigenous peoples to Christianity.

This chapter examines how the musical performance of coloured community members in Kroonvale reveals the history of encounters between various peoples in this region and how these origins combine to form the particular sound of congregational singing in this community. I assert that the music is a combination of disparate sources, including Khoisan and Xhosa indigenous practices, mission Christianity, and British and Dutch colonial influences. Using James Scott's theory of "hidden transcripts," I argue that the oral/aural history of church music in this region is embedded and archived in its sound. By exploring this auditory history as an act of musical archiving, I emphasize the necessity of listening carefully to the sonic manifestations of history.

Hiding Histories in Sound

Scott defines the term "hidden transcript" as "a critique of power spoken behind the back of the dominant" (1990, xii). In other words, the "hidden transcript" is the "discourse that takes place 'offstage,' beyond direct observation by powerholders. The hidden transcript is thus derivative in the sense that it consists of those offstage speeches, gestures, and practices that confirm, contradict, or inflect what appears in the public transcript." Scott defines the latter term as "a way of describing the open interaction between subordinates and those who dominate" (2, 4–5). Examples of genres where the hidden transcript can be located include "rumors, gossip, folktales, songs, gestures, [and] jokes" (xiii). He applies his theory to various historical and contemporary situations of resistance to political power and dominance. While I analyze the possibilities of more recent expressions of anti-apartheid sentiment within this community later in Chapter 4, I wish to examine here the more subtle historical transcripts embedded in sacred song performance and revealed through careful listening.

My approach necessitates that I expand Scott's theory in two ways. First, I assert that the hidden transcript does not necessarily always happen "offstage" and away from the dominant group's watchful gaze. Scott suggests something similar to this idea when he states that hidden transcripts can appear as a "veiled discourse of dignity and self-assertion within the public transcript" and cites folktales and the carnival ritual among other examples (137–38).[2] The key element of these examples is that they are performed, both for the immediate community and also for any powerholder who happens to be present, a characteristic also found in the ritualized performance of weekly church services. Although the latter can be interpreted as private events when seen in relation to state politics,[3] they are also public in the sense that large numbers of community members attend and all guests (regardless of religious or political affiliations) are welcome. Thus, I interpret the "public" transcript here to be a formalized religious ritual consisting of predetermined liturgy, sermon, prayers, and sacred song performed for all those present.

Second, while Scott only briefly mentions the ability of song within oral tradition to act as a resistance medium (160–62), I believe that this preservation of oral history in Kroonvale forms part of a hidden transcript that disrupts and subverts dominant ideas about coloured people. I thus focus particularly here on listening very closely to the sonic manifestations of the rich history that belongs to this community. The Kroonvale religious music I describe below contains powerful statements about the various encounters between historical actors in this region. Far from being a people and music without history, identity, and culture (a designation implied and reflected by the official apartheid record), Kroonvale congregation members have ensured the survival of their past by archiving this knowledge within a community musical tradition. While not an overtly political statement, I nevertheless interpret the preservation of aspects of community history in seemingly innocuous church music as a way of countering the ethnic stereotyping experienced by this community.

The understanding of archiving mentioned above borrows from Carol Muller's work, which expands the traditional notion of the archive as a building that houses (mainly written) items (2002, 409). Muller draws on Jacques Derrida's interpretation, namely, "There is no archive without a place of consignation, without a technique of repetition, and without a certain exteriority" (1995, 11; quoted in Muller 2002, 409). In relation to music and with reference to Muller's ideas, I understand the "place of consignation" as the body and mind of an individual, the "technique of repetition" as a performance of a particular composition, and the "exteriority" as the context/place of performance. Muller suggests that "we begin to consider certain kinds of music composition as archival practice: as constituting valued sites for the deposit and retrieval of historical styles and practices in both literate and pre-literate contexts" (2002, 410). In order to substantiate her argument, Muller draws on the work of three composers, namely, Isaiah Shembe, Nathoya Mbatha, and David Fanshawe. The composer exhibiting the most similarities with my Kroonvale research findings, Isaiah Shembe, established the Nazarite religion in what is now known as the KwaZulu-Natal Province in the early twentieth century. As advancing colonial and western influences began to eradicate traditional Zulu culture, Shembe experienced a series of dreams and visions in which ancestral spirits "gave" him the melodies of songs that would become the Nazarite hymn repertory. Shembe archived Africanness in this repertory through preservation of the following aspects. First, he acknowledged the Zulu tradition of ancestors with the visionary origins of the songs; second, he imbued the practice of "rhythm" with a fundamental importance for the performance of this repertory; third, the texts reflect a certain period in the history of the Zulu people and thus preserve contemporary commentary on this era; and fourth, Shembe archived the notion of "reciprocal gift-giving" through these hymns, which via the ancestors, Shembe, and congregation members became internalized and preserved to "give" to future generations (413–17).

Muller's insights, together with their application to Shembe, provide a framework for examining the act of archiving music within an oral history context. The Kroonvale religious musical context, however, suggests that while Shembe archived a deep sense of Africanness firmly within the Nazarite hymn repertory, the Kroonvale community archived the sonic result of encounters between groups in this area. This, therefore, is an act of preserving an "Africanness" of a slightly different kind, a plural "(South) Africanness" understood in the sense of the disparate groups of people living on the eastern Cape frontier at the time. What resulted is a musical repertory that retains these hints of disparate cultures but, over time, became something else. Unique and particular to this community, this style coalesced to form the sound of coloured (Reformed) church music in Kroonvale.[4] Additionally, the fact that this repertory (mainly hymns of European origin) had already been composed by others suggests that musical style as well as musical composition can be understood as a type of archival practice. The existence of this particular performance culture suggests that coloured people developed their own responses to the special circumstances of their presence in South Africa; the way that people sing this sacred repertory holds the clues to these responses and the community's history. I believe that the sound of coloured sacred song is unmistakable and that the particular processes of archiving historical information within the hidden transcripts of hymn singing produced a unique musical tradition in this context.

Contemporary Church Music in Kroonvale

Due to their missionary origins and close proximity in the town, the early history of these three churches is intertwined. Even the two missionary societies that originally established the DRMC and the PSCC congregations could not initially be easily distinguished as both the LMS and Graaff-Reinetsche Zendelings Genootschap held services in Dutch. As a physical reminder of this shared history, the PSCC is only a few yards up the road from the URC (the former DRMC) in Kroonvale, with the ESCC also in sight. The original PSCC and DRMC buildings in Graaff-Reinet are also within walking distance of each other.

These churches are firmly rooted in the Reformed tradition, specifically that branch of Protestant theology influenced primarily by John Calvin. In modern usage, the word "Reformed" is reserved for the churches of Calvinist background as opposed to the Anglican and Lutheran Protestant denominations. One of the main features of the Reformed doctrine is that the Bible is seen as the source of authority instead of a church bishop or representative of the church hierarchy. According to Jonathan Gerstner, "All religious teachings and all practices must be either directly scriptural or derived from scriptural principles" (1997, 16).[5] This emphasis is seen in the physical layout of Reformed church buildings, as the central focal point is the pulpit, and not the altar as in Catholic and Anglican (Episcopal) churches. The sermon constitutes the main part of a Reformed church service, with music at the beginning and end. The format of a typical URC service is as follows (Basson interview, August 11, 2004):

1. Introit (opening hymn)
2. Welcome and announcements
3. Votum (introduction)
4. The greeting of the congregation with a blessing (*seëngroet*)
5. Hymn or Psalm of praise
6. Recitation of a short version of the Ten Commandments
7. Hymn of confession (*sonde belydenis*)
8. Bible reading to show that congregation has been pardoned (*vryspraak*)
9. Confession of faith (Apostolic creed)
10. Announcement of Scripture reading
11. Short prayer
12. Sermon
13. Prayer
14. Musical item performed by church choir

15. (Communion)
16. Collection/Offering (takes place to the accompaniment of a hymn)
17. Prayer of blessing for offering
18. Final hymn
19. Final blessing

This format is generally followed in most Reformed churches even though their theological bases and administrative infrastructures differ.[6] In 2004 and 2005, approximately 1,400 people belonged to the URC, although usually between 150 and 200 people attended the services each week. A similar number of people were present at PSCC and ESCC services, but official member figures at these churches were approximately 650 and 900, respectively. Attendance figures differed according to the nature of the service (more people attended communion or *nagmaal* services, for example) as well as the rhythm of the school year. During school holidays, children's Sunday School did not take place and fewer people went to church. A typical service at these churches featured the minister (or sometimes, in the case of the URC, a lay preacher) at the pulpit with the church council members at the front left, facing the congregation.[7] Members of the service organizations within the congregation (for example, Sunday School, youth, and men's and women's societies) sat together toward the front of the church, with family units and older teenagers sitting toward the back. After the first hymn, the church secretary (a member of the council) usually made important announcements before the minister continued with the service.

Although many Kroonvale residents remained loyal to one church for most of their lives, the shared missionary origins, Reformed denominational tradition, and language (Afrikaans) of the churches made it possible for many churchgoers to attend services other than those of their chosen denominations. Family members moved between churches for a variety of reasons, for example, easier transport, marriage to a member of another denomination,[8] special occasions, and church celebrations. They attended these events both according to community links and loyalties and to denomination choice. This meant that the repertory of all three churches assumed similar musical styles and melodies and developed into a local religious musical culture (see Figure 3.1).

Although they made use of different hymnbooks, the Congregational churches and the URC in Kroonvale followed a similar pattern of musical practices within worship services. The music comprised three main types, namely, hymns or *gesange* (PURL 3.1), contemporary worship choruses or koortjies (PURL 3.2), and pieces for performance by the church choir. Usu-

Figure 3.1   Sunday morning service at the PSCC. Photograph by author.

ally, church members sang gesange and koortjies in Afrikaans, although the choirs often sang in English. The PSCC congregation also sang in English for some of the Congregational Church hymns, as the denomination's origins in the London Missionary Society meant that one of their hymnbooks used to be *Sacred Songs and Solos* compiled by Ira Sankey.[9] Sankey hymns continued to be great favorites in the PSCC, even though *Sacred Songs and Solos* was replaced by the newer hymnbook, *Sing Hosanna!* in 1975 (Bezuidenhoudt interview, November 26, 2004). The ESCC also used *Sing Hosanna!* as its official hymnbook. The URC utilized the fourth edition of a book called *Nuwe Sionsgesange.* Before this, the denomination used earlier editions of this book titled *Sionsgesange.* Although originally compiled to standardize the hymn singing (a variety of hymnbooks were in use before this time), it is significant that this book, printed especially for the use of coloured members of the DRMC, appeared one year before the Afrikaner National Party came into power in 1948.[10] Apartheid's infamous policy of "separate development" for all ethnic groups even applied to the books used for religious worship.

In 2004–2005, all three churches had an organist, but the most regular organ playing took place in the PSCC. The organ presence influenced the singing style in this church as the congregation sang very regular hymn lines and followed the organist's lead. In contrast, the ESCC minister, Rev. Leon

Barendse, sometimes requested the organist, Marlene Jasson, not to play at all, as he preferred to let the congregation members express themselves freely (Barendse interview, November 11, 2004). The URC congregation sang confidently with or without organ accompaniment, as it had strong *voorsingers* (lead singers) who guided the hymn singing on a regular basis. Sometimes the organist performed on an upright piano for special occasions that included choir performances. In these cases, the church's organist played the piano to accompany the choir. On two different occasions I saw guitar and keyboards used, the first for a confirmation service when the newly accepted young church members sang a contemporary worship song accompanied by one of the pre-programmed rhythmic ostinatos available on the keyboard. A guitarist led the singing. The second occasion, a Christmas carol service, incorporated the use of saxophone, keyboard, and pre-programmed drumbeats. Both of these events took place at the URC (November 18 and December 12, 2004).[11]

In general the minister presiding over the service announced the hymns or requested that the congregation sing a koortjie. After this, the congregation members stood up, found the relevant hymn number in their books, and then waited for the lead singer or organist to begin before joining in.[12] Some congregation members of all three churches clapped or (more commonly) slapped their Bibles, hymnbooks, or special leather cushions held in front of the singer in time to the music.[13] These cushions had elastic sewn across the middle on one side so that a person's left hand could be held in position while the church member used his/her right hand to slap the other side of the cushion (see Figure 3.2). The percussive sounds provided a solid rhythmic base for the singing. Some churchgoers stepped from side to side or swayed in time to the music, while others remained completely still.

Khoisan Origins

Although first published in 1934, Percival Kirby's study is still one of the most detailed descriptions of San and Khoekhoe music. He states that the music is based on a pentatonic scale and includes both solo and collective singing. (Deidre Hansen describes San singing style as one containing yodeling and "the absence of actual words" [1996, 297]). For both groups, dancing is very important, and all-night ceremonies in times of a new or full moon are also common. The Khoekhoe adopted the hunting bow of the San as a musical instrument, which in turn was adapted by the San as well. Khoekhoe musical bows are known variously as /gabus and /kha:s and the San name for their musical bow is /khou.[14] The Khoekhoe also played reed flutes in harmony, a practice later adopted by the South African Tswana people.[15] Similarly, the

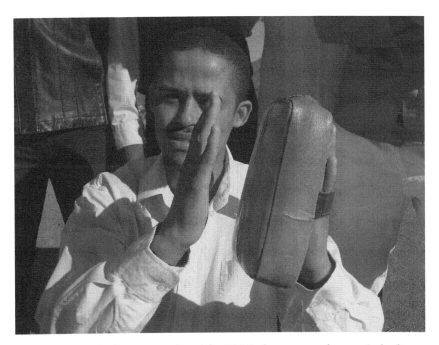

Figure 3.2   *Mitch Plaatjies, member of the ESCC, demonstrates the use of a leather cushion to produce additional percussive sounds. Photograph by author.*

Khoekhoe mouth bow, known as the *gorá*, now survives particularly among the Sotho people as their national instrument and is called the *lesiba*. San percussion instruments include ankle rattles and antelope skin stretched over a hole in the sand that rendered a percussive sound when danced on. The Khoekhoe made a type of drum (/*khais*) originally from Cape slave origin. A clay pot served as the base of the drum with an animal skin stretched over it. The Khoekhoe played this instrument by beating it with their hands (and not with a stick as in Cape slave communities) (Kirby 1935/1953, 12–13, 135, 142, 171–92, 211–12; Kirby 1986, 2:275–82; Levine 2005, 228–53).[16]

The question of how much Khoisan culture (including musical practices) survives in the Kroonvale community is a difficult one to answer. Alan Barnard suggests that while there are identifiable Khoekhoe links in the contemporary communities of the Rehoboth "Basters" in Namibia, the Griquas, and the coloured people of the northwestern Cape, the remaining aspects of coloured heritage, for example, Dutch, Indonesian, and African, do not demonstrate such clear links to these indigenous South African ancestors (1992, 198).[17] For instance, the sound of the music I heard during my research suggested stronger connections with Xhosa music and the hymnody of missionary Christianity. This does not mean that the Khoisan heritage is entirely absent, however. Elizabeth Elbourne and Robert Ross, for example, describe the transition of Khoekhoe rituals to Christian practices as follows: "Sacred dancing was central to worship, the Khoikhoi dancing at night, especially before a full moon, to the accompaniment of sacred songs. Christian converts abandoned dancing at night, and refused to sing Khoikhoi songs, but often substituted all-night religious meetings and Christian hymns" (1997, 33). Thus, Khoisan converts absorbed the tradition of all-night singing gatherings into their Christian practices. Gerhard Kubik's study of the San influence on the Bantu-speaking peoples of southern Africa furnishes another example of possible Khoisan influence. He suggests that the musical practices of the San can be traced in Xhosa music (1988, 42; see also Olivier and Fürniss 1997). The connections with Xhosa music that I noticed in Kroonvale religious music could therefore already contain San musical features.

Suggestions of Slavery

Even though the majority of the slave population lived in Cape Town and its surrounding arable farming districts (Armstrong and Worden 1989, 134), this discussion would be incomplete without a consideration of the slaves' possible influence on church music in Kroonvale. In the Graaff-Reinet region, slaves, like the Khoisan, worked as shepherds and herders for farmers' livestock or provided domestic help in the kitchens of colonial farmhouses.[18] In addition to their lower numbers in the eastern Cape, slaves' work and living circumstances made it difficult for them to develop a culture of their own.[19] Using Cape Town as a case study, Kerry Ward and Nigel Worden argue that these circumstances as well as the lack of written records about the lives, memories, and experiences of former slaves contribute to an absence (and in some cases, a "forgetting") of slave history and origins (1998, 204, 207).[20]

I believe that this situation is similar in Graaff-Reinet, especially since the practice of slavery existed there over a much shorter period of time (c. 1760–1834) than at the Cape.[21] One important contrasting feature in the Graaff-Reinet area, however, is the strong influence of colonists' Christian beliefs on the slave population as opposed to the predominance of the Muslim religion among Cape slaves.[22] Most colonists did not baptize their slaves because baptized slaves were entitled to their freedom and could not be sold (Elphick and Shell 1989, 191). Despite this reluctance to allow their slaves formal participation in the Christian religion, many colonists insisted on their slaves' and servants' attendance at prayer meetings. For example, in 1812, traveler William Burchell mentioned a gathering of all the members of a colonial household as well as slaves and "Hottentot" servants, for a New Testament Bible reading and explanation (1822/1953, 2:123–24).[23] In addition, we know that Andrew Murray (1794–1866), minister of the (white) Graaff-Reinet Dutch Reformed Church, requested slaves and servants to be present whenever he conducted worship services at outlying farms (Henning 1975, 95).[24] Slaves formed a significant proportion of the early DRMC school classes, with an 1820 report mentioning attendance of "52 slaves and 90 Khoi" (Minnaar 1987, 111). As those attending school lessons would most likely be expected to attend church services, this suggests that slaves joined the converted Khoisan people in the DRMC congregation. The most convincing evidence for the presence of slaves and, later on, former slaves, in the nineteenth-century services is that the DRMC church records report a "teameeting" event held annually on December 1 to celebrate the anniversary of the emancipation of the slaves.[25] The records mention this every year since 1884, and the tradition persisted until the early 1950s, when apartheid's hold tightened and, as Dominee Basson told me, the congregation "could not celebrate their freedom anymore" (communication, October 4, 2005).[26] Unfortunately, this information, while providing important context, does little to assist us in locating evidence of the slaves' legacy on the Kroonvale sacred singing tradition. We can only assume that as slaves and their descendants joined these mission congregations, they adopted the missionary and Khoisan influences they experienced while participating in the church services.[27]

Missionary and Colonial Origins: Religious Music on the Frontier

There is a strong musical legacy of missionary and colonial influence on coloured people's church music in Graaff-Reinet. This comprised psalms, hymns, Afrikaans *liederwysies*, and the tradition of the voorsinger, or lead singer. Initially, psalms were the only type of religious music to be sung in colonial South Africa. As Barry Smith reports:

> By 1655, when evening prayers were said at the Cape fort, they were no doubt accompanied by two or three verses of psalms sung from the 1566 Psalter of Petrus Dathenus, the hymnal of the Reformed churches of the Netherlands, a translation of the French Genevan Psalter of 1562. A later version of these psalms, published in 1775, became the official hymn book in the Dutch Reformed Church in South Africa, and stayed in use for more than 150 years. (1997, 316)

Books of this nature no doubt accompanied trekboers on their journey away from the Cape, and psalms also comprised the main religious music sung on the frontier. The nineteenth-century revivalist trend in the United States and the United Kingdom, however, supplemented psalm singing in South Africa with two volumes of devotional songs set to secular tunes. By the 1860s, a thin volume called *De Kinderharp* containing Dutch translations of American and English sacred songs circulated, and *Hallelujah!* (1883), a volume printed in Holland, followed thereafter.[28] As we know that at least some servants attended colonist family prayer services, there is no doubt about coloured people's exposure to the psalms and revivalist tunes of the time.[29]

Many of these tunes also appeared in the hymnbooks used by the coloured mission congregations. These groups had their own book, published in the mid-nineteenth century by the Rhenish Missionary Society as *Geestelijke gezangen ten gebruike van Evangelische gemeenten uit de heidenen in Zuid-Afrika* (Spiritual songs for use by the Evangelical congregations formed from the heathen in South Africa), but it is unclear whether the early coloured Graaff-Reinet congregations used this book. We do know, however, that the DRMC, the PSCC, and the ESCC used the Afrikaans edition of a book containing older psalm melodies, German and Dutch tunes, titled *Evangeliese gesange*. The Dutch Reformed Mission Church records only mention this book in 1934, although it is likely that the congregation used the earlier Dutch edition (known as *Evangelische gezangboek*) before this time (DRMC records, September 12, 1934).[30]

Afrikaans liederwysies constitute another important source of early hymn melodies in both settler and most likely in mission congregations of the region. Liederwysies are substitute melodies for official hymn melodies. These could be printed melodies of other psalm or hymn tunes used instead of the official printed melody for that specific text, or melodies from oral sources. Willem van Warmelo explains the origins of the latter type as follows:

> The liederwysie gradually came into being: from the exultant singing of a half-forgotten Psalm melody, from the folk tune that continued to be remembered, an own improvisation, or also from the memory of a melody from this cousin or that neighbor, who in turn heard it from another cousin or neighbor. Many liederwysies are products of contamination, assembled from hackneyed [melodic sources] and developed in the imagination of fellow sufferers [a reference to the hardships of the Afrikaner Great Trek], so that the original melody sometimes cannot be traced back and it is difficult to research what first was and what developed later. (1958, 18)[31]

Some of the Afrikaner settlers wrote these melodies in homemade manuscript books, sewn together with the same twine used to stitch boots (Olivier communication, June 1, 2006). During his travels, John Campbell mentioned that his host one evening, a Mr. Roos from the Caledon area, "produced a small manuscript book of hymns, which the family seemed to prize as more precious than gold. They formed a circle, and sung three or four hymns without intermission" (1815, 22; quoted in van Warmelo 1958, 16). Van Warmelo categorized the liederwysies he researched into those based on psalm melodies, those based on secular songs, and those that could not be traced back to any preexisting melodies. Gawie Cillié also wrote a book on the subject and grouped his findings according to melodies used for various psalms and hymns from popular nineteenth-century hymnbooks and then those melodies for which he could not trace the origins. In contrast to van Warmelo's earlier view that liederwysies only originated in isolated rural areas, Cillié stated that they could be located in cities and towns as well (1993, 3). Thus, together with the *Evangelische gezangboek* and other nineteenth-century hymnbooks, liederwysies and older psalm melodies constituted the main source of melodic material used for the singing of hymns.

In Kroonvale, I believe that the heritage of liederwysies contributed to the use of "unofficial" hymn melodies for church hymns. For example, during my fieldwork, I recorded four different versions of "Juig aarde, juig" of which only one was sung to the official melody (see Figures 3.3–3.6; PURLs 3.3–3.6).[32]

Figure 3.3 uses the official melody, titled "Old Hundredth," which is notated in both the keyboard editions of the URC and Congregational Church hymnbooks.[33] The English editor, Ravenscroft, named this melody as such in 1621 because it was inseparable from the text of the 100th Psalm (Routley 1983, 58). Figures 3.4 and 3.5 are not from the official hymnbooks, but each seems to show a vestige of connection to the official melody. The first phrase of Figure 3.3 ends on the mediant, thereby highlighting it.[34] Similarly, the melody of Figure 3.4 also tends to focus on the mediant. In addition, the first and second phrases of both examples show a parallel relationship as the second phrase contains the same melodic idea in a sequence pattern. Figure 3.5, however, is more bound on the tonic and emphasizes the melodic pattern of the tonic-leading note-tonic; this sets it apart from the official tune. Additionally, its opening use of the lower dominant note followed by the tonic and mediant suggests liederwysie origins, as Willem van Warmelo states that this is a common shape used to begin this type of melody (1958, 24).[35] Yet, the third phrase of Figure 3.5 also highlights the mediant, a characteristic of the official tune's opening phrase. Figure 3.6 is the melody of "Senzeni na," a well-known anti-apartheid resistance song (see Chapter 4). It features a similar tonic-leading note-tonic movement to Figure 3.5 as well as the use of a sequence relationship in the first two phrases, corresponding to Figures 3.3 and 3.4. From these examples, it appears likely that the general shapes of official hymn melodies, along with the tradition of

Figure 3.3 *"Juig al wat leef" (Rejoice All Who Live), from congregational singing at the PSCC, February 13, 2005. (Melody: "Old Hundredth," Afrikaans text by J. D. du Toit.) Transcription by author.*

Figure 3.4 *"Juig al wat leef," from congregational singing at the ESCC, July 17, 2005. Transcription by author.*

Figure 3.5 *"Juig aarde, juig" (Rejoice Earth, Rejoice), from congregational singing at the URC, August 15, 2004. (Afrikaans text by E. Hartwig.) Transcription by author.*

Figure 3.6 *"Juig al wat leef," from congregational singing at the combined Congregational Church broederband service, ESCC, February 17, 2005. Transcription by author.*

liederwysies and music from contemporary oral sources, had an impact on the formation of unofficial tunes. I also believe, however, that the format of the hymnbooks provided opportunities to introduce unofficial melodies. Both official hymnbooks for the Congregational churches and the URC have a chorale book edition, which is a larger book containing all the hymn melodies in staff notation. While church organists usually played from these editions, congregation members sang from books containing the hymn texts only and thus were never obliged to follow the official melody.[36]

Another colonial settler tradition is that of the voorsinger (lead singer), who usually began the hymns and led the congregation through strong, confident singing. Cillié explains that the role of the voorsinger in the Afrikaans religious tradition was originally linked to the role of the teacher, but later on referred to someone with a strong voice who knew his hymnbook very well (1983, 4). This definition aptly describes the voorsingers I heard during my fieldwork. Willem Kayster, a retired teacher and one of the voorsingers in the URC, mentioned to me in an interview that he knew more than three hundred hymn melodies from memory (August 18, 2004). I also heard many women voorsingers during my fieldwork experiences. Dominee Basson told me that this was a more recent trend, and Willem Kayster commented astutely that sometimes if a woman started the singing, the congregation members found her statement of the soprano melody easier to recognize as a familiar hymn tune (Basson interview, August 4, 2004; Kayster interview, July 4, 2006). As a voorsinger merely needed a strong confident voice, however, the congregation usually followed regardless of whether the singer was male or female.

Xhosa Origins

While hymn singing has a very long history in this religious community with the combination of missionary and colonial influences I've discussed, the singing of koortjies (according to community members) is a far more recent phenomenon that began in the later decades of the twentieth century. Rev. Jacobus Bezuidenhoudt mentioned that congregations in Cape Town sing koortjies to tunes from the American gospel book, *Loving Praise,* whereas Graaff-Reinet koortjies differ as they are in Afrikaans (interview, December 8, 2004). June Bosch remembered singing English choruses from earlier hymnbooks at the PSCC in the 1950s and suggested that these choruses originated in schools and Sunday Schools, before moving into official church services where people translated the verses into Afrikaans.[37] While it is likely that some of the lyrics originated from American books as well as from lines of English hymns and other sacred songs, the singing style of koortjies in

Kroonvale, however, is very similar to this description by David Dargie of the songs of Xhosa people's mission congregations:

> Many songs are not hymns arranged in verses but choruses of fre-
> quently repeated single-line texts or simple verses more closely related
> to the cyclic songs of African music than to the stylized structures of
> Western hymns. Such songs, called "amakorasi" or choruses, are sung
> with beating of hymn-books (and also, the beating of cushions held in
> the hand), with clapping and some body movement. (1997, 325)

Koortjies in Kroonvale demonstrate these characteristics mentioned by Dargie, namely, repeated lyrics in the texts, percussive elements, and African
call-and-response and cyclic forms (see Figure 3.7; PURL 3.7).[38]

Usually, congregations sang exactly the same text (or a few verses in Afrikaans and then a translation of the original lyrics into English or Xhosa), repeated
this for a few cycles, and then sang one final cycle, the latter often accompanied
by a halt in percussion before the koortjie ended. Congregation members never
sang these pieces for very long in formal church services and limited the number
of cycles to four or five repetitions. In contrast, many more repetitions of koortjie
verses took place during the period of time before the minister entered the
church in order to begin leading the Sunday worship service.

Another influence on this music (which most likely reached the Kroonvale
churches through interactions with Xhosa people) is the tradition of the African
Independent religions (see also Chapter 4). Although aspects of these rituals
such as healing, summoning the spirit (Comaroff 1985), drumming and sacred
dancing (Muller 1999), and use of hymn singing to cut sermons short (Kiernan
1990) are absent, the presence of percussive aspects such as hand clapping
and hymnbook slapping together with dance steps and the African aesthetics
of call-and-response and cyclic repetition do suggest musical borrowings from
these churches. As I observed during my fieldwork, the influence of percussion and dancing seems to have originated in the male and female groups of
the *broederband* (band of brothers, the name used for a church men's society)
and *vrouevereniging* (church women's society), respectively, and then gradually
moved into the formal Sunday services (see also Dargie 1997, 324).

Sacred Sounds

The singing style used by the congregations for both hymns and koortjies is
very similar. Marius Barnard, who grew up in the Karoo town of Beaufort
West, describes the sound of his father's Dutch Reformed Mission Church

Figure 3.7 *"Jesus is so lief vir my" (Jesus Loves Me Very Much), from congregational singing at the ESCC, June 26, 2005. (Composer and author unknown.) Transcription by author.*

congregation as follows: "The congregation sang as a whole but also as individuals. The better known, the more melodious the hymn, the stronger the congregation; the less well known the hymn, the more prominent the individuals" (1975, 28). This account, written in the 1970s, but referring to the early to mid-twentieth century, is (thus far) the only description I could find on the sound of coloured congregational singing in the Karoo. It suggests a full congregational sound when members sang a familiar hymn, but that stronger individual voices (perhaps voorsingers) became more prominent otherwise, and it certainly applies to what I heard at church services in Graaff-

Reinet. One of the most noticeable features, however, in all three churches was that members never sang in unison; rather, they harmonized freely in a highly individual way, which was roughly based on the SATB voice parts.[39] They sang melodies in parallel intervals and changed range as they wished, according to their individual singing voices. This harmonious sound constituted a very dense texture and timbre, and it was often very difficult to isolate the original soprano line of the hymn melody. In addition, this singing style meant that no two verses of a koortjie or hymn were alike. Singers constantly changed voice parts and harmonies and/or clapping patterns, and this contributed to a sense of gradual build-up to a "groove" of full volume, harmony, and percussion, only ending in a *decrescendo* on the final phrase of the piece. This technique demonstrates a characteristic of African music, in which each repetition of a pattern is slightly different from the previous one (Turino in Nettl et al. 1992, 165; Levine 2005, 21–22).

As the form of each hymn or koortjie became cyclical through either repetition of the melody for subsequent verses or repetition of both melody and text, this style also resulted in the increased prominence of the voorsinger as an independent voice within the piece. Instead of initiating the song and then singing together with the congregation for the rest of the hymn or koortjie, the voorsinger's role became more like the "call" of the call-and-response format typical of much African music making. For example, in this rendition of a popular hymn *Worstel mens* (Wrestle, Sinner), the voorsinger, a man singing in a falsetto voice, not only began the hymn but also continued with embellishments and a call toward the end of every line to which the congregation responded with the next line of the hymn. The voorsinger thus provided a powerful momentum throughout the piece. This is a complex example of how the Afrikaans voorsinger tradition and the African call-and-response aesthetic combined and became virtually indistinguishable. The difference in rendition of the first and second verses (as mentioned earlier) is also clear in this example (see Figures 3.8a and 3.8b; PURL 3.8).[40]

In addition to the voorsinger's role and the difference in rendition between the verses, one can also observe here some slight changes in voice parts and the slow beginning and then regular occurrence of the hand clapping. However, the notation is ill equipped to indicate the particular timbre of this performance. Sung at full volume, the effect was of a solid block of sound that completely enveloped the listener. Each listener experienced a different complex blend of sound according to his/her physical location within the church space; this ensured a subjective sonic experience for all those in attendance. Depending on where one sat in the congregation, the surrounding singers emphasized certain melodic lines, which contributed to the treatment of the hymn's "main" melody as one of various and constantly

Figure 3.8a "*Worstel mens*" (*Wrestle Sinner*), *from congregational singing at the combined Congregational Church* broederband *service, ESCC, February 17, 2005. (Composer unknown, Afrikaans text by G. B. A. Gerdener.) Transcription by author.*

changing harmonic strands. In this case especially, the open fourths and fifths between the voice parts contributed to a ringing sound that often dominated the overall effect. Two additional aspects of this music made it unique. First, the effect of scooping between pitches (notated above in bar 6 of each verse) also occurred between smaller intervals throughout the piece, and because each singer chose to slide between different pitches in comparison to his/her fellow congregation members, this added to the existing rich texture. Second, the particular Afrikaans pronunciation and accent typical of coloured South Africans lent a specific sonority and timbre to each syllable. These aspects clearly identify this singing as forming part of a distinctive religious musical culture. Congregational song in this community thus incorporates recognizable elements of music from other groups and molds these to form a particular musical aesthetic.

Figure 3.8b   *"Worstel mens" (Wrestle Sinner), from congregational singing at the combined Congregational Church* broederband *service, ESCC, February 17, 2005. (Composer unknown, Afrikaans text by G. B. A. Gerdener.) Transcription by author.*

To return to Scott's theory and its application here, it is clear that this musical tradition survived and became what it is today through its continuous, regular performance on a weekly basis. This performance often took place in front of a (white) minister who could be viewed as a representative of the dominant authority and power. In addition, the "public" setting of the church building meant that the hidden transcripts embedded in this music were clearly in the public domain, although, of course, those in power rarely chose to notice them. The fact that this music tradition survives today is due to this community's preservation of its oral history and records of encounter within this music, in the face of colonial and apartheid marginalization and negative stereotyping. While authorities generated their contradictory and racially biased definitions of colouredness as an ambiguous, in-between category, this community preserved its own identity, culture, and history in its religious music, which remains as a testament to its more than two-hundred-year history in this area. To summarize, hidden transcripts, whether in plain sight or spoken behind the back of the dominant, form an important vehicle for construction of coloured identity and a sense of culture and history in Kroonvale.

Conclusion

Traces of encounters between Khoisan, slaves, Xhosa, colonist, and missionary in this music not only ensure the preservation of an auditory history of this community, but also indicate a statement of defiance to the dominant power structures inherent in colonialism and apartheid. The "hidden transcripts" of congregational singing in this community suggest a refusal to comply with the existing negative perceptions that coloured people had no cultural history or identity. Instead this community archived its history and thus preserved its musical identity within the sound of its sacred song. What resulted is a sense of the complex history of this group within South African society, one which has been sadly neglected in the written record and that would otherwise be very difficult to retrieve.

The descriptions of coloured congregational singing in this chapter suggest two final ideas for contemplation. First, the community's sonic archive not only provides a sense of its musical history but also potentially reveals new insights in the areas of oral history, community memory, and cultural identity. I believe that there is a depth of knowledge embedded in these hidden musical transcripts that demands additional investigation of this community's auditory history. Although such hidden transcripts of preservation can be interpreted as a survival mechanism (especially during apartheid) and a way of undermining stereotypes of coloured people, they now have the potential to serve as important archives of memory, heritage, and cultural identity in the context of postliberation South Africa. Second, there is an ongoing need for careful listening and attention to the narrative subtleties hidden in sound. As John Blacking observed about the religious music of Venda Zionists, "The key to understanding this lies not so much in *what* people sang, but *how* they sang, and in particular how they sang hymns of European origin" (1995, 213). As scholars continue to investigate the historiography of South African music research (Olwage 2002; Lucia 2005), it is clear that previously ignored or marginalized genres not only offer rich insights and deeper understandings of the incredibly diverse musical offerings in this country but also present opportunities for broadening our current perception of South African music history.

4

"Senzeni na"

Interrelationships Between the Music of Mission and Independent African Church Denominations

On the evening of February 17, 2005, I arrived at the ESCC for the opening service of the United Congregational Church of Southern Africa's Broederband Conference.[1] Earlier in the week, an invitation to participate in the mass choir from one of its members meant that I did not sit in my usual place at the back of the church, but rather, with the ranks of singers who faced the congregation. Dressed to comply with the women singers' uniform of black skirts and white blouses, I soon stopped feeling exposed and listened to the powerful koortjies sung by the broederband (church men's society) members. I tried to absorb and learn the music, humming along with the choir members. The cyclic repetition of the songs meant that I could learn the melodies relatively quickly, but the words were harder to follow. Then I heard the words of "Juig al wat leef" (Rejoice All Who Live), a popular hymn, and soon realized that the melody differed to the renditions of this hymn I had heard previously. When I found myself humming along to a familiar tune, it took me a few moments to ascertain that it was the tune of "Senzeni na," the apartheid resistance song with the heartrending lyrics, "What have we done? Our only sin is being black." I mentioned this experience in an interview with the leader of the URC choir the following day. Mr. Kayster sang along with me for a few lines of "Senzeni na," and then he said, "I remember growing up with that tune being used as a church tune and then I saw it was being used in the struggle!"[2]

Despite its religious origins, it is compelling that a song so iconic of the anti-apartheid struggle with its lyrics of almost unbearable suffering can, after ten years of democracy, be sung to the words, "Rejoice all who live, rejoice before the Lord."[3] With the relaxed yet solidly rhythmic pace, punctuated by hand-claps, this rendition had a cheerful yet firm resolve. In a place like South Africa, the fact that a church-going community sang this melody to hymn texts before the height of the resistance struggle and still performed it as a hymn after apartheid is not unexpected. Tunes conceived for religious purposes and resistance songs are often very similar, if not identical. An example of this is Enoch Sontonga's composition (c. 1897), *Nkosi Sikelel' iAfrika*, which forms part of the current South African national anthem.[4] A complex relationship exists between religion and politics in this country (Villa-Vicencio 1996; de Gruchy 2005), and it is no surprise that music is also involved.

What is unusual, however, is the presence of a freedom song melody in the Congregational Church repertory, when the denomination originated as a traditional mission church. Usually, when authors interpret certain styles of musical expression and performance as resistance to apartheid South Africa, they refer to Independent African church denominations, such as the Zionists. This observation suggests a need to examine the music of Kroonvale congregations in the wider context of Christian religious music in South Africa. In this chapter, I examine the subtle messages introduced in religious performance style by Kroonvale congregations and I interpret these messages as expressions of anti-apartheid sentiment. I discuss these observations within a theoretical framework that incorporates notions of embodied difference, a critical approach to studies of musical "resistance," and a historiographical investigation of research on South African Christian (black and coloured) religious music.[5] Within this context, and drawing on my fieldwork observations, I assert that Kroonvale church music (in other words, music with mission church origins) also contains messages of a shared future and a post-apartheid vision of the country. I believe that congregations began to incorporate these messages in the music particularly in the later decades of the twentieth century and that these actions should be understood within the context of Black Consciousness philosophy and the height of violent anti-apartheid struggle. I argue that, especially during this period, a more permeable boundary between the music of mission churches and Independent African churches developed in the Eastern Cape Province.

"Coloureds Don't Toyi-Toyi": Anti-Apartheid Gestures

I borrow this rather provocative subtitle from Shannon Jackson's work in the context of mid-1990s Cape Town (2005). She observed post-apartheid responses at the University of the Western Cape, a university built in 1959 specifically for coloured students, which, in the 1990s, gained many black students.[6] The resulting tension due to demographic changes on campus led to many protests, with black students expressing this sentiment by toyi-toyiing. (This is a type of dance where people move in a tight military-like formation along a street, lifting their knees high in time to an accompanying song or chant, sometimes brandishing placards and/or traditional weapons.[7]) Watching black students participate in this kind of protest across the campus, coloured lecturers and students expressed fear and disgust at their "undisciplined and violent nature" (Jackson 2005, 210). "That's not the way *we* handle *our* problems" commented a bystander (211). Jackson interprets the statement, "coloureds don't toyi-toyi," made to her on several occasions, as a distancing of coloured people from black people, "as if to toyi-toyi is really an African thing and, since coloureds don't toyi-toyi, they must not by extension consider themselves African" (211).[8] The implied statement of difference between coloured and black people in this comment is not new. As Zimitri Erasmus states, "Coloured identities . . . are formed in hierarchical relation to both white and black African identities; they are experienced and constructed as less than white and better than black. On the one hand, the meaning of being coloured is shaped by the lived experiences of white domination. . . . On the other hand, it is shaped by complicity with these racist discourses through its creation of an inferior black African Other . . . and complicity with the exclusion and subordination of black Africans" (2001, 24). Although this quotation addresses the topic of coloured identities in Cape Town, community members I spoke to agreed that this type of ambivalence also exists in Graaff-Reinet. June Bosch and Anziske Kayster mentioned, however, that Graaff-Reinet's people are more understanding of each other because they live physically closer to each other in a small town and often have both coloured and Xhosa relatives (Bosch communication, October 14, 2006; Kayster communication, October 18, 2006).

While noting the ethnically conscious distinction made between black and coloured protest styles (a point to which I return later), Jackson is interested in the implied assertion of embodied difference in this statement, in other words, why these staff members and students believed so firmly that coloured bodies did not move in the typical toyi-toyi formation. What reasons exist for the accompanying belief "that coloured . . . [people] are, by their very embodied difference, capable of more secular, civic and therefore moral expressions of political conviction" (2005, 211)? She delves into the history of Cape Town in order to answer this question and argues that inscription of certain laws and beliefs onto bodies during this lived history forms a possible solution. For example, the exposure of emancipated slaves to the colonial rhetoric of home and family resulted in a "moral ordering of space" in which the domestic, private household and movement of people within that space formed the basic stable unit for the production of a civic-mindedness and a reserved public identity (218).[9] By stressing the need to investigate the history of this type of consciousness, Jackson asserts that scholars often neglect "tacit and diffuse domains of meaning" when they rely on "voting practices, voluntary behaviour and verbally expressed political positions" as their primary data. This results in an emphasis on "consciousness and consciously volunteered information" (209). By examining the statement, "coloureds don't toyi-toyi," Jackson therefore moves beyond its acceptance as an incontrovertible truth and investigates the historical reasons for its formulation. Similarly, I interpret this assertion as an accepted truth believed by certain people at a certain time, which encapsulates a discursive formulation of coloured identity and political consciousness.

Observing Tswana Zionism during the apartheid era, Jean Comaroff argues for a similar attention to subtle resistance strategies, in other words, for acknowledgment of what Jackson calls "tacit and diffuse domains of meaning." Comaroff explains that "we must look beyond the conventionally explicit domains of 'political action' and 'consciousness'; for, when expressions of dissent are prevented from attaining the level of open discourse, a subtle but systematic breach of authoritative cultural codes might make a statement of protest which, by virtue of being rooted in a shared structural predicament and experience of dispossession, conveys an unambiguous message. In such contexts, ritual provides an appropriate medium through which the values and structures of a contradictory world may be addressed and manipulated" (1985, 196). Despite their differing contexts of study, both these authors are critical of accepting only conventionally understood strategies of resistance and offer ways of investigating other signs, namely, those embedded in non-verbal statements and ritual. The work of these authors broadens the discussion of "resistance" beyond consciously volunteered information, and this is particularly applicable to my experiences in Kroonvale. Whenever I observed instances that could be interpreted as anti-apartheid sentiment in the three Kroonvale churches, community members I spoke to seldom agreed with me that these actions had political references. As mentioned above, Mr. Kayster, while noting the use of "Senzeni na" "in the struggle" also reminded me of his childhood associations with this melody's church/religious origins. There could be a number of reasons for these general community views, namely, a reluctance to admit to an outsider that these aspects could be symbols of overt political resistance, a need for distancing from the African National Congress and, by association, black South Africans (discussed above), and also a deep fatigue with the constant politicization of everything South African from sport to religion. Mainly, I received the impression that members merely thought that this was the way they had conducted their church services and church attendance for many years and that these musical and other characteristics simply formed part of their church tradition.

Yet, the intriguing use of "Senzeni na" I heard that evening warrants further investigation, especially if it is interpreted as a subtle, nonverbal statement of political consciousness. I believe that performance of this protest tune to a religious text created a powerful sense of shared experience and suffering during apartheid, both for individual congregation members and the community as a whole. What could not be spoken in words for fear of interrogation by apartheid police could be sung in the religious context and thus experienced, interpreted, and appreciated by all those present.

These observations demand a critical approach to what constitutes "resistance." For my purposes here, I associate the term "resistance" with overt verbal and physical signs of protest (such as political speeches and the toyi-toyi). I refer instead to the nonverbal signs I observed in Kroonvale as subtle expressions of anti-apartheid sentiment rather than direct protest in this context. By doing this, I also remain partially faithful to the viewpoints expressed by community members who were reluctant to identify resistance politics in this music and church tradition. Following Comaroff, I nevertheless believe that making use of these nonverbal signs offered one of the very few viable recourses for communities to express dissent at the time. The use of "Senzeni na" and any other nonverbal gestures, then, should first be understood within the context of apartheid and the function of the church in the South African political environment.

Church and State Connections

Against the background of McCarthyism in the United States, the South African government placed a ban on political meetings of certain parties in 1950. This aimed ostensibly at preventing the spread of communism. According to Rodney Davenport and Christopher Saunders, the Suppression of Communism Act "made the Communist Party unlawful. It empowered the Minister of Justice to declare any kindred organizations unlawful too, and to 'name' the office-bearers and active supporters of such bodies (subject to their right to make contrary representations), and to prohibit named persons from taking part in their activities. He could also restrict the movements of named persons and prohibit any gatherings likely in his view to further the ends of communism" (2000, 384–85). After the 1960 Sharpeville massacre in which police killed sixty-nine people and injured 180 people who were participating in a nonviolent protest, the government banned the African National Congress (ANC) and the Pan Africanist Congress (PAC). It also declared a state of emergency, which allowed the state to impose various restrictions, including a ban on public gatherings. This did not apply to religious services, however, and as Archbishop Desmond Tutu stated, "prior to February 1990 we often held political rallies under the guise of church services. Such actions were politically necessary and theologically correct" (Tutu in Villa-Vicencio 1996, 276).[10] Similarly, religion and politics fused in the funeral services held in the black communities for comrades killed by political violence. These became highly politicized occasions, with opportunities to sing protest songs, hand out leaflets, and make public speeches. Police often clashed with funeral attendees and "a rhythm of shootings at funerals, followed by further funerals and further shootings, occurred all too often during the next few years [after the 1976 Soweto riots]" (Davenport and Saunders 2000, 451).

Religious infrastructure could also be used as political domination, for example, in Graaff-Reinet, as elsewhere in South Africa, the apartheid government managed to control the church denomination to which the majority of South African coloured people belonged. It did this through the Dutch Reformed Church, the official church of the apartheid state. According to John de Gruchy, the separate spaces for coloured, black, and white services originated in a Synod resolution dating from 1857. Although this document stated a preference for all members of the Dutch Reformed Church to worship in the same congregations, due to the "weakness of some (i.e., whites), it was permissible to hold separate services [in separate buildings] for whites and blacks" (2005, 8). What originated as an exception to the rule, however, soon became standard practice, assisted by missionary beliefs that this allowed for better religious work among the indigenous peoples (8). In 1881, the Dutch Reformed Mission Church (or Sendingkerk) for coloured people became a "daughter" organization within the Dutch Reformed Church hierarchy, followed later by the Dutch Reformed Church in Africa, for black people. These actions "provid[ed] an ecclesiological blueprint for the Nationalist policy of separate development" that followed (9). The Afrikaner church rarely appointed coloured ministers to the mission church, which meant that the white ministers presiding over these congregations supervised the content of weekly services.[11]

In the English churches, separate worship venues also existed, for example, the London Missionary Society (LMS) churches for coloured people with separate Congregational Church buildings for white people. In theory, however, these settler churches joined with the indigenous people's churches in 1864, when the LMS and Congregational churches combined to form the Evangelical Voluntary Union.[12] As de Gruchy states, "By the end of the [nineteenth] century it was not uncommon for black priests to be members of synod, though the Anglicans were behind the Methodists, Presbyterians, and Congregationalists in this respect. As the years passed, it became increasingly significant that these English-speaking churches were becoming more multi-racial in character" (2005, 22).[13] This tendency is illustrated in the appointment of a black minister for the PSCC congregation in 1886, Rev. S. Sihali and its first coloured minister, Rev. J. W. Stawel, in 1918 (Minnaar 1987, 95). More recently, Rev. Frederick Emmanuel Hufkie (1918–2001) became the minister of the PSCC from 1984 (before this he acted as principal of the Spandau High School in Kroonvale). Hufkie was a well-beloved figure in the community, and people told me that he would buy food at church bazaars to give to the poor and would help anyone, regardless of their church denomination (Barendse interview, October 27, 2005; Jasson interview, November 3, 2005). He was also an outspoken man who often delivered political sermons. Security police arrested and imprisoned Hufkie on two occasions: for seven months in 1976 and for six months in 1985 (*Graaff-Reinet Advertiser,* July 27, 2001). An eighty-year-old PSCC member recalled when police took Hufkie away from Spandau High School. "That was a very sad day," Marjorie Visagie said, with tears in her eyes (interview, March 8, 2005). By arresting Rev. Hufkie, the apartheid government made it even more clear that open resistance would not be tolerated, even in a rural Karoo town.[14] Despite the multiracial character of the historically English-speaking churches then, the apartheid government maintained strict control.

The Subtle Signs of Dissent

Conversations and sermons in Kroonvale and elsewhere, therefore, could always be heard and reported to the authorities, with often devastating results. Singing hymns, however, offered opportunities to express shared sentiment and a sense of community belonging, despite apartheid oppression. John Blacking suggests a similar interpretation in his work on Venda Zionists conducted in the 1950s and 1960s. He argues that their religious music revealed a sense of black South African political consciousness.[15] In order to substantiate this theory, he draws on his interpretations of the style and sound of the music, for example, the use of percussive sounds such as drumming and handclaps, call-and-response structures, and similarities to indigenous Venda forms such as *malende* and *tshikona*. Blacking asserts that "the way in which the Zionists sing, and much of the music that they sing, expresses opposition to white domination and reinforces the Africanist view of the political future of South Africa" (1995, 199). Later, he adds that "their hymns were not protest songs, but nevertheless they protested" (218). Despite their application to a different religious denomination and its music, I am strongly indebted to Blacking's ideas of listening carefully to the sound of performance, paying attention to its style, and using these observations in order to interpret statements of political sentiment.[16] Following his example, I outline below some nonverbal gestures within religious music performance in Kroonvale that can be interpreted as expressions of anti-apartheid feeling.

The native language of most coloured people, Afrikaans, prevented them from using language as a vehicle of protest, unless they were willing to risk arrest or, at the very least, harassment by police officials. Coloured people shared Afrikaans with the National Party's apartheid government and the majority of its police officials; all dialogue could therefore be completely and mutually understood.[17] When koortjies entered the repertory, however, congregations often sang English and Xhosa verses in addition to singing verses in Afrikaans. By choosing to sing in English or Xhosa, coloured people in Kroonvale could make certain political statements that did not need to be expressed explicitly in the musical lyrics. English, the first language of some white South Africans and the second language of many coloured, black, and white Afrikaans-speaking South Africans, connected coloured people to other South African groups. As the language of American popular music, Hollywood movies, and the British motherland, English linked those who spoke or sang it to a wider community that stretched beyond Graaff-Reinet's rural isolation and South Africa's general international isolation (see also Chapter 5).[18] Alternatively, by singing in Xhosa, coloured people could acknowledge their parentage (many Graaff-Reinet coloured people have one black Xhosa-speaking parent and one coloured Afrikaans-speaking parent) and/or a subtle statement of their identification with the African National Congress's anti-apartheid struggle. Therefore, I believe that the choice of language for songs at religious services was often politically and socially motivated.

Through language choice, coloured people thus stated their loyalties to, and connections with, other ethnic groups; they also did this through use of melody. For example, by singing the tune of "Senzeni na" with Afrikaans hymn lyrics during apartheid, the congregation members could voice their feelings through melody alone. Anyone who knew the Xhosa lyrics of "Senzeni na" would share the communal, nonverbal statement of anti-apartheid loyalties, completely protected by and hidden underneath the standard Afrikaans hymn text. The colonial influences of liederwysies also encouraged the practice of utilizing unofficial melodies and assisted toward making the use of alternative melodies very much a standard part of church services. Ministers most likely did not subject alternative melodies to any particular scrutiny because their use already constituted part of the congregation's singing tradition. The oral transmission and use of songs not printed in the hymnbook thus served as vehicles for members to choose and insert their own melodies

into the official written repertory. This created opportunities for congregations to insert protest songs as these alternative melodies or simply introduce
music of different origin into the religious performance tradition.[19] This is
especially ironic, given the highly text-centered emphasis in the Reformed
Church denomination. Many community members expressed to me the
necessity that texts remained clearly audible above the sound of musical
accompaniment, and that sermons were biblically based and theologically
sound. Unspoken incorporation of unwritten melodies is a particularly rich
commentary on the inability of official texts (and by extension, the official
apartheid legislation) to have the final word. By replacing the written melodies with orally transmitted tunes, the congregations inserted ambiguity into
the formal, weekly church services.[20]

At a broederband service at the URC on August 8, 2004, I observed
another nonverbal sign of anti-apartheid sentiment that forms a part of this
community's religious performance style. Toward the end of a koortjie, I
saw the voorsinger of the church service raise his right hand and gradually
close his fist to signal that the congregation should end the singing with the
customary decrescendo on the final line of the hymn (see Figure 4.1). This
raised right fist is the sign of "Amandla" (Power [to the people]), commonly
used during anti-apartheid political rallies. The broederband members themselves would probably not agree that this is a political statement, but rather
a very utilitarian way of conducting the congregation. In fact, two church
ministers told me that the gesture means *hou vas* (hold tight), which refers
to the gradual closing of the right hand toward the end of a hymn or koortjie
verse (Barendse interview, July 6, 2006; Basson communication, July 4,
2006). Hidden in plain sight, no one could contest the fact that the "hou
vas" gesture functioned in a practical sense to cease the music and allow the
religious message to be heard. Yet, the use of this physical gesture, so iconic
of the anti-apartheid struggle, is open to additional interpretation; I believe
its presence in 2004 is a residual sign of the permeable boundary between
church and politics in the apartheid context.

The presence of these signs within this religious music performance style
suggests that it offered a vehicle for expression of communal, nonverbal, anti-
apartheid sentiment. Yet, simultaneously, I also interpret these nonverbal
aspects within a wider context, namely, as a result of influences from Christian Xhosa religious practices. I have already mentioned above that Xhosa
and coloured people in the Graaff-Reinet area often share relatives and, of
course, live closer to each other geographically than in large urban areas such
as Cape Town or Johannesburg. Most likely as a result of these interactions,
certain elements of Xhosa musical style (such as percussion, handclaps, call-
and-response structures, and cyclic forms) entered the Kroonvale repertory

Figure 4.1 *Rev. Leon Barendse, minister of the ESCC, demonstrates* hou vas *gesture used to cease* koortjie *singing. Photograph by author.*

some time ago. Sources of these influences included the use of koortjies and the more informal worship styles of church women's and men's groups that met at separate occasions during the week with no minister present. The use of "Senzeni na" and the "Amandla" gesture also indicates the use of more informal worship styles within weekly church services in Kroonvale. According to David Dargie, the infusion of influences from the church women's and men's groups within Sunday services also occurred in black South African churches with missionary origins (1997, 324). In addition, certain elements of African musical influence in Kroonvale are similar to those Blacking identified in the music of Venda Zionists. This suggests a link between the Kroonvale religious musical tradition and the music of Independent African religions with their associated "Africanized" religious practices. Together, these findings suggest far more permeable boundaries between the music of Independent churches and (black and coloured) mission churches than previously implied in the scholarly literature.

Independent Church, Mission Church

The following discussion relies mainly on historiographical evidence and some ethnographic data where available. As mentioned previously (see

Chapter 1), the dearth of ethnographic sources on coloured Christian religious music makes it impossible to draw on empirical studies of the music
performed in different religious denominations in coloured communities.
Hermann Giliomee states that in the early twentieth century the majority of coloured people belonged to the Dutch Reformed Mission Church or
Sendingkerk (2003, 389). More recent data suggest, however, that this is no
longer the case, especially since the end of apartheid. For example, those
who identified themselves as "coloured" for the purposes of the 2001 population census held in the Graaff-Reinet area reveal Dutch Reformed and Congregational allegiances, but many people also belonged to Pentecostal and
Apostolic churches (Statistics South Africa 2001).[21] The number of available
denominations and their members, of course, will neither remain static nor
constitute the same combination in each town or city and thus much work
remains to be done on the investigation of coloured people's religious music
in different areas of South Africa. My research on Dutch Reformed and Congregational church music in Kroonvale remains a micro-study, especially in
this respect, and the suggestions offered here are tentative. Similarly, on the
topic of black mission church music, very little ethnographic work exists, and
thus I rely on passing comments in the context of work on Independent African religions.[22] One scholar, however, David Dargie, has conducted research
on the church music of Xhosa mission congregations as well as Xhosa Zionists, and his work thus offers an important point of departure for the ideas
expressed later in this section.

De Gruchy states that at the turn of the twentieth century in South
Africa, black South African Christians had three choices of religious affiliation (he does not mention coloured people's religious choices, most likely due
to their assumed Sendingkerk membership). These included membership of
mission churches with black membership but white control; membership of
churches with multiracial congregations but white leadership domination
and paternalism; and membership of African Independent churches (2005,
40). From the 1880s, the latter denominations seceded from mission and
multiracial churches in order to form congregations with black leaders and
a more African style of worship. Bengt Sundkler, a Lutheran missionary,
categorized these denominations as forming two distinct groups, namely, the
Ethiopians and the Zionists. Zionism offered a syncretic blend of African
and Western Christianity, and Ethiopians followed the style and practices of
the mission churches, but with a philosophy of "Africa for Africans" (1961,
53–55). Despite these differences, Independent African religious groups
shared a common desire for black leadership and a need to escape white
control and discrimination within church structures (de Gruchy 2005, 44).

Musically, this desire for independence took the form of "Africanizing" the church repertory, for example, by introducing influences from indigenous practices, body movement, and percussive sounds to accompany the singing.[23] This represents an important departure from the accepted norms and inherent taboos of mission church worship style, as missionaries typically forbade dancing, drums, and any other indigenous influences among their converts.[24] Writing about Independent African religions in South Africa is therefore rich in ethnographic description of how these religious groups inserted African values and aesthetics within the modified church repertory. Carol Muller, for example, describes Isaiah Shembe's insertion of indigenous Zulu values into the Nazarite hymn repertory as a way of archiving threatened traditional knowledge (1999; see also Chapter 3). With reference to Xhosa Zionists, Dargie writes about the use of running in a circle as a way of retaining physical movement in religious rituals and circumventing the missionary ban on dancing (1997, 323–24; see also Dargie 2010). Blacking's theory of the politically conscious expressions inherent in musical style also forms part of this discourse. The importance and significance of these denominations lie in their ability to express an African political consciousness in their worship and singing styles that developed despite white Western mission influence.

In contrast to the rich body of scholarship on Independent African church music in this country, there is an almost complete absence of ethnographic work on mission church music. In my opinion, this situation arose because of the following two reasons. First, mission church denominations have been constructed as inferior "others" to those of Independent African churches. Related to this, an enduring perception exists that because mission church music adheres more strictly to the style of Western religious music it does not furnish material of sufficient musical interest to warrant further study. Blacking's work on the music of Venda Zionists, for example, implies that mission church congregations (and by association, their music) are conservative and unAfrican; in other words, they constitute a sphere from which to escape. Venda Zionist members informed Blacking in the 1950s and 1960s that mission services were "dull and send you to sleep" (1995, 208). In addition, "Venda Zionists . . . saw themselves as . . . more enlightened than mission Christians" (203). Blacking thus assumes that traditional mission church membership did not satisfy its members' needs, hence the move toward Zionism (202).[25] Authors generally interpret Independent African religions as offering protection, safety, and a sense of belonging to their respective congregations (Kiernan 1974, 1977).

Second, the perception of mission church music as conservative and based on Western religious practices created an assumption that no room for anti-apartheid sentiment existed in these repertories. Thus, the music of mission churches became a politically incorrect choice of research topic in contrast to the more "authentic" African Independent religious music with its associations of black nationalism. In his work on the historiography of South African indigenous choralism, Grant Olwage analyzes the absence of writing on this genre as the result of scholarly attention paid instead to narratives of resistance (2002, 30). He states that "stories of black musicking as resistance, in South Africa as elsewhere, have assumed the stuff of a master narrative" (29).[26] Following Olwage's insights, I believe that the work on Independent African religions also falls broadly into a "resistance paradigm" of writing (41 n. 41), and that an instance of scholarly neglect occurred because of the perception that mission churches adhered to Western musical style only. Although my work in the current chapter and in the previous chapter on "hidden transcripts" also belongs in the "resistance paradigm" to some extent, its focus on the mission church music of coloured people attempts to broaden this discourse.

As a way of reexamining narratives of resistance in the historiography of South African Christian religious music studies, I thus argue that the implied difference between mission churches as conservative and Independent churches as innovative constructs a more artificial separation between the two than what I believe is necessary. A study of ethnographic descriptions of Independent African religions, for example, hints at a much more fluid situation in reality. For example, Blacking observed that Venda Zionists could sing in both mission and Zionist style according to the particular situation and context (1995, 213). (Unfortunately, however, he does not describe what "singing in mission style" sounded like [214].) If Venda Zionists could sing in both styles in the 1950s and 1960s, then I believe that the possibility for these musics to influence each other existed, and over time, this mutual influence became a distinct reality. Muller describes two "contrasting forms of religious worship" in the Nazarite religion, namely, *inkhonzo*, "based on Western Christian services, and *ukusina*, or religious dance" (1999, 72).[27] What is important to note here, despite the recognized separate times and spaces of the Nazarite worship styles, is that together they constituted the recognized markers of Nazarite religious practice and members could and did participate in both types of ritual.

The ability of Independent African church members to sing in different styles is important evidence of the more fluid relationship between Independent and mission church music for which I am advocating. Dargie's work on Xhosa mission and Zionist congregations in various Xhosa communities of the Eastern Cape also confirms this phenomenon. For example, he states, "A single song may, in fact, be considered both a Zionist song and a Methodist song, depending on the method of performance. What was originally a mission song—or even something very High Church out of the Anglican *Hymns*

Ancient and Modern—can be totally transformed by the method of performance. . . . Western hymns are Africanized in performance in many Zionist
congregations and also in many mainline, traditionally mission churches by
the use of drumming, rhythmic instruments and body movement" (1997,
325–26). He also points out that many church members often attended both
mission and Independent church services on a Sunday (326).[28] This evidence
suggests that similarities of repertoire and "Africanized" style of performance
took place within both mission and Independent contexts. Dargie's observations of coexisting mission and Independent musical styles emphasizes that
the two should not be viewed as mutually exclusive, especially in the latter
half of the twentieth century. This period coincided with the proliferation
of Black Consciousness philosophy and violent anti-apartheid protests. The
Black Consciousness context of a collective solidarity (comprising coloured,
Indian, and black people) formed against oppressive apartheid laws brought
people together under a common banner of protest against white political
control. In my opinion, this awareness of belonging to a general "black" South
African group infused mission and Independent church gatherings with
similar sentiments. In 1994, when previously separate denominations such
as the black and coloured Dutch Reformed Church members joined to form
the Uniting Reformed Church, this also opened the way for shared services,
guest performances by local church members, and of course, the occurrence
of musical influences. These historical and social circumstances, I believe,
provided a suitable context for these musical permeations to occur.

Conclusion

A historiographical analysis of a selection of available sources on South
African religious music demonstrates the construction of a division between
the music of mission and Independent churches. The absence of ethnographic evidence on both black and coloured mission church congregations
assisted in forming this perceived contrast. This chapter proposes that a
more similar style of (black and coloured) Christian religious singing in the
Eastern Cape of South Africa exists than what previous research implies.
My findings suggest the presence of certain connections and similarities
of style between the music of mission church and Independent African
church denominations, and I believe that this is particularly true during
the latter decades of the twentieth century. Dancing, percussive sounds,
call-and-response, and cyclic forms in the Kroonvale repertory as well as
nonverbal signs such as language use, the "Amandla" gesture, and unofficial
melodies for church hymns also indicate this influence. A significant need
exists for more ethnographic research on the topic of Christian religious

music in churches with mission church backgrounds, in order to test these preliminary findings.

Shannon Jackson's work, in the Cape Town context, calls for a more nuanced understanding of political dissent and consciousness in order to interpret certain nonverbal signs in this repertory. While I respect the general community view that politics is not linked to religious practice, I do not interpret these factors as neutral aspects of religious culture in this community. Instead, I view them as expressions of anti-apartheid sentiment, which are influenced by the "Africanized" sounds of mission and Independent African church music. To return to the point I mentioned earlier in this chapter on the perceived difference between black and coloured protest styles, my observations in Kroonvale suggest instead that certain crossovers of musical boundaries occurred. In addition to producing a fluidity in religious musical styles, this also reveals a subversion of existing preconceptions of difference between the ways in which black and coloured people expressed anti-apartheid sentiment. These musical borrowings and use of nonverbal signs took place despite the notions of embodied difference between black and coloured people's ways of expressing political dissent.

This evidence also implies that a more sensitive and careful approach to locating resistance and resistance narratives in South African music should be utilized, for three reasons. First, attention to resistance narratives in South African music tends to neglect certain genres because they become inscribed as nonresistant. Scholars therefore do not perceive them as worthy of study. As Olwage states, "Narratives of resistance are always stories of erasure" (2002, 30). The comparatively small body of ethnographic work on the music of mission church congregations in relation to available studies on Independent African religious music serves as an example of how mission church music became neglected in the scholarly record. The second reason for a more careful approach to locating "resistance" is that attention to overt musical statements of protest may ignore more subtle and nuanced musical gestures that contain anti-apartheid sentiments. With South Africa's long history of oppression, the idea of "resistance" should be carefully interrogated and precisely defined, so that the multiple meanings and strategies located in various musical repertories are not collapsed into a potentially misleading and overarching category. Third, the association between resistance and difference may succeed in producing studies that are intent on keeping that difference firmly inscribed. Instead, research can focus on paying attention to possible encounters and connections, which influenced the development of certain musical genres.

The musical style of the Kroonvale congregations where I conducted fieldwork not only reveals the need for additional research on Christian black and coloured music in South Africa, but also that nonverbal signs within performance should be carefully analyzed within the broader context of church, state, and anti-apartheid protest in this country. This music and the style in which it is performed offered an important way of understanding the permeable boundaries between politics and religion in South Africa, especially in the latter decades of the twentieth century. It is in the sound of Kroonvale congregational singing that I also heard the individual freedom and collective democracy that has characterized many South African hopes and aspirations before and since the official end of apartheid in 1994.

5

Singing the "Queen's English"

Church Choirs in Kroonvale

O n November 30, 2004, I attended a typical rehearsal of the interdenominational "Ladies' Choir."[1] From 3:30 p.m. onward, choir members
arrived at June Bosch's house and arranged themselves according to
voice groupings of soprano, second soprano, and alto in the sitting room. Much
conversation ensued with news and gossip being exchanged and discussed.
About forty minutes later, Mrs. Bosch suddenly straightened up from her position on the piano stool and with a few of her verbal admonishments, the talk
gradually ceased. "Okay ladies," she said, "nou moet ons sing" (now we must
sing). After she announced a song title, choir files rustled as the members found
the relevant page. With a brief piano introduction, the music began. Sol-fa
notation transformed into sound, as clear three-part harmonies filled the room.
When satisfied with the rehearsal, the choir leader announced that she and a
few helpers would serve tea and biscuits. Afterward, as I bent down to take
Shirley's teacup, the soprano met my eyes and we both giggled. Even ten years
after the end of apartheid, the idea of a white woman serving a coloured woman
(and not vice versa) filled us both with a delicious sense of irony.

Talk, tunes, and tea became a weekly habit for this group. Love of music and
singing as well as catching up on community news constituted an important
incentive for attending choir rehearsals. By meeting once a week to sing, in
June Bosch's words "good music," the "Ladies' Choir" members furthered a
tradition of choral performance that has its roots in South African colonial
and missionary history. An important factor, however, is that these women

stated their affiliation to a certain class of people who know and appreciate this type of repertoire. The choir members, either working or retired teachers and nurses, belonged to the ranks of Kroonvale's middle class. Rehearsals and the music performed on these occasions formed ways for members to state their position in a society that did not always recognize them as educated, qualified professionals.

In this chapter, I argue that the music of church and church-affiliated choirs states a sense of belonging to a middle-class status group in Kroonvale. In order to make this statement, choir members utilize language choice (as manifested in their preference to sing in the "Queen's English,"[2] the language of the British colonial motherland), musical literacy (in other words, tonic sol-fa), and a certain accepted repertoire of sacred and secular music in their rehearsals and performances. I assert that the church-related choral singing tradition in Kroonvale articulates a sense of social status through collective musical performance and functions as a manifestation of the quest for coloured respectability. During apartheid, performing this music subverted stereotypes of coloured people as members of a working-class group only. The notion of "class" and its applications to music, however, requires careful consideration.

The Complexities of Class and Music

As a term of description and categorization, "class" is a very contested issue.[3] Since the 1980s, cultural theorists have significantly expanded on the traditional Marxist conception, namely, the functioning of a working class and a dominant class within a capitalist system. According to Sherry Ortner in her discussion of class in the United States, this notion in American discourse is "extraordinarily elusive" (2003, 10). One of the reasons for this, Ortner argues, is that class is often completely subsumed by discourses of race and ethnicity (1998, 4). As an example, she describes her interviews with the primarily Jewish members who graduated from her high school in 1958. Ortner endeavored to focus the conversations on class, but her interviewees tended to talk about their Jewishness (in the sense of an ethnic identity rather than in terms of religious belonging) as a dominant part of the interview (6). This inclination toward highlighting the primacy of race and ethnicity obliged researchers to either ignore class altogether in their work or, in order to de-emphasize race, to focus only on the economic aspects of class (2). As a way of solving this problem, Ortner proposes two overlapping approaches, the first is to regard class as socially and historically constructed and the second is to understand the constructed nature of class as working within a context of power structures and their accompanying ideological formations (4).

Pierre Bourdieu specifies that a class formation is a mostly homogeneous entity that is

> defined not only by its position in the relations of production, as identified through indices such as occupation, income or even educational level, but also by a certain sex-ratio, a certain distribution in geographical space (which is never socially neutral) and by a whole set of subsidiary characteristics which may function, in the form of tacit requirements, as real principles of selection or exclusion without ever being formally stated (this is the case with ethnic origin and sex). (1984, 102)

A person's class position, therefore, cannot simply be reduced to income and/ or occupation; in addition, it "shapes one's sense of self, one's tastes, one's picture of the world and its possibilities" (Ortner 2003, 13). Both Ortner's and Bourdieu's ideas indicate that it is impossible to talk about class without mentioning factors such as gender, race, geographical location, history, and generation. I suggest here that musical taste also constitutes one of these factors (Bourdieu 1984, 18). Ideas of class in South African society are no less complex and ambivalent than those Bourdieu implies above and those Ortner outlines in the American context. Following Ortner's two related approaches, I begin here with my understanding of the power ideologies at work in the South African context and then present my interpretation of the historical and social constructions of class in the coloured community of Kroonvale.

The power structures and ideologies that affected class formation in South African society are rooted in Cape colonial history. Richard Elphick and Hermann Giliomee argue that the legal categories of people imposed by the Dutch East India Company at the Cape gave rise to "a social structure in which race and class were closely correlated. . . . It remained fundamentally constant, though altered in detail, throughout the period 1652 to 1840. However, in the late eighteenth and early nineteenth century a series of crises began to challenge the long-established social order, and, to defend it, Europeans evolved an ideology of racism and indulged increasingly in racially discriminatory practices" (1989, 522–23).[4] These discriminatory practices continued throughout the next century in various guises and culminated in apartheid policy, which formally categorized people according to ethnicity only, in other words, no room remained for class distinctions.[5] As David Coplan states, "Racial discrimination . . . promoted class levelling" (2007, 131).

For the purposes of this chapter, I adopt the premise that apartheid infrastructures and discourses caused a construction of class as equal to race in

South Africa, and this formulation also affected the Kroonvale community. In other words, class categories became mapped unquestioningly onto racial categories, with white people regarded as middle or upper class and coloured, Indian, and black people relegated to at best, lower-middle or, more commonly, working-class membership. That class distinctions existed within these communities did not interest the government, and in fact, it tended to view middle-class people who were not white as impudent. Bloke Modisane, a black journalist who worked for *Drum* magazine in the 1950s, bluntly summarized this situation as follows: "There is a resentment—almost as deep-rooted as the prejudice itself—against the educated African, not so much because he is allegedly cheeky, but that he fails to conform to the stereotype image of the black man sanctified and cherished with jealous intensity by the white man; such a Native must—as a desperate necessity—be humiliated into submission" (1990, 94). Black men who had gained a mission education, with its accompanying connotation of elite status, constituted a problem category because they refused to conform to the stereotype of a black person as an uneducated laborer.[6] The existence of a connection between education and middle-class status among black people in South Africa is also clear in Modisane's narrative.

Historically, there is a deeply entrenched link in South Africa between mission education, middle-class respectability, and the choral repertory of anthems, hymns, and light semiclassical or Victorian secular pieces. Grant Olwage's discussion of the disciplining powers of choralism on the working class of Victorian England as well as the South African colonial population explains this by analyzing the connection between the Victorian choral repertory and the colonial project. He describes a concert held in 1861 by a "group of Fingoes and Hottentots" that sang "staples of the Victorian repertory" in Grahamstown (a town in the Eastern Cape Province). Apparently, "the review . . . was not so much concerned with the choir's performance as with the effect that practices of choir singing had on its black members. In short, the utility of choralism was its civilizing potential, where civilizing, . . . was synonymous with disciplining" (2005, 25, 26).[7] Veit Erlmann states that the South African choir, which toured England and North America in the late nineteenth century, consisted of

> devout Christians, most of them educated mission graduates from the Cape and members of exceedingly prosperous farming communities. . . . In other words, the group comprised people whose careers were exemplary of the tiny stratum of educated Africans and whose vision of proper relations between the colonizers, and their subjects were based on the firm belief in a common core of Christian values,

the "uplifting" role of education, and in the need for some form of enlightened African self-rule. . . . To sing in a choir, to play the harmonium or the piano was to submit proof of one's place in a civilized community. (1997, 172–73)

By singing in choir formation, converts not only proved their civilized status but also found a vocal place in the social fabric. Both confining (in the "disciplining" sense) and empowering (in the social mobility sense), choral singing exemplified the values of aspiring middle-class mission converts and the "civilizing project" of the missionaries who trained them.[8] In the eastern Cape, mission communities, especially those for coloured people, adopted the discourses of Christian civility in order to form a particular notion of respectability. As Elizabeth Elbourne and Robert Ross explain, "Christian respectability was indubitably, for some [Khoekhoe and slaves], a means of gaining self-respect, of reconstructing community, and of restoring the honour lost by servitude" (1997, 48). Faced with the consequences of cultural annihilation together with prejudice concerning their origins, I believe that coloured people in Kroonvale chose to deal with the legacy of mission Christianity and its discourses of middle-class respectability in a specific way. Part of this strategy included choral music. In her reading of *Writing Black* (1981), an autobiography by Richard Rive (a South African writer classified as "coloured" by the apartheid regime), Desiree Lewis states, "Subjects who are labelled coloured cannot enlist the same signs or signifying logic used in ideologies like Negritude or Black Consciousness, ideologies which invert negative evaluations yet retain a binaristic and essentializing logic. For many coloured subjects, therefore, authority can be claimed by . . . looking to other signifiers to inscribe dignity, respectability and social superiority" (2001, 146).[9] I believe that the quest for respectability, with its accompanying implicit need to express a distance from a shameful past of slavery and servitude, thus forms an important context for understanding class constructions in Kroonvale.[10] That this discourse was at work even before the apartheid era is clearly implied in the following "letter to the editor," which appeared in 1926:

Building Plots for Coloured Folk

We feel dishonoured by the frequent remarks that the hire rooms and specially those occupied by coloured people are an eyesore and disgrace to the town. We recognize that there is a difference between you [Europeans] and us [coloured people] and there must be a distinction in our dwellings. Therefore we pray you to help us to bring that distinction into practice. We feel the Location is no place for the *more respectable people of our class socially*. We are in daily contact with all classes and races of people, which merely has a bad effect on our children, and in many instances makes them unfit to take their proper places for which they are being trained.

> David Hector, Chairman
> Solomon Gates
> Abraham West
> Jappie J. Marais
> Graaff-Reinet Location, March 29th, 1926
> (*Graaff-Reinet Advertiser*, April 3; emphasis mine)

This example illustrates that class distinction, dictated by discourses of respectability and shame in the middle-class coloured community of Graaff-Reinet, has a long history. In addition, this excerpt implies that respectability would be easier to maintain if coloured people did not live in the same place as black people. Thus, these "key defining terms of middle class coloured experience" (Erasmus 2001, 13) can be located in Graaff-Reinet and music, specifically choral music performance, became one of these signifiers with which to inscribe a sense of societal belonging and status. This genre was used to further the ends of respectability and class status within the community. I believe that this musical mobilization under the banner of class (for all its missionary and colonial restrictions and its accompanying European paternalism and discrimination) could be utilized as a discourse to disrupt the prevailing stereotypical narratives of coloured people's place within society. This appears to be the case in the stories told to me by Kroonvale choir members, especially when understood framed within a broader historical background of South African ethnic groups and educational opportunity.

Education and Status in Kroonvale

Due to PSCC commitments one Tuesday afternoon (February 8, 2005), many women excused themselves from the "Ladies' Choir" rehearsal and only three people (including me) arrived at the usual time. Instead of singing, the rehearsal was canceled, though the three of us stayed to have tea and chat. The presence of a smaller group allowed the conversation to turn to more intimate subjects like apartheid and various personal experiences. June Bosch related the following story:

My relative, Ellen, and I went to the GKW [a general store] one day. I was engaged but not yet married. I picked out the few things I needed and then we went to the cashier's desk at the back of the shop. As the white lady added up the amount I owed, she said under her breath "sê dankie miesies" (say "Thank-you ma'am" [to me]). Ellen paused and asked slowly, "What did you say?" The cashier didn't repeat the statement. Ellen grabbed my left hand and slammed it on the counter, displaying my engagement ring. "This lady, to you, is Mrs. Bosch," Ellen shouted, "and her boss is the Department of Education. And it is not us, the customers who should be saying thank you to you, but the other way around, because we keep your chimney fires burning!" Ooh, and my hand was so sore!

Caroline Meyer, a retired teacher who sings alto in the choir, narrated a similar experience:

> I was five months pregnant with my fourth child and I went to the Bergers store to buy pantyhose. I noticed that the young Afrikaans girl at the counter was calling all people who were not white by the insulting names of Outa [a general term for an older working-class black man] and Aia [similar to "Outa," but for a black woman]. I was so nervous that she would call me "Aia" as well. When I reached the head of the queue and she called "Aia," I took no notice. She called again "Aia, ek praat met jou" (Aia, I'm talking to you). I turned around slowly and said, "Dame, praat u met my? (Lady, are you talking to me?) She said, "Ja, want ek weet nie wat jou naam is nie" (Yes, because I don't know your name). I said, "Maar dame, ek weet ook nie wat u naam is nie, maar ek noem jou 'u' en 'dame.' As 'n mens geleerd is, dan weet 'n mens hoe om met mense te praat wie u nie ken nie" (But, Lady, I also don't know your name, but I'm calling you "you" [the polite form] and "Lady." If a person is properly educated [in manners], then one should know how to talk to people when one doesn't know their names.) At this point, the manager appeared and said to me, "Mevrou Meyer" (because he knew my husband and me) "is daar 'n problem" (is there a problem)? I told him of the insulting terms of address used by the young girl, and he offered to fire her on the spot. "Shame," I said in front of her. "Look at her, what chance does she have of finding another job or having a career? At least I am employed as a teacher. Let her keep her job." Later that day, via one of my relatives, I heard how angry this [exchange] made the girl![11]

Hinging on the use of offensive apartheid terminology for working-class black people and the terms of address used in Afrikaans ("u," the formal form of address, and "jou," the informal form, are similar to the use of "Sie" and "du" in the German language), this encounter highlights the frustration of an educated middle-class professional, who because she is coloured was deemed unworthy of respectful address by the white shop assistant. In the former story, it is clear that Ellen became angry mainly at the patronizing attitude of the shop assistant stating that Ellen and June should call her "miesies" (ma'am). To an outsider, "miesies" appears to be a neutral term, but in apartheid South Africa, all nonwhite citizens were expected to use it to address all white women, regardless of the latter's education and status. Furthermore, the use of "miesies" immediately implied an employer-employee relationship and therefore placed those forced to use the term in a position of servility. Thus, Ellen used June Bosch's future status as a married woman and the fact that she already had an employer (the Department of Education) to demonstrate that they did not have to address the store assistant as if she was their superior. In both stories, the implicit assumption of a white South African woman of her own superiority, on the basis of whiteness only, constituted the worst possible insult.

The South African educational system also sought to entrench these notions of white superiority. The Bantu Education Act (1953) ensured that nonwhite South Africans gained an inferior standard of education. On average, the government spent ten times as much on each white student as on each black student; the funding provided for coloured and Indian students fell somewhere in between, which again shows the far-reaching affects of the apartheid racial hierarchy and forces of discrimination. Within this system, therefore, slightly better schools and facilities enabled coloured people and those of Indian descent to gain a better education than that of black South Africans. Although tertiary institutions such as the University of Cape Town, the University of the Witwatersrand (in Johannesburg), and the University of KwaZulu-Natal permitted a few nonwhite South Africans to register and attend classes every year, financial constraints and the constant threat of government interference meant that most coloured people attended teacher's training colleges directly after they had finished school. Besides obtaining a teaching qualification, coloured people could also train as nurses (in the case of women) or artisans (in the case of men).[12] Many sacrifices ensued, as Patrick Hector, a URC choir member who is now a government educational development officer, told me, "Isn't it ironic that there was a good teacher's training college right here in Graaff-Reinet, but as it was for whites only, I had to go to Port Elizabeth to be able to qualify as a teacher" (communication, December 6, 2004).[13] Other sacrifices were financial, as often one spouse worked while another studied through correspondence (for example, at the University of South Africa) and vice versa until both earned their bachelor's degrees (Bosch communication, August 19, 2004).

Gaining an education in a country that institutionalized inferior training for its nonwhite citizens was an achievement against all odds. Therefore, it was clearly subversive if a coloured person had a higher educational qualification than a white store assistant. But, there is another reason why education and respectful terms of address play such a key role in the stories that opened this section. Lewis explains that

> racial domination is challenged not by speaking the language of "race," but by sidestepping this language and speaking the language of culture and civility. . . . The emphasis on class status is therefore emphatically discursive as it positions both addressee and addresser through messages about class authority and formal education. (2001, 145)

By emphasizing class and education, therefore, coloured people disrupted the dominant apartheid discourse of non-Europeans as inferior and forced these disjunctures into the consciousness of their interlocutors. This is particularly clear in the stories quoted above. The question that presents itself at this point is what this means for musical performance, and how musical repertories are formed to complement these statements of middle-class belonging.

Contexts of Choral Performance

Over a hundred people arrived at the ESCC for the opening of the United Congregational Church of Southern Africa's Broederband Conference on February 17, 2005. People had traveled from as far as Windhoek, Namibia (1697 km/1055 miles away) to attend, and the atmosphere was one of excitement and great energy. The mass choir formed specifically for the event comprised members of the ESCC, PSCC, and URC choirs in addition to members of a church choir from Aberdeen (a Karoo town about 56 km/34 miles from Graaff-Reinet). To add to the formality of the occasion, a choir uniform of black skirts/trousers with white blouses/shirts had been decided upon and the PSCC minister, Rev. Jacobus Bezuidenhoudt, conducted the choir. After the Master of Ceremonies announced each choir item, Rev. Bezuidenhoudt gestured to the choir to stand and played the starting pitches on the electric organ. The choir sang these pieces in a reverent, slow tempo, with careful English pronunciation and attention to phrasing. Its members held the sheet music in front of them in order to read the tonic sol-fa notation. Demonstrating a marked contrast in style and sound from the spontaneously sung koortjies that comprised the musical repertoire throughout the rest of the event, the texture in Schubert's "Holy, Holy, Holy" and much of "Zion, City of God" (by G. Froelich) was mainly chordal and homorhythmic. A solo sung by Mrs. Marjorie Visagie in "Zion, City of God" changed the texture briefly to that of a melody with chordal accompaniment in a repeated rhythmic pattern. After appreciative applause and some affirmative shouts from the congregation, the Master of Ceremonies formally thanked the choir, and the service continued.

These and other performances that I attended are part of a well-established tradition of church choir performance in Kroonvale (see Figures 5.1a, 5.1b, and 5.2; PURLs 5.1 and 5.2).[14] The formation of choirs for church singing among coloured people probably dates back to the early nineteenth-century period of missionary activity in this area. Unfortunately, the first mention of the DRMC choir in the records only dates from 1893, but it possibly existed many years before this.[15] Herbert Daniel Liebenberg (n.d.) reports that the PSCC choir performed for the first time in 1883, at a service celebrating the church's independence from the London Missionary Society. It is almost certain that these early choirs began by singing hymns from the London Missionary Society and the Dutch Reformed Church traditions and gradually extended their roles to one of performance within the structure of the weekly service. For example, a meeting of the DRMC council in 1910 reports a request from the choir that it perform a hymn while the monetary collections are made.[16] This culture of performance extended to participation in annual choir festivals (both local and regional) by DRMC choirs and also tours by the PSCC choir members that left Graaff-Reinet to give concerts in many places in South Africa (see Figure 5.3).[17] In 1967, for example, both the PSCC and ESCC choirs won prizes in a church choir competition held in Grahamstown (*Graaff-Reinet Advertiser*, March 16, 1967). By the time I began fieldwork, the tradition of festivals and tours seemed to have ceased. Choir members explained to me that travel was too costly and the ministers who had organized these events in the past were no longer present (Basson, Bosch, and Visagie communication, March 8, 2005).

While church choir members often fulfilled the important role of being *voorsingers* who began the hymns and *koortjies* for the rest of the congregation to follow, the choir performance slot within the service attracted the most emphasis. At these moments, the congregation sat still and listened to the performance, as an audience would in a concert hall (see Figure 5.4). In other words, the rhythmic texture of clapping, stamping, and hymnbook slapping combined with the stepping and swaying motion I described in the previous chapters did not accompany the sounds of choral performance.

Preparation for the performance of these pieces took place in weekly rehearsals at the respective churches. In 2004–2005, presiding ministers announced these choir performances. The URC choir performance generally occurred after the sermon, while the PSCC choir usually sang two items per service, one before the Bible reading at the beginning of the service, and one after the sermon toward the end (PURL 5.3). Of the three ESCC choir performances I heard, one took place after the sermon, one at the end of a service, and the third was a guest performance at the URC.[18] The music performed consisted of well-known pieces from the choir's particular repertoire of anthems and other religious works, transcribed into tonic sol-fa notation. Congregations often greeted special guest performances by local choirs from neighboring churches and schools or visiting choirs from other regions with murmurs of appreciation and enthusiastic applause.

The interdenominational "Ladies' Choir," mentioned at the start of this chapter, comprised members of both the PSCC choir and the URC choir. Prior to this formation, a "Ladies' Choir" comprising a similar list of members existed under the leadership of Mrs. Alice Loff and subsequently Mrs. Rhoda Hufkie, wife of the Rev. F. Hufkie (Bosch and Visagie communication, March 8, 2005). June Bosch, a retired organist of the PSCC, formed this particular choir in response to member requests in 2003.[19] Many of the songs performed by the "Ladies' Choir" were religious in nature, for example, anthems arranged for three parts and African American spirituals, such as "Deep River." But the choir's repertoire also comprised many secular songs, namely, pieces popularized by Frank Sinatra (for example, "My Way"), Pat Boone (for example, "April Love"), and Nat King Cole (for example, "Autumn Leaves").

The mixture of religious anthems, spirituals, and secular songs in the "Ladies' Choir" repertoire bears testimony to the diverse exposure of the Graaff-Reinet population to many local and foreign influences.[20] Nineteenth-century missionary hymns and hymn singing combined with the tours of performance groups to this Karoo town began a long series of musical interactions. In addition to religious musical influences, eighteenth- and nineteenth-century European and American secular musical influences also reached this area. Minstrel and vaudeville tunes joined the ranks of the foreign repertoire that was heard in performance by visiting foreign artists, imitated, and finally localized through performance and re-creation by resident musicians and singers. When the famous Christy Minstrels visited Graaff-Reinet in February 1869, the local music store, Essex, Rabone and Co., did not delay in offering a two-volume publication of 120 Christy Minstrels pieces for sale (*Graaff-Reinet Herald*, January 30, 1869). Suppliers of sheet music (of which John Lewis Viner was the best-known and largest music business active from about 1859–1903) (Henning 1975, 205) made various secular and sacred pieces readily available, and by the sheer amount of sheet music in the archives of the Reinet House Museum there can be no doubt that this music was purchased, performed, and enjoyed, at least by those who could afford it or who could borrow it from friends.[21] Later on, Graaff-Reinet boasted one

Figure 5.1a   *"Zion, City of God," by G. Froelich.*

Figure 5.1b "Zion, City of God," by G. Froelich.

Figure 5.2 *"Holy, Holy, Holy," by Franz Schubert, from* The New Oxford Easy Anthem Book, © *Oxford University Press, 2002. Reproduced by permission. All rights reserved.*

bioscope (the old South African term for cinema) in the 1920s, and by the 1960s, the town had two cinemas, known as GEM and Plaza, respectively. During the latter decade, Westerns, classics, along with Elvis Presley movies (for example, *Fun in Acapulco, GI Blues, Blue Hawaii*) were the order of the day (*Graaff-Reinet Advertiser*, March 7, 1963, June 17, 1963, and October 1, 1964). More recently, choristers themselves created musical and social networks through common choir, denominational, or family membership, which allowed them to obtain the sheet music of pieces they heard and enjoyed in performance. Thus, people circulated well-known pieces for church services and other events as needed. Exchange of musical recordings and the advent of radio also enabled this process.[22] Choir members who taught music at local schools also drew repertory from their personal collections of teaching materials. Many coloured people owned musical instruments such as piano, organ, guitar, or concertina, and they used these to accompany family "sing-along" evenings. These occasions often took place on Sunday evenings after church, and some people even used brass instruments for accompaniment (Bosch communication, August 19, 2004, and July 5, 2006).

During the 1940s, 1950s, and 1960s, a lively dance band culture existed in the town. Advertisements for show dances and balls often appeared in the local newspaper. Although it is unclear how many members of the coloured community were permitted to attend these functions, Villa Louther, Graaff-Reinet's best-known musician, remembered sitting at the front of the hall at one of these events and trying to learn the saxophone by watching the band musician's fingers move on the instrument (interview, June 23, 2005).[23] He also remembered that as a young boy who grew up in Sunnyside (a Graaff-Reinet suburb next to Kroonvale), hosts and hostesses of neighborhood parties paid him sixpence to turn the records on the gramophone player a little faster than the speed produced by the weak electricity connection (interview, June 23, 2005). Thus, through recordings, live dance bands, sheet music, cinema, and radio, together with rote-learning at home and at school, popular contemporary religious, secular, and light classical tunes became well known to the generation of people who still sing in church choirs today. This music formed the sonic background against which church choir members would perform expressions of middle-class belonging.

Respectable Sounds

In the latter decades of the twentieth century, church choirs gradually expanded their repertoire from anthems to other sacred works in the context of Sunday church services and from semiclassical to other light, secular pieces in the context of choir festivals and the interdenominational "Ladies' Choir." These changes took place gradually because in the Graaff-Reinet area, as in many other missionized regions of South Africa, the Christian way of life initially demanded a rejection of secular influences. This fact, and its accompanying ideas of appropriate music, provides the first of three ways in which choral musical performance became coupled with middle-class coloured respectability and values.[24] For example, Rev. A. Compaan, minister of the Dutch Reformed Mission Church from 1865–1914, launched a steady

Programme

1.	Moonlight	Eaton Faning	Choir
2.	Let Me this Day	Peter Warren	Ladies' Choir
3.	Come back to Sorrento	..	Mrs Rhoda Hufkie
4.	Behold the Lamb of God	Handel's Messiah ..	Choir
5.	Heimwee Kokkewiet	Le Roux Marais ..	Mrs Petronella Martin
6.	May Morning	Lui Gi Denza ..	Ladies's Choir
7.	Serenata	Enrico Toselli's ..	Mr G. Hufkie
8.	The Heavens are Telling	"The Creation":Haydn ..	Choir
9.	Mother Macree	..	Mrs Marjorie Visagie
10.	The Orchestra Song	..	Choir
11.	Fold your Wings	Ivor Novello ..	Ladies' Choir
21.	Once Upon a Time	..	Mr G. Hufkie
13.	I want to be Ready	Negro Spiritual ..	Gents' Choir
14.	The Lord is My Shepherd	Franz Schubert	Choir
15.	Deep River	Negro Spiritual ..	Ladies' Choir
16.	Give us this Day	..	Mrs Elizabeth Louther
17.	N'kosi Sekilele	Enoch Sontanga	Choir
18.	Sluimer Beminde	Le Roux Marais ..	Ladies' Choir
19.	The Trout	F. Schubert ..	Ladies' Choir
20.	Caro Mia Ben	Giordani ..	Mrs Petronella Martin
21.	Laughing Song		Ladies' Choir
22.	The Sea hath it's Pearls Pinsuti	Words by Longfellow, music by	Choir
23.	Ek Hou My Oë Opgerig	Psalm 121	Ladies' Choir
24.	There is a Prayer	G. A. Blackburn	Choir
25.	I heard a robin singing	Conrad Leonard	Ladies' Choir

Figure 5.3   Program of Concert Tour Performance in Kimberley, September 3, 1972. Courtesy of Mrs. Marjorie Visagie.

Figure 5.4   PSCC choir in performance. Photograph by author.

campaign of punishment for those church members who participated in any kind of dancing.[25] This included, by implicit association, the music used for its accompaniment. The church records of this time are peppered with items such as the following:

5 February 1896

The young sister Maria Hermans, found guilty of dancing, was given a severe warning to keep away from such un-Christian gatherings and [she] promised to improve. . . .

17 August 1908

Anna Meyer, Hendrina Jacobs and Aletta Jacobs, three young sisters found guilty of tickey draai [a type of dance]. The first [sister] was excused with a warning because it was the first time, but the other two had previously been warned and were placed under 3 months of censure. (DRMC Records, vol. 2)[26]

This censure included the removal of members' rights such as baptism of children, confirmation, and the right to communion. Respectable behavior that did not include dancing was also expected from choir members. On

August 5, 1924, ten years after Rev. Compaan's departure, the Rev. P. P. Joubert notated fifteen rules for the church choir, three of which were:

8. Members who are found guilty of immoral behavior will be cut off for at least 12 months.
9. Members who are found guilty of drunkenness will be cut off for at least 6 months.
10. Members who participate in dance parties will be dismissed for at least 3 months. (DRMC Records, 3:191)[27]

Dancing is equated here (albeit with less punishment) with drunkenness and sexual immorality as a crime worthy of dismissal from the choir. By disapproving of dancing and its accompanying music, an alternative type of musical repertoire, namely, hymns and anthems, sung while keeping the body still, became acceptable.[28] Marjorie Visagie, a Congregational Church choir member who remembered music evenings with her father sitting at the organ, reinforces this practice in a comment: "Did you ever sing popular songs?" I asked, and her reply was "[no], not when he was playing" (interview, March 8, 2005). For this church member's father, hymns and church music constituted the only acceptable music for family song evenings. Thus a certain type of behavior and musical repertoire came to mark churchgoers, including choir members, as a distinct social, in this case middle-class group. A value judgment became attached to this repertoire; it is seen as classic, traditional, and being of good quality.

Sometimes, the preference for this type of music led to conflict between contemporary requirements of worship style and choir members who hankered after the anthems of the old days.[29] For example, Mrs. Visagie told me that in those days "we sang good music. It's different now because we have all these koortjies." I asked her whether she liked singing the latter and she replied, "No, I don't sing them." "Why?" I asked. "[Because] we have a perfectly good hymnbook that isn't used," she answered (interview, March 8, 2005). Koortjies and tunes belonging to the "praise and worship" genre have therefore, to some extent, replaced these older pieces. Choir members designated some of the "praise and worship" pieces as "Sunday School music" (in other words, children's music) with the connotation that they are simple and easy to perform, in contrast to the anthems, which are thought of as more difficult and complicated (Bosch communication, March 2, 2005). The implication here is that anyone can sing this newer type of music, whereas those in the choir have the skills necessary to sing more complex classical pieces. Kroonvale church choir members have to possess a certain vocal ability and training before they can gain the elevated status within the church as having a role other than a normal congregation member.[30] Choosing and singing this type of repertoire is, therefore, the first step in achieving respectability through choral performance.

The second musical manifestation of respectability and class associations, besides the choice of the repertoire itself, is that choir members need reading skills in tonic sol-fa notation in order to rehearse and perform these pieces. A London missionary, Christopher Birkett, introduced this system of music notation in South Africa at Fort Beaufort in 1855 (Coplan 2007, 46).[31] It was taught according to the method of John Spencer Curwen and used to train Christian converts to sing European hymns in four-part harmony. Tonic sol-fa training spread quickly to various mission stations throughout the country in the second half of the nineteenth century. According to Olwage, "By the end of the [nineteenth] century, a sixth of all black pupils at African's largest mission institution, Lovedale, in the eastern Cape, were being examined for and awarded sol-fa certificates" (2005, 31). By the early twentieth century, Zulu people in Natal who had converted to Christianity made use of tonic sol-fa for their musical performances and printed editions of religious and secular pieces (Erlmann 1991, 60).[32] In Graaff-Reinet itself, a certain Mr. Kidd formed a singing class for teaching theory and practice of music using sol-fa. After very negative reviews following the group's concert in August 1861, the group disbanded in the same year it had begun (Henning 1975, 193). Nevertheless, this indicates that sol-fa was not unknown in the Graaff-Reinet area and at least some members of the public admired its merits. By the 1930s if not before, many black and coloured South Africans learned tonic sol-fa notation at school (education in staff notation was reserved for white schools).[33] Choir members prided themselves on their ability to read in this musical language, and, as Marjorie Visagie said, "it's a better way to sing instead of just listening [learning by rote]" (interview, March 8, 2005). I believe that aside from the perceived efficiency of tonic sol-fa as a method of learning music, choir members granted the much-beloved "difficult" pieces extra status because they were read in this notation and not acquired through oral transmission. This perception about musical literacy parallels the emphasis in the Reformed tradition on the authority of the written (biblical) text and therefore places choir members apart from the more general congregational practice of subverting "official" versions of hymn melodies through performance of alternative tunes (see Chapters 3 and 4).

The third aspect of performance that aspires toward respectability is the enunciation and pronunciation of the English language. June Bosch pointed out to me that when the "Ladies' Choir" performs, all of its members are aware of the right diction and enunciation to sound more "English" (communication, November 16, 2004). As a retired teacher of many subjects, including English, correct pronunciation and usage is close to Mrs. Bosch's heart. She professes a love for the "Queen's English," and this, together with her training in music and her experience of choir leadership, forms her high standards of what is expected in the sound of sung language. When a white English-speaking Graaff-Reinetter commented in surprise on the choir's excellent diction at a performance they gave in the town, Mrs. Bosch was equally taken aback by the assumption that coloured people did not have the necessary training or background in English enunciation. While relating this incident to the choir, she said, "But we [the "Ladies' Choir"] *know* how to sing proper English" (choir rehearsal, November 30, 2004). "Proper" English here of course refers to British English, which is a reminder of the deep impression of Graaff-Reinet's colonial history on the people in the area.[34]

British colonial influence therefore constituted an important factor in the choice of language for choral pieces.[35] While the members of the PSCC choir sang in English because of the LMS background and influence, it is intriguing that the URC choir members (from a traditionally Afrikaans con-gregation) also sang English songs.[36] Although Graaff-Reinet's colonial back-ground and culture constitute an important reason for this language choice, I also regard the force of apartheid in everyday life as partially responsible for these circumstances. It was expected that coloured and black people spoke Afrikaans when they communicated with white people. English, associated with mission education, marked those coloured and black people who spoke it as receivers of a better education than the one offered by the government. The government viewed such people at best as precocious and at worst as a threat to the country's stability.[37] By singing in English, these choirs simulta-neously exhibited their higher educational status and ability and their refusal to comply with the apartheid stereotypes of coloured and black people.[38] In addition, the use of English as an international language connected people to a global community.[39]

The combination of tonic sol-fa, the ability to sing in properly enunci-ated English (but also songs in Afrikaans, German, and Dutch when avail-able), and the type of religious, classical, and semiclassical repertoire that is beloved of these choirs constitutes a certain type of literacy. Not only do members need the ability to read in a certain language for singing purposes, but they should also be able to read the language of tonic sol-fa and "read," understand, and appreciate the musical language of this particular repertoire. A certain amount of education and training is required for all of these, which marks choir members as belonging to the middle class of Kroonvale.

Scholars in the South African music field are generally cautious in their opinions about whether people's class status directly affects musical perfor-mance culture. For example, Erlmann suggests that one of the limitations to studying music as class articulation is the problem of ignoring the importance of individuals' agency. He states, "South African black performance culture cannot be based on the notion of organic and homogeneous class cultures. Rather, the myriad performance genres grow out of the constant mobilization, manipulation, and appropriation of the most diverse symbols and cultural resources by different social actors. . . . In this view, performance cultures are processes of active structuralization of social relations rather than institutions annexed to social classes" (1991, 179–80). Coplan echoes this view as follows, "The historical relationship between social experience and performative consciousness is not only complexly indirect, but mediated by a kind of endless dialectic between forms of resistance and accommodation and the various syntheses incorporating both" (1995, 161). While Christopher Ballantine also voices the problem of confining musical performance to strict class divisions, he describes a particular ideology perpetuated by white liberals and black middle-class people in the urban areas that pathologized jazz and *marabi* (an early twentieth-century keyboard style) and regarded Western classical music and/or choral music as respectable genres for consumption (1993, 11–12, 75, 80). In fact, all three of these highly regarded scholars in the field of South African ethnomusicology imply that musical performance cultures should not be directly correlated to class alone, yet they do tend to name class formations (such as middle class, elite, migrant, or working class) and the accompanying musical ideologies in their writing.

The issue here is that despite the fluidity of musical taste and the consumption and creation of different genres by people from various backgrounds, writing on South African musical genres nevertheless constructed class and social status narratives surrounding categories such as "urban," "rural," "Westernized," "traditional," "middle class," "worker," "migrant," "mission-educated," and "Christian." Deborah James suggests that, particularly in the 1980s, following the publication of Coplan's seminal work *In Township Tonight!*, researchers of South African music began to investigate the class associations as part of their attention to specific genres (1990, 314; see also James 1997). For example, in the context of her own work, James explains that in Bapedi or Northern Sotho society, a clear class distinction existed between Christian and non-Christian, with music preferences as one of the most important determining factors (1999, 8). These inscriptions of class values onto music genres were also subject to change. Ballantine explains the gradual acceptance of jazz by middle-class Africans in the 1930s after it became more "refined" by the newer Swing tradition popular in the United States (1993, 84). This means that various genres became inscribed with the ideologies of various class formations at various historical junctures. The question that arises is what cultural work these musical genres and their associations of class status achieved, especially for those making the music. More specifically, what did performances of choral music provide for middle-class choir members in Kroonvale?

Conclusion

Choral music performance offered three discursive and social opportunities for choir members. First, as an extension of the stories quoted earlier, I interpret the performance of religious choral music in this community as an additional way of undermining apartheid stereotypes of race and class. Performance and appreciation of this repertory disrupted narratives that insisted on collapsing race and class categories. Second, participation in church choirs also created a sense of pride and dignity for those involved, as they relied on certain skills and abilities in order to be choir members. The choice of repertoire, requirements of musical literacy, and use of language became musical markers of respectability. This provided a platform for a collective statement of middle-class belonging, in keeping with the members' sacrifices and struggles in order to obtain the best education available in the circumstances. Finally, choir membership offered an enjoyment of collective musical performance in the company of like-minded individuals and friends with similar goals and aspirations. Thus, choir members in Kroonvale formed a repertory of music, in this case often of European origin, which nevertheless functioned as a way of re-creating and actively formulating a sense of belonging to a particular status group within the broader community.

The significance of these interpretations for South African musical studies is that they accept the reality of class inscriptions onto musical genres and endeavor to highlight the intersections of class and music in a particular repertory located in a specific community. Moving beyond the apartheid context of racial categorization, the evidence presented here attempts to highlight class statements as an alternative way of understanding church choir performance in Kroonvale. The fact that coloured people in Kroonvale (and most likely elsewhere in South Africa) became forced by external circumstances to use the "language of culture and civility" in order to "sidestep . . . the language of race" is a disturbing legacy of South African attitudes toward race and ethnicity (Lewis 2001, 145). The paternalism and discrimination inherent in apartheid assumptions of race equaling class emphasize the struggle faced by middle-class and educated coloured, Indian, and black people. The Kroonvale generation of middle-class choir members (who belong mainly to the older generation today) utilized their exposure to contemporary musical repertories and ideas of musical respectability as a way of undermining these assumptions and dealing more explicitly with these issues. Musical performance served as a vehicle for these expressions.

Ideas of class status and their signs in music continue to change and reform in response to contemporary historical, social, and political circumstances. Community choir members lamented that new recruits were becoming increasingly difficult to find; young people, while they enjoyed listening to church choir performances, generally did not show an interest in choir membership. This suggests a new contextualization of choir performance and its particular adherence to a generation of people who came of age during the height of apartheid oppression. Respectability, shame, and class issues are part of this community history and are constantly being negotiated in Kroonvale as elsewhere in the country. As Ortner states, "People are never wholly constructed by their class position, or indeed by any other single aspect of their identity" (2003, 13). Thus, the musical embodiment of class status in this community is subject to change and constant renegotiation, while at the same time partially shaping the lives of its contemporary residents. Through singing, the many choir members of Kroonvale state the intersecting aspects of their particular identities as individuals, and they continue enjoying the pleasure of musical performance in the company of good friends.

6

Mothers of the Church

Women's Society Music and the Politics of Gender

'n Hen wat kraai se nek word omgedraai. Daars net 'n haan mos op 'n kerktoring—baie kerke—het jy al gesien?

[A hen that crows gets its neck wrung. There are only roosters on church towers—many churches—have you seen this?]

—Joyce Grootboom, 2005

Die man is die dak van die huis.

[The man is the roof of the house.]

—COMMUNITY PROVERB

On July 3, 2005, I attended a communion service at the ESCC. The organist played hymns as background music before the service began, and, sheltered by the sound, the congregation became unusually talkative. After a shout of "stilte!" (Afrikaans for "silence!"), the vrouevereniging (women's society) and the jongsusters (young women's group) began a series of koortjies, thereby forcing the congregation to sing instead of to discuss the news of the week. The congregation sang dutifully and order was restored. Later in the service, after communion, the vrouevereniging and jongsusters members again took charge of the situation. This time, they rose to their feet, formed a line and danced around the church singing a loud, joyful koortjie, "Die engele roer die bad om siekes gesond te maak" (The angels stir the pool to heal the sick).[1] Led by Suster Hendriks, a short, wiry older lady with lively, mischievous eyes, they wound their way around the church aisles. For those few minutes, the women of the church controlled the space.*

Gender has long been a site of contestation in private and public life in South Africa. At first glance, the quotations that open this chapter support the notion of a strict patriarchal system in Kroonvale within which women are expected to remain subservient and in the private sphere of the household. There is a clear separation between men's roles and women's roles in this community. Yet, my fieldwork narrative demonstrates that in the sacred space of the church, women can and do control aspects of the service without infringing on the traditionally powerful role of the male minister. Despite the strict division of gender and labor roles in this South African community, there is nevertheless space for the expression of individuality and creativity for women, both at Sunday church services and at weekly prayer meetings where they meet alone.

Although significant improvements have taken place in the struggle for gender equality and empowerment in this country, many communities still expect women to remain subordinate to men. Phillipe Denis identifies this situation as a major obstacle in oral history studies, stating that "women are particularly reluctant to speak on their own. . . . [They are] culturally conditioned to let their husbands, boyfriends, employers, or ministers . . . speak on their behalf" (2003, 213, 214). This chapter examines the ways in which Kroonvale women's society music and practices claim independent space and recognition for members within the church context.[2] By comparing the function of music in the official church services with how music works within women's prayer meetings, I argue that music serves as a vehicle of female expression, creativity, and independence from traditional South African patriarchal systems.

Gendered Spaces

Women's often subordinate role in South African society has a long and complex history; what Belinda Bozzoli calls "a patchwork quilt of patriarchies" existed in nineteenth-century South Africa (1983, 149). Cherryl Walker explains that we can reduce these various forms into two systems, namely, the African system and the European settler system. The former involved women as a pivotal center of society because of their reproductive capabilities but simultaneously saw them as possessions. The latter was largely influenced by Victorian values, in which women remained in the home where they raised children and managed the household. Both these dominant systems enforced the control of women and thus worked together to reinforce various patriarchal forms in the country (1990, 1).[3]

Within these patriarchal systems, South African women seldom resorted to open acts of defiance. A famous exception to this is their well-documented activism during the antipass campaign in the 1950s. Yet, some scholars have interpreted this period of resistance as primarily against state interference in women's family and domestic lives, which remained located in an essentially patriarchal framework (Walker 1982; Wells 1982). Feminist theorist Julia Wells characterized this type of resistance as "motherism," a concept she defines as the strategic use of women's roles as mothers in order to fight social injustice.[4] She states, "Motherism is not feminism. Women swept up in motherist movements are not fighting for their personal rights as women, but for their rights as mothers. Since concepts of the sanctity of motherhood are so deeply entrenched in the social fabric of most societies, this strategy often proves effective where other attempts to generate social change fail" (1991, 4). The concept of motherhood is questioned by Walker who warns against assumptions of a unified understanding of this term and calls for "a more deeply historicised understanding of motherhood in South Africa" (1995, 418, 423). She argues for a three-dimensional understanding of the term, which incorporates "mothering work—the practice of motherhood . . . the discourse of motherhood, embracing the norms, values and ideas about 'the Good Mother' that operate in any one society . . . [and] motherhood as social identity," which includes the construction of motherhood as identity and self-image within a specific social group (424). Her inquiry into the meanings of this term reveals differing discourses of "motherhood" within South Africa that often separate and then converge in various historical contexts. Her work suggests that the "motherist" movements cannot be dismissed as essentially conservative. Women do not merely exist in a patriarchal framework that defines them only as mothers, sisters, or wives; they also knowingly develop new strategies for empowerment (428). Often, however, these strategies form part of how patriarchal systems work, by allowing a certain amount of resistance to male domination on condition that this is confined to accepted roles with the system, for example, women's additional power within the private domestic sphere of the household. Walker summarizes this as "the dialectic between female resistance to and acquiescence in their subordination is a [common] theme" (1990, 31).

These notions suggest that despite the seemingly conservative bases for resistance, South African women made use of the resources and "motherhood" rhetoric available within patriarchal systems in order to gain political ground of their own. As some women from certain groups are not always comfortable speaking for themselves, I believe that closer study of both religious contexts and an assessment of nonverbal practices (including music) can reveal subtle ways and means of disrupting the male-dominated order. The church constitutes an important context for this type of practice as it is simultaneously private (a space for personal spiritual contemplation and worship) and public (a space where fellow community members gather, away from the private sphere of home and family).

My interpretation of the church context builds on Carol Muller's notion of the church as "feminized" space in the context of her work with the followers of the Nazarite religion.[5] Muller states that the spaces of "the family, religious homes, and some musical repertories . . . have conventionally been defined as sacred and feminine"; these spaces provide shelter and protection from the outside male-dominated spheres of the military and the state, as they did particularly in apartheid South Africa (1999, xviii; see also Franco 1985). In the church context, I believe that women can apply their domestic skills, including the attributes of mothering and nurturing, not only in the care of their own families but also for the good of the wider church family. Thus the church becomes an extension of the private, domestic sphere and a place of safety for community members. However, I believe that the church also offers a more public setting for the appreciation of women's (usually invisible) domestic activities. In Kroonvale, for instance, the community saying, "The man is the roof of the house," encapsulates an acceptable woman's role. This saying illustrates the firm belief that family members are subordinate to the man of the household who has the final word on all matters. In the community churches where God, not man, is the roof of the house, I believe that opportunities arise for a subtle reordering of gender norms and expectations and that the women's singing also reveals these tendencies.

An additional theoretical insight following from these ideas is that the church events and gatherings are themselves gendered differently. For example, I regard the Sunday church service as a public space in the sense that it is dominated by a male minister, attended by men, women, and children of the community and takes place in a formal setting. In contrast, I interpret the more intimate women's gatherings, usually held on Thursdays with no other congregation members present, as belonging to the private sphere. Thus, the church space is constituted differently depending on the day of the week, the type of event, and the event's attendance by certain sections of the congregation. In addition to these gendered spaces, the simultaneously private and public spaces offered by the church provide opportunities for the recontextualization and reinterpretation of expected gender roles within this community. After providing a brief historical background of the women's society tradition in the next section, I discuss how their practices and music provide evidence for these theoretical ideas.

Kroonvale Women's Society History
and the *Manyano* Tradition

I stumbled upon the Kroonvale women's society prayer meetings when I made an appointment to interview the ESCC minister, Rev. Leon Barendse. Due to important church business, he did not arrive at the agreed-on time, 3:00 p.m. on a Thursday. Instead, the women's society members invited me to join their prayer meeting. It was one of those scorchingly hot, dry Karoo days. Open windows in the church helped the hot air to circulate and brought only slight relief to those of us sitting in the pews. The members of the women's society, dressed in the customary uniform of black skirt, black sandals, white blouse, black jacket and white or black head-scarf, fanned themselves with their hymnbooks.

The oldest member of the society at that time, Ouma Calla, led the service from a small table and chair in front of the pews. After a few koortjies, Ouma said a prayer of thanks that everyone could be present, and all the women joined her in saying the Lord's Prayer. After the next song, another member rose to her feet and labored over the words she read from the Bible, asking for our patience with her reading as she had not brought her glasses. After her reading and subsequent sermon, the society sang a koortjie and then another member delivered a sermon. Ouma requested that two or three members say prayers, which they did. One woman in particular delivered a highly emotional prayer, her voice rising and falling in volume and pitch, with a particularly gritty timbre when she spoke about the forces of evil. Her prayer culminated in sobbing, and the society sang a hymn so that she could regain her composure. After the final blessing, the women began singing a cheerful rhythmic koortjie to signal the end of the meeting.

Although I did not know this at the time, it is customary at the end of a prayer meeting for each woman to walk to the front, shake the leader's hand, and stand next to her until everybody has shaken each member's hand and formed a line.[6] I remained seated until a few women motioned to me to stand up and shake Ouma Calla's hand. The members patiently guided me through this process with eye contact and gestures until I too had participated in the correct manner. Still singing, the society members danced out of the church. Without skipping a beat of the koortjie, the women around me nodded their farewells and guided me into the minister's office, where he was waiting to begin our interview.[7]

Almost by accident then, I attended my first *biduur* (hour of prayer) that Thursday afternoon (see Figure 6.1). According to Deborah Gaitskell, Thursday is also the day throughout South Africa for women's prayer meetings in many denominations because, during apartheid, Thursday afternoon was the traditional afternoon off for domestic workers. In fact, it is often said that "Thursday is the women's day, as Sunday is the preacher's" (1995, 226).[8] What I observed in Kroonvale is, therefore, very similar to a deeply entrenched ritual among South African black women. Known as *manyano,* a Xhosa word for "union" and used to refer to the Methodist women's groups as well as to this kind of group all over the country, this tradition dates back to the nineteenth-century period of missionization and colonization in South Africa.

Figure 6.1   *Rev. Leon Barendse and members of the women's society outside the ESCC. Photograph by author.*

It is problematic to assume that the term manyano can be applied without question to the Kroonvale women's society tradition. Whether this can be done is particularly difficult to determine as very little written evidence exists on Christian coloured women's religious identities and practices. My research suggests that many similarities exist between what I observed in Kroonvale and what is described in the literature on the black Christian women's meetings, hence my use of this material here is a way of contextualizing this type of tradition. However, Helen Scanlon's work on Western Cape women seems to draw a distinction between African women's manyanos and church women's organizations such as the Women's Home and Foreign Mission Society of the African Methodist Episcopal Church with its largely coloured working-class membership (2007, 126). Thus, I use the term manyano below with these reservations in mind.

The tradition of African church women's meetings emerged by the 1830s, when the wives of missionaries organized regular women's gatherings to teach black women converts to sew. By the 1880s, these practical lessons had changed to meetings for the "unstructured times of shared 'testimony,' exposition of biblical verses and extemporaneous prayer that have been the life-blood of church meetings for thousands of African women over the past century" (Gaitskell 1990, 255–56). Although originally a way of educating African women converts to be good Christian wives and mothers in the Victorian sense, these meetings began to serve the purpose of converting new "heathen" members, preaching for religious devotion and temperance, preaching against indigenous beer, and holding meetings to visit and pray for the sick (256).

While it is clear from these sources that African Christian women's unions existed and continue to do so, there is a relative paucity of information about the history of similar groups in the coloured community of Graaff-Reinet. Nevertheless, the following deductions suggest that the tradition has a long history in this area. First, despite its rural isolation, Graaff-Reinet did not operate in a vacuum apart from the rest of South Africa. If meetings of African women all over South Africa were well entrenched by the 1880s, it is unlikely that these meetings did not take place in Graaff-Reinet. In addition, as both coloured and black people lived in the same area before the 1960s, it is possible that they would have shared these meetings and their associated cultural practices. Second, the many references to church bazaars in Graaff-Reinet's historical records indicate that this tradition cannot be overlooked as perhaps a forerunner to or coexisting phenomenon with women's society groups. From the mid-nineteenth century in Graaff-Reinet, various church denominations held bazaars to raise funds. The women of all these congregations played an important role in the preparation, organization, and gathering of food and other items sold at these occasions. Third and finally, the relevant church records as well as current members themselves provide evidence of a long tradition of women's society activity in Kroonvale. For instance, an announcement of a women's prayer meeting to be held in the "Location" appears in the DRMC records on February 6, 1899. A reference to a women's *werkgezelschap* (work society) follows a year later, as do regular allusions to the women's society in records up to the present day (DRMC Records, February 12, 1900).[9] Virginia Christoffels, a PSCC member, mentioned to me that this church's women's society celebrated their eightieth year of existence in 2005, which would place its establishment in 1925 (interview, October 28, 2005).[10] The ESCC women's society celebrated its sixty-fifth anniversary in November 2005. This primary material in the archives and oral history sources suggests that the tradition of weekly women's prayer meetings in the coloured community of Graaff-Reinet dates back to the late nineteenth century, if not before.

Praying, Preaching . . .

Gaitskell's work reveals three shared characteristics with the prayer meetings in the Kroonvale church denominations on Thursday afternoons. Mia Brandel-Syrier also noted these in her study of African women's societies in the Johannesburg area (1962, 27, 35–36, 44). First, the women wear distinctive uniforms. Gaitskell describes the composition of these as "complex cultural borrowings"; for example, according to her, the British military uniforms of red, black, and white originally influenced the Natal Methodist women's uniform (1990, 261).[11] In the Eastern Cape, it is traditional to wear black skirts,

*Figure 6.2   Women's society meeting, ESCC. From left: Suster Speelman, Suster
Saptoe, Suster Barendse, Suster Reid, and Suster Haarhoff. Photograph by author.*

white jackets or blouses, and white or black berets or some other type of head
covering, which might have been influenced by the nuns who worked with
some earlier women's groups in this region (261). The Kroonvale women's
society members dressed in these colors during 2004 and 2005, but when I
attended a biduur in 2010, I noticed that the uniform has since changed to
black skirts, black blouses, and a blue jacket (see Figure 6.2). I have also seen
members wearing badges with the official Congregational Church emblem
of a white dove and olive branch against a light blue background, as part of
the uniform. Suster Kalse explained to me when I asked about these badges
that they cannot be worn on just any occasion; they are only meant to be
worn, with serious intent, for religious occasions (communication, November 3, 2005; see also Hendrickson 1996; Muller 1999). In addition to the
physical covering of the body to demonstrate their membership, it is generally
expected that women prepare themselves mentally for the meetings through
Bible reading, meditation, and prayer.

A second characteristic Gaitskell mentions is that the women come
together specifically in their roles as mothers (1990, 251). She explains:

Motherhood was central to African women's personal and cultural
identity as well as their social and economic roles long before the

advent of Christian missions in South Africa. But church groups served to transform, elevate and entrench the importance of marriage, wifehood and motherhood for women. They were among the powerful ideological forces contributing to the ongoing centrality of the notion of motherhood in African women's organisation in the twentieth century. (1990, 271–72)

This characteristic is also noticeable in Kroonvale women's society meetings. During sermons and prayers, I often heard members addressing each other as *mammas* or *moeders* (mothers). Members are usually of the mother or grandmother generation and hold the respected status of being the elderly of the community. In this protective role, they meet not only to preach and support each other but also to visit the sick and the bereaved, to cater for church functions, and to provide much-needed financial support to the church as a whole. Rev. Barendse told me that a few years ago the women's society of the ESCC settled the R15,000 mortgage debt on the parsonage (interview, October 27, 2005).[12] For women who mostly survive on meager monthly pensions with no regular work this is no mean feat.

In addition to working within and for their churches, contemporary women's societies from various denominations and places meet together at certain times. Each year, for example, the women's society of a church holds an anniversary that celebrates another year of the society's existence. As part of this celebration, women's groups from all over the Eastern Cape region travel to the church where they hold an all-night "social" on the Saturday night. Each group performs a number of songs and then gives a monetary donation to the church. The anniversary celebration culminates in a communion service on the Sunday morning. There is also the fundraising tradition of the *pennieslaan* (penny-slam), which is mentioned in church record books from the late 1970s (DRMC records, September 23, 1977; PSCC records, November 21, 1980, November 18, 1983, March 27, 1987, April 24, 1987).[13] On these occasions, members proceed to the front of the venue while singing and dancing and slam small change onto the table in time with the music. These events are held within one women's society, or they can invite other societies to join them (van Jaarsveld interview, November 10, 2005; Kayster interview, July 4, 2006). Another type of biduur, the *sametrekking* (gathering) meeting, is held once a month in Kroonvale. This is a gathering of women's society members from different local denominations and an invited guest speaker usually preaches on a selected biblical text or a current issue relevant to the community, such as family, divorce, marriage, or HIV/AIDS. Thus, it is clear that women's society members take their role as mothers very seriously, not only in caring for their own families but also in being "mothers of the church" in their roles of holding meetings and organizing fundraising events within the broader church community.

The interplay between orality and literacy, which I observed at contemporary Kroonvale prayer meetings, is the third characteristic Gaitskell mentions about manyano traditions. Her description of this phenomenon in the following quote can be applied equally to the prayer meetings I participated in during my fieldwork.

> The praying and preaching style of the manyanos could certainly repay investigation by a specialist in traditional African female oral literature, since published accounts of female story-telling and praise poetry provide suggestive insights. In manyano preaching, a verse of Bible passage is used as the basis for a variety of preaching performances or individual testimonies. This does not seem entirely unlike the process by which a "core image" of a folktale is "expanded during performance by the exercise of the imagination into a work of literary art." The same process of blending "tradition and creativity, memorization and improvisation, the communal and the individual," is at work. Both the teller of folktales and the manyano preacher are almost invariably mature women, often of the grandmother generation, and in both cases the audience determines the duration of the performance, the speaker concluding when the listeners no longer participate, respond or agree, or perhaps launch into a diverting song. (1995, 225–26; Cope 1978, 193, 199)

Most members brought their Bibles and hymnbooks to the meetings and used these intermittently. Members placed great value on these texts and often spoke to me (before and after meetings) in terms of Bible quotations or references to certain passages. This was the case despite the fact that, according to Sabina van Jaarsveld (chair of the URC women's society), many members of her generation could not read (interview, November 10, 2005). I presume this is because of inadequate educational opportunities and financial constraints during apartheid.[14] Due to this reality, some women asked others to read the Bible for them before they preached the sermon on the featured excerpt. However, once the preaching began there was no hesitation and women expressed themselves freely, urged their fellow members toward better behavior, and told stories of their personal lives as illustrations. Murmurs of assent, nods of approval, rapt concentration on the speaker's words, and statements of "*dankie Jesus*" (Thank you, Jesus) demonstrated support for the preacher's message. Women memorized and internalized these texts and combined them with stories of their life experiences and other words of wisdom to create sermons at the meetings. This malleability of text is in direct contrast to the usually heavily text-centered approach in the Reformed religious tradition.

There is evidence of subtle play within the three characteristics of women's society traditions as discussed above. For example, while the choice of clothing worn as uniforms is directly related to the historical circumstances of colonialism and missionary activity, the women use these uniforms in order to function as "markers of identity" (Muller 1999, 85). For Sabina van Jaarsveld, the uniforms show solidarity so that the women's association with the church is clear (interview, November 10, 2005). In addition, they also serve to eliminate differences in social and economic status so that the group maintains its internal unity (see Brandel-Syrier 1962, 222). In terms of the importance of motherly roles, the women emphasize care and nurturing for their families and other church members, but at the same time, they assume a traditionally male role when they provide financial support for the church and lead the organization of other church fundraising events. The interplay between orality and literacy discussed here shows an adherence to the scripture and liturgy of the church denomination, yet these written texts are mainly used as a point of departure for women to express their individual interpretations. The three general characteristics of the women's society tradition thus reveal a technique of playing with expectations within a certain framework. This technique is nonthreatening to the wider community, yet serves as a way for women to carve out a clearly recognizable, independent space for themselves within the church context.

One of the main reasons for this nonthreatening appearance of women's society groups is that their meetings take place on Thursday afternoons, usually with no men present. This allows the women a certain measure of liberty in the way they structure and hold these gatherings. As Gaitskell explains, "Women's marginality gave them a new freedom to experiment and learn from other denominations, making Christianity their own, because there was not such a fixed conception in each denomination of female as opposed to male ministry" (1990, 264). In relation to the more formal Sunday morning church services, however, these meetings function as subsidiary events within the official church schedule. Gaitskell characterizes the subordinate position of women in church as follows:

> Just as formal religious leadership in traditional society is male, in both family and tribal ancestral veneration, while the charismatic diviner is generally a woman . . . so in the mission churches the prayer women provide a less regulated counterpart to the formal authority of ordained ministers and paid evangelists. The women prophets and

healers of the independent churches fill a similar role and are just as unthreatening in any permanent sense on the whole to male dominance. The obligatory tribute to women as the "backbone" of the church confirms the notion of a supportive, unobtrusive, female role. (1995, 227)

While Gaitskell's views highlight that women's societies forge an independent and individual tradition which is nevertheless allowed to be subsumed by the official male-dominated church practices, she does not include an interpretation of how music functions at women's society meetings. In the following section, I focus on how the singing at prayer meetings provides a sense of women's creativity, mutual support, and independence in relation to the music at official Sunday church services.

. . . And Singing

Koortjies and hymns comprised the musical repertoire sung at these meetings. At their prayer meetings, members often chose to sing the favorite hymns and koortjies of the particular church congregation and its minister. Members knew many hymns and koortjies from memory, and instead of referring to their hymnbooks, they often used the books to provide percussive rhythmic punctuation by holding the book in one hand and slapping it with the other in time. Other members brought the leather cushions (mentioned earlier in reference to Sunday services) to provide rhythmic accompaniment to the singing. Slapping the books and cushions in combination with deliberate foot stamping added a resonant thudding timbre to the rhythm, which differed completely from the (less common) sound of clapping hands. Aside from slapping the books/cushions and sometimes stamping in time to the music, members also stepped from side to side and often danced where they stood in the pews.

As members used identical hymn and koortjie texts to those of Sunday church services, one cannot analyze these alone for evidence of women's freedom of expression.[15] It is more important here to listen to the women's singing style at their Thursday afternoon meetings.[16] Despite the similarity of repertoire, I believe that the purpose and presentation of the music at the meetings differed.[17] On Sundays, for instance, the minister formally announced the hymns, and the congregation stood and sang from their hymnbooks. At prayer meetings, members did not announce hymns and koortjies; they sang at any time. Even if they did not know or remember the words or ran out of written verses in the hymnbook, members employed a variety of vocables and the singing continued. This introduced a certain flexibility in the singing—members chose when to repeat verses or simply when to stop singing actual words to the melodies. Biduur participants also tended to sing more koortjies than formal hymns, which aided the flow of the event. At Sunday services, the minister often requested koortjies and the congregation obliged; in women's meetings, it was far less necessary to ask people to sing. Singing seemed to flow spontaneously and seamlessly.[18] Women's society members (especially the lead singers) were experts at covering silences with singing, supporting a woman who was preaching,[19] signaling to the preacher that she should end her sermon, singing for her to walk back to her seat, singing for the next speaker to walk to the front, singing to allow women to regain their composure after an emotional sermon or prayer, and generally perceiving good moments to begin songs throughout the biduur. Every aspect of a meeting was covered and protected by song.[20]

Three-part harmony constituted the basic foundation of the singing in women's society meetings. This often resulted in harmonizations that would be considered incomplete in the traditional Western sense (successions of second-inversion chords, for example), yet the fact that women seldom provided a fourth, bass voice gave the singing its unique sound and texture. In addition, several other features characterized the music as belonging to this particular group. The closer overall range of women's voices (in comparison to the addition of men's and children's voices at Sunday services) gave the singing a particular sound, and the equal emphasis on all the melody lines meant that the "main" melody (that is, the soprano part) of the hymn or koortjie constituted only one strand of a variety of contrapuntal lines within the overall chordal texture. Each woman chose her own way through the harmony of the song, depending on the pitch of her usual speaking voice and the melody lines she had become accustomed to singing for many years. The range of the singing therefore voiced the solidarity of the women's society (similar to the visual aspect of the identical uniforms) and yet allowed each woman a respected and individual place within that sound. The combination of women's vocal ranges and the different melody lines resulted in a very rich, sensual harmony. In general, women's society music took a freer approach to the improvisation of call-and-response melodies and harmonies than the singing at Sunday church services.[21] Additional features included scooping at the ends of phrases and the use of breath (for example, sighing and sobbing), which contributed to the overall richness of the sound.

The use of nonverbal sounds can be characterized as examples of *écriture féminine,* a concept theorized by French feminist writers as a particularly feminine mode of writing, in other words, "writing the [female] body" (Citron 1993, 53–54). As Renée Cox explains, "A music modeled on feminine writing would engage the listener in the musical moment rather than in the structure as a whole. . . . In sung music, vocalization would be relaxed and make use of nonverbal . . . sounds" (1991, 333–34). Cox characterizes these aspects as a manifestation of *jouissance,* the pleasure experienced in the pre-Oedipal stage of a girl infant's relationship with her mother (1993, 334). Although aware of concerns that these concepts merely perpetuate gender essentialism as well as the problems of mapping European feminist aesthetics to women's singing in Kroonvale, I believe that the style of their singing contains not only nonverbal sounds but also a sense of spiritual joy or jouissance inherent in their free and playful approach to the church repertoire. To give an indication of this type of sound, I have transcribed a very popular church koortjie from the Dutch Reformed Church tradition, "Wees stil en weet dat ek is God" (Be Still and Know that I Am God). This was a favorite at many church services as well as prayer meetings that I attended, and this rendition can be compared to a rendition of this koortjie at a Sunday morning service (see Figures 6.3 and 6.4, respectively; PURLs 6.1 and 6.2).

From the sound of "Wees stil en weet dat ek is God," especially when sung at women's society meetings, there is a sense of languishing in the particular richness of the women's vocal timbre. The slow tempo and reverent style make this koortjie a unique addition to the atmosphere of a biduur, even though this koortjie is probably sung at least twice a week if not more in Graaff-Reinet's Reformed Church community. To me, there was a definite difference in sound between the freer rendition of this koortjie at the women's society prayer meeting and the rendition of the same koortjie at the Sunday service. In Figure 6.3, instead of retaining the phrase structure of "Wees stil en weet dat ek is God" by pausing to breathe at the end of each phrase, women improvised different voice parts and held notes longer so that the music became more continuous. The lead singer assisted as well by providing a "call" (bar 4) to which the women responded with the second phrase. In Figure 6.4, the congregation paused for breath at the end of every phrase, resulting in a few seconds of silence. The lead singer sang alone only at the start of the piece, which, together with the strict adherence to the homorhythmic texture of crotchet and minim note values, contributed to a sense that the congregation sang the music in the style of a traditional European Christian hymn. Nonverbal elements in Figure 6.3 included the use of vocables in the lead singer's part (bar 4) and in the moving quavers in the lowest part (bar 6). In addition, the slide between pitches (bar 10) in the women's society rendition is far more pronounced than the same place in Figure 6.4 where only the women singing the alto part contributed this element. The music of women's societies therefore conformed to the general repertoire and style of singing in this community, yet it had a freer, more intense and improvisational sound. It is this playful approach that contributes to the

Figure 6.3 *"Wees stil en weet dat ek is God" (Be Still and Know that I Am God), from women's singing at the Women's World Day of Prayer service, ESCC, March 3, 2005. (Composer and author unknown.) Transcription by author.*

sense of spiritual joy or jouissance to which I alluded earlier. In addition, I interpret this simultaneous adhesion to and departure from the community singing style as a nonverbal manifestation of a well-known concept in African performance studies.

Poetic License

On November 12, 2005, I attended my first social at the ESCC women's society anniversary celebrations. With the minister's permission, I brought my camcorder to the event. Up until that point I had not used it at the church, as ministers

Figure 6.4   "*Wees stil en weet dat ek is God," from congregational singing at the ESCC, June 26, 2005. Transcription by author.*

generally preferred audio to visual recording equipment because it caused less distraction for the congregation. Sitting with the women's society members and observing the way a Saturday night social works was a fascinating and rewarding experience (PURLs 6.3 and 6.4). Although my camcorder and I were the objects of much curiosity, I soon became thoroughly immersed in the singing and the practices within this tradition.

The next morning, I arrived at the church in the pouring rain (incredibly rare for the Karoo) for the communion service and hurried to prepare my recording equipment. Just as I had settled down with mini-disc player and camcorder running, a women's society member tugged at my sleeve and said that there was something important in the church hall that I needed to record with my camera. Reluctant to leave the church and music behind, especially so close to the start of the service, I followed her with my camcorder and tried to hide my surprise and confusion when I realized that the women required me to record the preparation of food for the postservice refreshments (PURL 6.5). Women's society members opened cans of fruit salad and placed their contents into a huge bowl. Other women were busily making fried chicken. I dutifully recorded all the activities taking place in the tiny kitchen, conversed briefly about the welcome rainy weather, and made my exit, just in time for the church service to begin.

Although I soon became involved in the beautiful singing at the church service that morning (PURL 6.6), this interlude repeatedly tugged at my memory. By calling my attention to their labor, the women's society members reminded me that without their work and sacrifice that morning (after having remained awake all of the previous night to provide food at the social), there would be no refreshments after the service and many people would leave hungry.[22] Thus, my trip to the church hall that morning forced me to acknowledge the work of food production as equally important to the service itself.

From my own background as a white, Western, feminist-influenced woman, this event and the prayer meetings I witnessed made it seem obvious at first to interpret the women's society tradition in Kroonvale as conservative and indicative of women's ongoing subordination in the face of South African patriarchal society. However, there is a contradiction in the roles of women in this community that I found difficult to reconcile to this view. As mentioned earlier in relation to Gaitskell's interpretation, women worked within a subordinate domestic role (for example, the covered heads in church of the older generation of women because of the belief that a woman could not go bareheaded into a church, the food preparation for church functions, the emphasis on mothering, nurturing, and so on). Yet, I observed a subtle play with these expectations in the very events that seemed on the surface to be so subordinate. Examples here are the dominant organizational role of women at church fundraising events, the women's society's significant financial contributions to the church, and the singing and control of the church space as mentioned at the start of this chapter.

It is in these actions and sounds of their singing that Walker's notion of the dialectic between acceptance and rejection of stereotypical gender roles takes place in the religious practices of these women. The women's society tradition constitutes a unique utilization of motherhood rhetoric to further its members' goals of community care and loyalty to the church, but also it ensures that these important roles are properly acknowledged and appreciated by the wider church congregation. The discourse of motherhood, understood within the differently gendered spaces of the church context, therefore provides women's society members with a distinctive vehicle for expressing their simultaneous adherence to and departure from community gender norms. The sounds of their singing form an important way of expressing this dialectic. Denis's statement (mentioned earlier) that many women are culturally conditioned not to speak for themselves indicates that one cannot judge women's independence from and struggles against South African patriarchies by the spoken word alone. In southern Africa there is a long history of praise poetry and other performance genres that allow the performers to state their objections to their circumstances in song. This type of criticism would not usually be allowed in normal speech. In the context of my research I wish to suggest a new way of approaching the notion of "poetic license" in order to broaden the understanding of this term to include nonverbal actions such as musical style.

Hugh Tracey first adopted the term "poetic justice" in relation to music in his book on the Chopi musicians of Mozambique. He explained it as follows: "African music . . . performs a highly social and cathartic function in a society which has no daily press, no publications and no stage other than the village yard in which publicly to express its feelings or voice its protests . . ." (1948/1970, 3). Leroy Vail and Landeg White borrowed this notion for their book on southern African praise poetry. However, they used the term "poetic license" and defined it as follows:

> There have, in fact, been many writers who have noted the phenomenon that the various forms of oral poetry in sub-Saharan Africa are licensed by a freedom of expression which violates normal conventions—that chiefs and headmen may be criticized by the followers, husbands by their wives, fathers by their sons, employers or overseers by their workers, officials and politicians by their underlings, and even Life Presidents by their subjects, in ways that the prevailing social and political codes would not normally permit, so long as it is done through poetry. (1991, 43)

Here I would like to extend this idea to include nonverbal forms of aesthetic expression, in other words, not only "poetry" understood in its strictest sense but also other aspects of performance that can nevertheless be characterized as a commentary that counters the prevailing status quo. The choice of clothing, flexible approach to liturgical text, recourse to the role of motherhood and all its attendant symbolic meaning, as well as the elements of musical style discussed above all indicate to me that the women's society tradition in Kroonvale comments nonverbally on the roles and expectations of women. In terms of practices, this is done by blurring the boundaries between the strictly envisaged ideas of women's and men's roles in the community (for example, when women take the lead in organizational and financial matters). Regarding music, the women introduce a freedom of expression above and beyond the usual musical practices in this religious tradition and thus recontextualize these expectations as well. On the surface, women comply with their expected gender roles as expressed in the sayings mentioned at the start of this chapter, but their actions instead suggest a strong awareness and knowledge of their strength, independence, and authority in the church environment. The sound and style of their singing is a poetic and aesthetic expression of this knowledge and its resultant freedom. Thus, the expanded type of nonverbal poetic license is inherent in the music and practices of women's society tradition in Kroonvale and provides evidence of women's subtle defiance of the patriarchal systems still entrenched in many South African communities.

Conclusion

Just as the church provides a space for the assumption of and subsequent creative play with expected gender roles, the women's singing at meetings also exemplifies this creative approach to existing social norms. Close listening to their singing reveals sonic evidence for the creative space provided by church women's society organizations. It is here, in the differently gendered spaces of the church context, that women's responses to and commentaries on long-entrenched South African patriarchal systems can be found in their singing style and use of improvisational and nonverbal sounds. Song thus empowers and liberates the members of women's society meetings while simultaneously drawing them together in a shared sense of community and solidarity. This shared sense is also largely due to the motherly roles that the women assume within the community. As "mothers of the church" the women utilize this traditional female role not only as a vehicle for self-expression but also as a way of gaining recognition for their activities. All this takes place without unduly disturbing the norms of the community.

The women's society members with whom I conversed seldom spoke directly about themselves. Instead, they preferred to use sayings and biblical texts and often repeated statements made by the church minister. A possible interpretation of this is that they may have consciously or subconsciously chosen to limit what they spoke about to me and that this approach forms part of a culturally based strategy to deal with the patriarchal framework within which they live. As South African society changes and more communities become sensitive to gender equality, it will be interesting to observe whether the Kroonvale women's society music, actions, and conversations become more openly stated. In the future, it might become possible to hear in women's words that which I heard in their singing. In the meantime, the independence shown by Kroonvale women in the church context reminds us that the women of this community never completely accepted the roles imposed on them by various patriarchal systems. They are constantly playing with these expectations through their meetings and the intricate individual interweaving lines of their singing. With South Africa's particularly long and shameful history of women's subordination, the struggle for equality and empowerment needs to join those against crime and HIV/AIDS as being of equal and paramount importance. The sounds of the singing at women's prayer meetings and their claiming of the church space as their own form an integral part of this process.

7

Conclusion

Reflections on Karoo Sonic Spaces

The effect of the sun, combined with that of the red saline
dust, had inflamed my eyes to such an extent that I dared
not keep them open. Six hours of slow travel brought us
to Zout pan, salt spring. . . . When we had had dinner and
an hour's siesta, we set off again and soon crossed the dry
bed of the Wolf Rivier, after which we called at the Visagie farm. At least we could breathe there: the Karroo was
behind us. . . .

—Delegorgue 1838/1990, 1:23–33

Just opened is an exclusive-use villa, the Mountain
Retreat . . . at Samara Private Game Reserve near Graaff-
Reinet. Dramatic mountains, 28 000 hectacres [*sic*] of
Karoo bushveld and cheetah encounters come standard—
as well as a private ranger for guided walks, a chef special-
ising in Karoo classics and a dedicated housekeeper. Electricity is limited, which adds to the authentic wilderness
experience.

—British Airways travel magazine, January 2010, 31

The typical outsider view of the Karoo as uncomfortably hot, dusty,
and arid is a perception dating back to travel accounts of the nineteenth century, such as the one above by the French naturalist, Adulphe Delegorgue. In contemporary South Africa, this urgent need to leave the
Karoo behind persists. In the minds of many non-Karoo residents, Graaff-
Reinet is simply a place to refill the car's gas tank, obtain cheap takeout food,
and at the very most, stay one night at a local bed and breakfast. Many travelers, of course, drive straight through the town, impatient to leave the Karoo
behind and continue their journeys toward the sea.[1] However, if visitors linger
for a while longer, the region's charms (not always visible from the monoto-
nous national roads) unfold quietly and with great subtlety.

Due to recent media attention focused on the area (see the excerpt quoted above), many people's general perception of rural Karoo towns as merely refueling points has gradually changed to one that can be described as at best nostalgic and at worst as "new age." Glossy travel magazines in shopping malls with titles such as *Getaway* and *Country Life* describe the beautiful scenery, healthy lifestyle, friendly yet eccentric rural people, and fresh air of the Karoo in glowing terms, while at the same time pointing out such practical considerations as lower crime rates and cheaper property prices. In 2005, for instance, plans existed to build an African Dream Center in the Graaff-Reinet area, where "visitors will trek into the centre 'to get a feel of the land.' They will sleep around a communal fire, and their dreams will be analysed by a team of resident psychologists" (*Eastern Province Herald*, November 4). Although I share the concerns of some Graaff-Reinet residents that this area will soon be reduced to a gigantic health spa for the rich and famous, it is also positive that the Karoo is gaining more appreciation from both local and overseas visitors.

This media attention, however, serves as a reminder that the Karoo context has changed for both outsiders and insiders, and it continues to do so. Many surrounding sheep, goat, and ostrich farms have been sold to wealthy local or foreign landowners who removed the internal fences (originally constructed in order to work with livestock) for the purpose of establishing large game farms. The latter served the purpose of attracting trophy hunters who yearned to add the horns and skins of African animals to their collections. Many farmworkers adjusted to this new development, with its similarities to stock farming, but itinerant sheep-shearers suffered tremendously, as their source of livelihood dissipated with the onset of game farming in the area.[2] The steady rise of tourism and the hospitality industry, both in the town and surrounding region, serves to further diversify the contexts in which people in the Graaff-Reinet area live and work.[3]

My own perspective of Graaff-Reinet and its surrounding Karoo landscape also changed when, at the beginning of 2006, I moved 547 miles/880 km away to the Gauteng Province. I found myself in the center of the South African economic and business powerhouse, the "place of gold." Being on the periphery of the Karoo in a place where people predominantly regarded the Karoo as peripheral meant that my new surroundings and acquaintances exposed me to the viewpoints of non-Karoo residents. Many Eastern Cape, Western Cape, and KwaZulu-Natal residents joke about the stereotyped mass exodus of financially able Gauteng residents every December to the coast, and now, for the first time in my life, I was potentially a member of this group. The harsh and strident sounds of urban existence now accompanied my everyday routine, and they constantly reminded me of the great distance between the city of Pretoria (Tshwane) and the Eastern Cape. I could barely reconstruct the smells and sounds of Graaff-Reinet and the Karoo in this new context. Only when I listened to my field recordings could I remember and relive those days of driving to church on crisp Sunday mornings, rather nervous of what to expect, of repeating koortjies to myself on my way home, trying to remember the tunes and piece together the lyrics, of the fantastic sunsets, the ominous thunderstorms, the indescribably lovely smell of the Karoo plants immediately after rain, and most of all, my encounters with the people of Kroonvale.

Encounters from Afar

My academic and scholarly perception of church music in the Karoo has also experienced changes. In September 2009, I presented a guest lecture at a workshop on vernacular culture in Oudtshoorn, a Western Cape town well known for its ostrich farms. This event took place under the auspices of the ABSA Bank–sponsored Klein Karoo Nasionale Kunstefees (Little Karoo National Festival). The KKNK is well known as an annual Afrikaans-language festival. As coloured people constitute Oudtshoorn's majority population, the festival organizers wished to explore ways of making the event more inclusive of all Afrikaans speakers. This workshop provided a platform in which to discuss these possibilities and celebrate the rich vernacular culture of the local coloured community. During informal conversations before my presentation at the workshop, I remember participants showing great interest in the koortjie phenomenon. After my lecture, which featured the diverse origins and musical encounters within this repertory, I sensed a waning of interest, however. I received the impression that the religious nature of this music did not resonate with those endeavoring to recapture authentic "Khoisan" cultural and vernacular heritage. As many researchers tend not to choose the predominant, politically correct topics of the day, the response at the workshop did not cause me undue distress, but it did provide a new perspective on my work.

The experience also reminded me of a guest lecture I had presented a year before, at the University of Stellenbosch. While speaking, I noticed three additional audience members sitting right at the back of the venue. They were obviously not students of the particular undergraduate seminar to whom I'd been presenting, but had been following the discussion with interest. Alex van Heerden, and the sisters, An-Lize and Letitia Davids, introduced themselves during the question period afterward. I already knew of Alex van Heerden, jazz musician and performer/researcher of indigenous

Karoo folk music in the northern Cape region. He also worked as a consultant for the Solms Delta Museum, located at a local wine farm, which funded various projects aimed at preserving the indigenous cultural and musical heritage of the area (Solms Delta 2010). An-Lize and Letitia came from a very musical family whom Alex had befriended as part of his research on vernacular genres of the region. The Davids sisters informed me that what they had just heard in my field recordings was rather conservative and old-fashioned, but that they also sang koortjies in their church, the True Gospel Pentecostal Church in Atlantis outside Cape Town. "In our church, we sing the koortjies much faster," they said. All those present begged for a demonstration, and after some encouragement, the sisters performed three koortjies with Alex accompanying them on the accordion. Soon the entire hall reverberated with the infectious melodies and lively handclaps. The sisters revealed two additionally interesting pieces of information about music in their church. First, they told us that gospel-style tunes had started to replace koortjies, and second, that their mother was saddened by this because the cyclic and repeating nature of the koortjies made her feel more spiritually connected during a religious service. In other words, koortjies became a vehicle for a trancelike religious expression, which the verse-chorus structure of the gospel tunes could not provide.

My mind buzzed with questions: Was the replacement of koortjies by gospel tunes limited only to Pentecostal and/or urban congregations? Did the older generation in general lament the advent of the gospel tune genre? Did a different repertory of koortjies exist in Graaff-Reinet and Cape Town (or anywhere else for that matter), or did similar tunes occur? But, question time was over, and we agreed to keep in contact in order to begin a conversation about our mutual research and musical interests.[4]

Even though a year separated these guest lecture occasions, both of them significantly changed my perspective on the sounds of church music in Kroonvale, and this continues to adjust as I receive comments and comparisons from various quarters. Fundamentally, my experiences in Oudtshoorn and Stellenbosch confirm that a significant amount of research remains to be conducted. I view this book as only the beginning and hope it can provide a departure point for conversations between congregation and community members, researchers, musicians, and other interested parties. This conversation will no doubt eventually produce a substantial body of scholarly literature on the music of coloured people's communities in South Africa.[5]

Reading the Transnational Moment

Currently, the South African music studies field incorporates an expanded notion of what "South African music" entails and an appreciation of new research topics and approaches. The more recent appearance of research work on coloured people's music thus takes place within an environment particularly receptive to changing contexts. Within the post-apartheid literary and cultural studies discipline, Sarah Nuttall theorizes this perception of change and its accompanying need for new approaches by identifying two critical standpoints of this period (2009, 17). She characterizes the first as

> neo-Marxist in inflection. Here, the dominant critical impulse has been to assert continuity with the past, producing a critique based on reiteration and return, and an argument in the name of that which has not changed in the country. Such critics employ categories of race, class, domination and resistance in much the same way as critics had done in the decade or so before. (17)

Writers from this standpoint generally acknowledge the changes taking place in the country but believe that the "issues of hegemony, resistance and race that marked an earlier critical idiom need to remain at the centre of our critical investigations" (17). Nuttall names Shaun Jacobs and Herman Wasserman (2003) and Barbara Harlow and David Attwell (2000) as examples. The second position is one of grappling with "an as yet nameless present" in order to portray a "more future-inflected politics." Scholars such as Leon de Kock (2004), Isabel Hofmeyr (2004), Michael Titlestad (2004), and Mark Sanders (2002) attempt to expand existing vocabularies in order to accommodate the "prognostics of change" (19).

Despite their apparent ideological differences, both these approaches share an ongoing engagement with the past (which the first group understands as an ongoing dominant force today and which the second group perceives as important to acknowledge in order to enable conceptualization of tomorrow). Additionally, both groups realize that the politics of mass resistance no longer constitutes the definitive, primary force within this new environment.[6] This comprehension is expressed as a sense of loss in the first group and a nostalgia for a clear idea of who constituted one's friends and enemies; the second group is less perturbed by this realization as it is already focused on finding new ways of interpretation and analysis (18–20). For scholars working from these standpoints, the liberation from the need to tell the stories of political struggle means that, however they decide to frame their interpretations of the post-apartheid present, they remain free to investigate the immense diversity and wealth of research possibilities in this country.[7]

According to my observations, the new writerly fascination with those ancestors of coloured people, namely, the Khoekhoe and San, should be understood as only one strand of this freedom. A visit to any large bookstore in a South African shopping mall reveals several new titles on this topic in the African nonfiction section, alongside the now mainstream biographies of prominent ANC governmental and political figures. In addition to Antjie Krog's translations of San poetry (2004) and Elana Bregin and Belinda Kruiper's poignant account of the San artist, Vetkat Regopstaan Kruiper (2004), recent publications such as Andrew Bank's research on the Bleek-Lloyd collection of San folklore at the University of Cape Town (2006), Neil Parsons's work on the circus performer with Khoisan origins, Franz Taibosh (2009), and Clifton Crais and Pamela Scully's "ghost story and biography" on the life of Sara Baartman (2009) beckon invitingly from the shelves. The last-mentioned work is a sensitive account of Sara (or Saartjie) Baartman's life, which reimagines and refigures Sara Baartman's place in South Africa, not as a tragic figment of the European imagination (the "Hottentot Venus"), but as a "living, breathing person" (2009, 6). Baartman was born in the Eastern Cape in the 1770s and left for Cape Town in the mid-1790s. She spent the last five years of her life on display in Europe, and after her death in 1815, her thoroughly dissected remains were kept in Paris for almost two hundred years. In 2002, after long negotiations between the French and South African governments, Sara Baartman was finally laid to rest outside Hankey, an Eastern Cape town near Port Elizabeth.

The story of Baartman's "homecoming" shows how a historical South African figure is reclaimed and reinterpreted in the context of a changing, post-apartheid present. Her story resonated deeply with the political and social situation in a newly democratic South Africa; her life became a metaphor for the overcoming of injustices suffered during colonialism and apartheid and anyone, regardless of his/her background, could identify with her as an important historical icon of a new, united South Africa. Now characterized as " 'Mama Saartjie,' the maternal figure of the new South Africa" (Crais and Scully 2009, 155), Sara Baartman soon became represented as a new mother of and from a new nation. Crais and Scully identify an inherent problem in the narratives of the time, however, because there is a tension surrounding the question of who is reclaiming Baartman and for what purpose(s). The debates about the suitable nature, place, and funeral rite of her return to South Africa showed some questionable sides of local and international politics, for example, the various lobby groups who wished to claim her in the name of feminism, indigeneity, African Renaissance philosophy, human rights, and/or nation-building. In these circumstances, politicians and governmental figures also remained ever mindful of the powerful sway held by the coloured people's vote in the Western Cape region (153–67). In the end, these intense debates obscured yet again the "living, breathing person" who was Sara Baartman. Like her restricted existence in Europe, she remains behind the bars of her grave near Hankey, kept there by those who recently engaged in various discourses on her behalf (168). The present thus allows for the construction of new and overlapping narratives, which can be liberatory, or in the case of Sara Baartman, necessitate additional critique.

The current South African context also furnishes a discursive space for the construction of new master narratives or perhaps the reuse of old ones in a new environment. The following serves as an example of how national rhetoric can ignore the fractured, multiple ways of being in contemporary South Africa as well as overlook the very same groups who were designated as "in-between" during apartheid. Jacob Zuma referred to "South Africans, black and white" in his most recent state of the nation address (2010). The jarring nature of this statement, with its modernist binary opposition and its implied divisive racial politics, is particularly disturbing. Although its intent appears to be inclusive of "all" South Africans, this declaration still echoes the much-maligned apartheid rhetoric of "separate development" and also fails to acknowledge the existence of coloured and Indian people's communities in the country.[8]

Leon de Kock, one of the scholars Nuttall includes in the group who attempt to find post-apartheid vocabularies, remains concerned about the formation of new master narratives (2001, 289). In his recent commentary on the state of "South African literature," de Kock believes that there is no longer the scholarly or writerly need to form a unified narrative of South Africa, to speak from a position of "we" and forced homogeneity (2005, 72–73, 77; see also de Kock 2008). De Kock revisits his notion of the seam as a metaphor for the crisis of inscription and representation faced by early colonial writers. They attempted to eliminate difference by suturing together various disparate narratives, peoples, and histories, but the stitch marks always remained visible as a testament to the impossibility of eradicating otherness (see Chapter 2). In the present era, de Kock suggests instead that there can now be multiple seams and/or no seam at all; the various fabrics are free to diverge (2005, 81).[9] This viewpoint makes it possible to avoid the formation of new and rigid master narratives.

Another way in which new master narratives can be avoided is by looking beyond national borders and breaking away from the notion of South Africa as a "closed space" (Nuttall and Michael 2000, 2–5). De Kock understands recent South African writing within a transnational context, which he believes is at once transnational as well as local (2005, 81). As an example, he explains that Afrikaans fiction writers such as Etienne van Heerden and Marlene van Niekerk "seem to be working within a much larger terrain, informed by historical re-reading which is deeply South African, and conventions of form which are, in the last resort, more broadly transnational than national" (2005, 80). De Kock believes that the present state of South African literature is one of "diffusion in two different directions, going more specifically local, getting more irreverently local, without apology . . . on the one hand, while also feeling utterly free to ride the big transnational waves wherever they may take you" (2005, 81). The location of current writing in South Africa within a transnational moment thus allows for the unhitching of the seam, the relaxation of the need to present a unified narrative, and a kind of reveling in the fluid, the syncretic, and the diffuse. Like Sara Baartman's life story, the new style of inscription spans several continents, times, and spaces, but nevertheless retains a strong sense of rootedness in South Africa. This book can thus be interpreted as situated in a post-apartheid, transnational moment that also simultaneously understands the sacred singing of the congregations in these three Kroonvale churches as a particularly local tradition.

A Sonic Sense of Place

When I visited Graaff-Reinet in January 2010, the whole of the Eastern Cape region remained in the grip of a severe drought. I joined the ranks of local residents anxiously scanning the horizon every day for signs of thunderclouds, yet, during my stay, I became increasingly aware of a sense of timelessness in that place. Regardless of human activity in that area, I knew that droughts would come and go and that, eventually, the rain would arrive. The parched and scorched veld merely waited patiently to become green again, while the human residents suffered the tests of endurance that literally come with the Karoo territory. I could not shake off a deep impression that the landscape had existed long before its human guests arrived and would exist long afterward.

The notion of place as the first point of departure, in other words, the idea that place contains space and time rather than vice versa, is expertly argued by Edward Casey (1996). He asserts that human experience begins with place, in other words, that place has attributes of universality. One of the important characteristics of places, he states, is their ability to "gather things in their midst" (24). Places gather things, people, experiences, memories, and histories. Bodies also carry culture into a place (34). Following this, I interpret sound as one of these items and believe that bodies carry sound with them into places. Places also have the ability to keep these items within their designated area, and this collection of items as well as its nature and constitution becomes distinctive of that place. The particular configuration of the Kroonvale church music I investigated then becomes one of many items belonging in Kroonvale, in the Graaff-Reinet area of the South African Karoo. The music thus reveals a sense of this place, of the gathering of people along with their sounds, possessions, memories, histories, cultures, and identities. These sounds have belonged here for more than two hundred years. I suspect that this place will shape its music for many years to come, and these sounds will continue to provide a sense of belonging, a feeling of being at home (Middleton 2000, 78).

My understanding of sonic spaces always started with the notion of a three-dimensional area filled with sound that is nevertheless rooted in this particular place. During my fieldwork, I constantly experienced the sound of the Kroonvale congregations as a physical presence that was uniquely theirs. Despite oppression and marginalization, this vocal presence refused to be silenced and carved out sonic spaces that can only be described as belonging to the coloured community of Kroonvale. In the preceding chapters I understand these sonic spaces variously as the space of frontier encounter, musical archiving, anti-apartheid expression, middle-class belonging, and creativity and independence. I also interpret the physical church building as public, private, and gendered space, depending on the context of its use. I believe that the coloured community in this town continually confirms the existence of its culture, identity, and history through the physical presence of the sound of their singing. This is evidence of a constant claiming, reclaiming, and articulation of space that occurs at each church event. In a wider sense, the Kroonvale congregations' sonic spaces speak of the unique histories and identities of coloured people in South Africa and furnish a constant reminder of a particularly unique indigeneity. The story of coloured people in South Africa is the story of encounter, creolization, and entanglement, aspects that have persisted throughout the country's history, despite the severe superimpositions of colonization, segregation, and apartheid. This is a particularly rich South Africanness, one that was present from the nation's earliest encounters and that our current theoretical, historical, and social situation is only beginning to appreciate.

Notes

CHAPTER 1

1. The typical vegetation of the Karoo (low-lying scrub bushes and drought-resistant succulents) covers about one-third of South Africa's total land area (153,000 square miles/395,000 square kilometers). It is split into three areas: the Great Karoo and the Little Karoo, in the areas of the Western and Eastern Cape Provinces, and the Upper Karoo in the Northern Cape region. Graaff-Reinet lies in the Great Karoo. Farmers raise livestock (mainly sheep, goats, cattle, and ostriches) or cultivate crops (mainly fruit and grains) as the principal trades of the area (Encyclopaedia Britannica 2010).

2. In 1959, the apartheid government further differentiated the "coloured" category into seven subdivisions, namely, "Cape Coloured, Cape Malay, Griqua, Indian, Chinese, 'other Asiatic,' and 'Other Coloured' " (Reddy 2001, 75). The use of the word "native" in the 1950 Population Registration Act shows how the "coloured" category was constructed as not indigenous in relation to black South Africans, when in fact the ancestors of many coloured people, the Khoekhoe and San, are now viewed as the original inhabitants of the country. In certain contexts, apartheid ideology also constructed black people as not indigenous (see note 5 below).

3. Within the field of geography, Graaff-Reinet can be categorized as a "central place." A central place refers to a market town that provides goods and services for the surrounding (rural) farming community. Thus, I should qualify the term "rural" with this explanation of Graaff-Reinet as a central place within a larger rural area (Encyclopaedia Britannica 2010).

4. In Nama, the predominantly surviving Khoekhoe language, "Khoekhoe" is a more recent spelling of the older term "Khoikhoi." Although some South African his-

torians still prefer the term "Khoikhoi," "Khoekhoe" continues to gain currency in contemporary scholarly literature as it bears a closer resemblance to the name's correct pronunciation (Newton-King 1999, 8 n. 25; Davenport and Saunders 2000, 8).

5. The name "Karoo" comes from a Khoekhoe word meaning "dry" or "thirstland," which is an additional testament to the Khoekhoe people's connection to this area (Westby-Nunn 2004, 146; Willis 2009). Attempts to date the arrivals of the peoples of South Africa on the land of the present-day nation remain infused with political ideology, especially because of the deeply contested issue of land ownership and the post-apartheid land-claims process. A myth "once held in innocence and long propagated, that the Bantu-speaking peoples arrived as immigrants on the highveld of the trans-Vaal at about the same time as the Europeans first settled in Table Bay, has been demolished as a consequence of archaeological research" (Davenport and Saunders 2000, 8–9). In recent times, this myth allowed Europeans to claim equal land access with the African peoples as both groups were constructed as "immigrants," which therefore designated the African peoples as "not indigenous." This ideological construction is similar in some ways to the Australian "terra nullius" doctrine, which designated the country as empty and unoccupied, thus allowing European settlers to claim land belonging to the aboriginal peoples. This was overturned in 1992 (Brett 2001).

6. "Bantu" refers to a large group of indigenous people with a series of related languages who migrated into southern Africa around the third or fourth century C.E. Although the term itself merely means "persons," the apartheid government often used it as a derogatory term for black people (Beck 2000, 11–17).

7. The zoologist Leonhard Schultze coined the term "Khoisan" in 1928, which Isaac Schapera used as a name for the Khoekhoe and San in his work two years later (1930, 5). South African historians adopted this term in the 1970s, largely due to various debates about the terminology and practices of the Khoekhoe and San (Newton-King 1999, 250 n. 28). In a recent work on post-apartheid revivals of Khoesan ethnic identity, Michael Besten introduces a hyphen between the two terms, explaining that "although the early hunter-gathering and herding indigenes of southern Africa had a shared ancestry and some cultural commonalities, there were differences in language, culture, livelihood and identity between the two. This configuration [Khoe-San] also takes account of the objection that the San should not be subordinated to, or subsumed within, Khoekhoe groupings" (2009, 135). While remaining aware of these concerns, I continue to use the term "Khoisan" for the purposes of this book, in order to avoid adding more confusion to the already-controversial terminology surrounding the Cape's indigenous peoples.

8. After the Union of South Africa in 1910, Graaff-Reinet formed part of the larger Cape Province. Since 1994, the old Cape Province has been divided into the Northern, Western, and the Eastern Cape Provinces (Beck 2000, 4). Throughout the book, I refer to the historical region of the eastern Cape frontier with a lowercase "e" for "eastern" and to the contemporary region of the Eastern Cape Province using uppercase letters.

9. The name, Graaff-Reinet, originates from the last name of the Cape governor at the time, Cornelius van der Graaff, and his wife's maiden name, Reynett (Westby-Nunn 2004, 15). Initially, Graaff-Reinet referred to a magisterial district or (to use the Dutch term) Drostdy, which included the actual settlement and a large surrounding area stretching all the way to the coastal city of Port Elizabeth. In 1804, Governor de Mist proclaimed a new Drostdy known as Uitenhage in the coastal half of the old

Graaff-Reinet area. By 1966, the original district of Graaff-Reinet comprised more than twenty different municipalities and today, the town and its immediate surrounds lie in the Camdeboo municipality area (Smith 1976, xvii, 60). Graaff-Reinet remains a popular tourist destination for both local and overseas visitors as it boasts more than two hundred buildings of historic interest and environmental sites such as the Camdeboo National Park and the Valley of Desolation (see www.graaffreinet.co.za).

10. A word on languages is also necessary here. At present the country has eleven official languages. Depending on the geographical location, white and coloured South Africans usually speak either Afrikaans or English as their native language; Indian South Africans speak English and sometimes a language from India; and the languages of black South Africans include Zulu, Xhosa, Pedi, Tswana, Sotho, Tsonga, Swazi, Venda, and Ndebele. The multilingualism inherent in the South African situation means that many citizens speak English, Afrikaans, or an African language as a second, third, or sometimes even fourth language (Beck 2000, 3).

11. A legacy of the Cape colonial government allowed all Cape Province men who owned property worth at least £25 or who earned this amount the right to vote. This right was removed from black men in 1936 and from coloured men in 1956. In the western Cape, a policy stipulated that coloured people would be given employment in preference to black people; this remained in force until 1978. Voting and employment rights constituted two of the main reasons for coloured political mobilization in the western Cape in the early twentieth century. For example, the African Peoples' Organization (established in 1902), with Dr. A. Abdurahman as president, fought for the rights of coloured people, but it gradually lost influence due to the continual erosion of these rights by the government (Goldin 1987, xiv, 32, 40; Beck 2000, 54; Davenport and Saunders 2000, 244, 467).

12. This residential area developed around 1857 after the Xhosa cattle-killing. This took place after Nongqawuse, a young girl, prophesied that the resurrection of ancestral spirits would occur with an accompanying supply of food from heaven. Xhosa people destroyed crops and slaughtered livestock, which led to widespread starvation and death. Many Xhosa people fled to the Cape Colony in search of work and food, and more than three thousand Xhosa people arrived in Graaff-Reinet at this time (Davenport and Saunders 2000, 142; Westby-Nunn 2004, 71).

13. This subheading is borrowed from a conference title, "The Burden of Race: 'Whiteness' and 'Blackness' in Modern South Africa," held in July 2001 at the University of the Witwatersrand in Johannesburg.

14. While the Cape population census of 1892 defined "coloured" as all non-European people, the census of 1904 distinguished between three racial groups namely, "white," "black," and "coloured" (Goldin 1987, 12–13). Mohamed Adhikari states, however, that the term "coloured" became standardized from the 1880s onward (2009, xi).

15. The New National Party is the contemporary name used (since 1998) for the previously white Afrikaner National Party. The Democratic Party, the Federal Alliance, and the New National Party formed the Democratic Alliance in 2000 although the latter withdrew from this organization in 2001 in order to join ranks with the ANC. In 2005 the New National Party disbanded completely (Davenport and Saunders 2000, 590; Weaver et al. 2009; Encyclopaedia Britannica 2010). The Democratic Alliance is commonly viewed as the (predominantly white) opposition party to the ANC. For a selection of studies that analyze the 1994 Western Cape election result, see Adhikari (2009, 19 n. 20).

16. "Boesman" is a derogatory term used by black people for coloured people. But, the complexity of the politics of naming means that not all people find this name insulting. For example, Vetkat Regopstaan Kruiper, a San artist living in the Kalahari, insists that he does not know what "San" means, but he likes being called "Boesman" because that is what his parents called him (South African Broadcasting Corporation 2005; see also Bregin and Kruiper 2004). Similarly, some people prefer the name "coloured," while others prefer "so-called coloured," "*bruinmens*," and/or "black."

17. Adhikari further divides the work of the essentialist school into three subcategories. The first, classified as "traditionalist," unquestioningly followed the apartheid state's hierarchical racial categories (with their implied levels of superiority and inferiority according to skin color). The second subcategory, the "liberal essentialists," believed that the very existence of coloured people as a group proved that people interacted with each other despite the artificial imposition of racial categories. Progressionists constituted the third subcategory; literature written from this ideological standpoint accepted the apartheid view of coloured people as inferior to white people but believed that coloured people nevertheless had the potential to become as "civilized" as white people and therefore deserve fair and just treatment as equal citizens in South African society (2009, 7–10). Adhikari's work not only provides an insightful historiographical analysis but also a useful overview of the literature on coloured people in South Africa.

18. Stereotypes of coloured people originated well before the apartheid era began. In his detailed analysis of the coloured stereotype in South African literature, Vernon February states that characteristics attributed to the "Hottentot" people by early travel writers became mapped onto coloured people (1981, 1). For a critical discussion of early writing about "Hottentot" people's "idleness" in South Africa, see Coetzee (1988/2007, 13–37).

19. The Mugglestone article is a particularly interesting case as it not only confirms the idea of coloured people's music as a mixture between black and white musics but also interprets this as a reflection of "claiming parity with White culture or asserting political alignment with the Black population" (1984, 153). Musical style thus becomes conflated with stereotypical ideas of coloured people's apartheid racial category as well as mapped onto their political affiliations.

20. The predominantly Afrikaans-speaking Cape Malay community comprises descendants of Muslim South and Southeast Asian immigrants and slaves, and "converts from among both the free and unfree [Cape colonial] population" (Jeppie 2001, 83). The Afrikaans intellectual, Izak David Du Plessis (1900–81), became "the most energetic proponent of a distinctive past and separate culture for these people," but used these ideas as a way of validating the heritage of the (white) Afrikaans-speaking person's language and culture (80, 86). Studies of Islam at the Cape reveal a little-known fact about the Afrikaans language. Its first written sources are in Arabic, as it was used in the early nineteenth-century Cape Colony to facilitate the conversion of slaves to Islam (Du Plessis 1986, 1, 2, 33). (Richard Elphick and Robert Shell state that Christianity did not spread as rapidly among the slave population because they were excluded from many of its rituals, such as marriages and funerals [1989, 191].) The origins of Afrikaans as a creolized Dutch used for communication between masters and slaves and its use in the Islamic community have often been ignored due to its associations with white Afrikaner nationalism during apartheid (see also Giliomee 2003, 215–20, 429).

21. Jonathan Drury's work is largely exploratory and poses questions on the topic of whether coloured Afrikaans folk songs exist as a unique category. He also specifically omits religious songs in his discussion (1985, 39). Matilda Burden's doctoral dissertation mainly presents transcriptions of songs she recorded in various coloured communities and frames these with a general discussion of the folk song category and its application to this musical repertoire. For general commentary on the historiography of the South African music studies field, see Olwage (2002), Lucia (2005), and Muller (2007).

22. In June 1976, approximately 15,000 Soweto schoolchildren marched in protest against a new law that required their language of instruction to be Afrikaans (Davenport and Saunders 2000, 449). Police opened fire to disperse the crowd and killed at least two people, including thirteen-year-old Hector Petersen. Within days, violent protests and rioting spread across the country (Beck 2000, 160–61). In the 1970s, Black Consciousness was a philosophical movement spearheaded by Steve Biko (1946–77) who believed that all South African black people (regardless of particular ethnic background) needed to free themselves from their self-conception as servants or inferior to white people. To present a unified, anti-apartheid stance regardless of imposed racial classifications, many coloured people regarded themselves as black during this period, even though "the Black Consciousness Movement tended towards a universal and single notion of being black which privileged black African experiences (narrowly defined)" (Erasmus 2001, 19). This identification with Black Consciousness philosophy continues in the post-apartheid era; for example, the coloured staff of the Bush Radio station in Cape Town "have always preferred to refer to themselves as black" and play a significant amount of kwaito music (South African hip-hop) on the air to "signify a more inclusive 'blackness' " (Bosch 2008, 78).

23. In 2008, the Documentation Centre for Music (DOMUS) at the University of Stellenbosch obtained a collection of archival documents relating to the Eoan group, an organization formed for opera, ballet, and theater performance among the coloured community of the Western Cape. Currently, an oral history book project is under way in order to gather ethnographic data about this group and its social and historical context (DOMUS 2010).

24. More than 60 percent of South Africa's coloured population lives in the Western Cape Province, which helps to explain the scholarly focus on coloured people's music in Cape Town. More recently, Boudina Coetzer from Rhodes University in Grahamstown, Eastern Cape Province, conducted research on the local *langarm* dance band, known as Coysan, which, together with this project, perhaps indicates the beginning of a trend toward research on the music of coloured people in other regions of the country (Coetzer 2005a, 2005b, 2005c).

25. A number of works have already successfully applied this theory to literary and ethnographic case studies in South Africa (Salo 2004, 2005, 2007; Lee 2009; Strauss 2009). While scholars in the South African context made use of creolization theory, terminology related to mulatto and mestizo cultures is rare. The historical explanation for this is that "the Cape, unlike Latin America, did not adopt or evolve a complicated system of socio-racial terminology to distinguish between persons of various racial backgrounds" (Armstrong and Worden 1989, 122). Thus, while I remain aware of the wide discursive usage of these terms in the American and Caribbean context, I do not use them here for reasons of regional, geographic, historical, and cultural speci-

ficity. For an analytical discussion of the "discursive complex" that is creolization in the Caribbean context, see Puri (2004, 50, 61–66); and for an analysis of creolization techniques in the storytelling styles of Madagascar, Mauritius, Réunion, Seychelles, and the Comoros Islands, see Haring (2003).

26. Ulf Hannerz's work on Sophiatown also makes use of creolization theory (1996, 1997). Sophiatown, originally a multiracial residential area in Johannesburg, was demolished in 1957 by the apartheid government, renamed "Triomf" (Triumph) and rezoned for white homes (Davenport and Saunders 2000, 396).

27. For additional commentary on this provocative work, see responses by Jacobs and Wasserman (2003, 16), Trotter (2009, 26), Barber (2001), and Nuttall (2002).

28. I believe that conditions of slavery (or similar contexts of coerced labor) shaped most interactions between peoples in South Africa to a substantial degree (in other words, not only at the Cape, but beyond). Yet, while subscribing to the notion of South African society as a creole one, I believe that these processes of encounter (and their accompanying degrees of coercion and/or equal connection) occurred differently in each community and in each geographic location. Therefore, it is essential to examine the different experiences and circumstances of each creolized community.

29. The small but significant body of literature on South African Indian music is worth mentioning here as it also deals with the traditions of a marginalized group in South African society (Jackson 1989, 1991; Goodall 1993). Due to the differing historical origins and cultural contexts of these communities, further comparison would require a separate study that is beyond the scope of the present book.

30. I understand the term "margin" here as a reference to the colonial and apartheid authorities' conception of coloured people as occupying a subordinate and unrecognized position within society. Thus, I do not intend to suggest the notions of "hybrid" and "in-betweenness" (and their connotations discussed earlier) when using this term.

31. I am aware that Erasmus states this theory with the context of Cape Town in mind, a city that historically housed the majority of the South African slave population. As will become apparent in Chapter 2, far fewer slaves lived in the interior of the country. However, the colonists quickly implemented a system of indentured labor for Khoekhoe and San people, which made the status of the Khoisan approximate to that of slavery in many respects (Elbourne 2002, 82). I remain sensitive to this particular distinction, however, as it constitutes an important regional difference at work in the formation of Khoisan identity in the Karoo.

32. Particularly with reference to slavery origins, South African scholars have stated that coloured people "suffer from a historical amnesia" and that "for the most part, they do not invest in a remote past" (Trotter 2009, 49; see also Ward and Worden 1998).

33. Nuttall's characterizations of creolization and entanglement overlap in some respects, for example the acknowledgment of violence and cruelty and the commitment to finding points of intersection between previously divided and separate entities. Entanglement (while it may incorporate past engagements) informs the present and incorporates interactions within broader (post-apartheid) South African society. Nevertheless, both concepts offer useful ways of examining coloured people's religious music.

34. While it is fair to assume (especially since the end of apartheid) that coloured farmworkers would insist on claiming a place in the front of the vehicle, this is not the

case in my experience. When I drove farmworkers to and from the town to do their grocery shopping, I found that members of the younger generation are comfortable with this arrangement, but some members of the older generation flatly refused to take a seat in the vehicle cab or became visibly uncomfortable and felt obliged to make suitable conversation for the duration of the trip. It is a tragic legacy of severe oppression in this community that even a simple vehicle ride into town can be fraught with the politics of race.

35. Part of my unease was also the adjustment to Graaff-Reinet and the Karoo as a place of work and a research site. For the first few weeks of my fieldwork, I felt very conscious of a rupture between the familiar, comfortable surroundings of the family farm and my trips to Kroonvale.

36. Gender complicates this picture even further, as it is rare to see woman farmers in this area. However, because gendered division of labor is common in these rural communities, it makes the separation of women and men on this journey slightly less problematic than if the farmers were men as well.

37. For an autobiographical account of a white, English-speaking South African who grew up in the Eastern Cape and had family connections in the Karoo town of Oudtshoorn, see Nixon (1999/2001).

38. Old Apostolic Church service, Kendrew, Graaff-Reinet area, November 6, 2005.

39. As not only my ethnic background but also my age and gender determined the dynamics of my research relationships, I believe that a completely different set of circumstances and research relationships would have applied if I had been a white older male. For example, Michael de Jongh's work with the Karretjie people of the Karoo Colesberg area suggests a very different set of research dynamics (2002).

40. Of course, the nature of my relationship with Graaff-Reinet means that I have visited the district fairly regularly since my intense fieldwork periods; some of the more recent information I provide in the text stems from these visits.

41. South African residents of the Eastern Cape Province can easily recognize whether a person speaks English or Afrikaans as his/her native language. Even though I tried to speak Afrikaans as much as possible, especially when meeting people for the first time, Kroonvale community members could hear that my first language is English and often switched automatically to English in our conversations. Exceptions to this norm did occur, as some people preferred to answer my questions in Afrikaans, and my interactions with the women's society of the East Street Congregational Church took place in Afrikaans only.

CHAPTER 2

1. "Transformation" is an umbrella political term for various strategies to redress the inequities of the apartheid past. Black Economic Empowerment (BEE) (the South African equivalent of affirmative action) is one example; another is the use of "transformation" in higher education circles in reference to "Africanizing" the curriculum. One of the first transformation projects the Reinet House Museum undertook to redress the glaring omissions in its existing exhibitions featured Robert Sobukwe (1924–78), the founder of the Pan Africanist Congress, who was born in Graaff-Reinet and later imprisoned on Robben Island for nine years. The exhibition was officially opened on

September 24, 2001, by his widow, Nosango Veronica Sobukwe, and in 2008, a commemoration ceremony of his death took place (Kayster 2008, 11). Sobukwe's biography
is one of the few items featuring the story of a locally born black South African that is
for sale in Graaff-Reinet (see Pogrund 1997).

2. "Muti" is a South African word, drawn from the Zulu language, meaning traditional or indigenous medicine (Oxford 2002b, 768). The 120-year-old rhino horn was
from an animal shot by the brother of a well-known figure in Graaff-Reinet history,
Rev. Charles Murray. The horn was originally used as a doorstop at various parsonages
in the Murray family and later donated to the museum (Westby-Nunn 2004, 84). A
somewhat eccentric choice of relic to an outside observer, nonetheless, rhino horns
and other animal artifacts are reminiscent of the vast herds of game that originally
roamed the interior of the country. The Graaff-Reinet incident is one of a spate of
rhino horn thefts at various South African museums (for example, the Iziko South
African Museum in Cape Town, the Transvaal Museum in Pretoria, and the King
William's Town Museum). Rhino horns are prized in China as traditional medicine
and in Yemen where they are carved into dagger handles. After the theft at the Iziko
Museum, Jatti Bredekamp, the chief executive officer, cautioned that horns were often
preserved by soaking them in arsenic and applying DDT regularly; the thieves and the
buyers thus risked exposure to these highly toxic substances (Iafrica News 2008; see
also Olivier 2004).

3. In contrast to other Karoo towns, Graaff-Reinet is fortunate to have this comparatively large written record, despite the need to treat these sources with caution.

4. For a detailed account of the causes and outcomes of the nine frontier wars
(known collectively as the Hundred Years War) (Mostert 1992, xxix), see Davenport
and Saunders (2000, 132–48).

5. The two competing cultures mentioned here comprise the Xhosa people and
the colonists, although colonists most definitely also encountered Khoekhoe people
during this period. While twentieth-century historians usually regard the eastern Cape
frontier as that area characterized by colonist-Xhosa strife in the more coastal territo-
ries near the Fish River, I adopt Hermann Giliomee's designation of the initial eastern
Cape frontier region as including Graaff-Reinet and its surrounding area, particularly
from the 1760s until 1812 (1989, 421–22). It follows from this interpretation that the
frontier encounter included three general groups, namely, Khoekhoe, colonists, and
Xhosa.

6. Legassick identifies I. D. MacCrone (*Race Attitudes in South Africa*, London,
1937) as the author of the first detailed formulation of this thesis (1980, 12).

7. Elizabeth Elbourne believes that even in an open frontier context, competition
for limited resources could supersede the trend toward cooperation (2002, 82). The
colonists usually bartered tobacco, copper, and iron in exchange for the Khoekhoe's
sheep and cattle. The Xhosa traded their livestock with the Europeans for copper, iron,
and beads (Elphick and Malherbe 1989, 8; Giliomee 1989, 432).

8. I use "hunter-robbers" to refer to people who lived primarily by stealing and
slaughtering the livestock of nearby groups (Elphick 1985, xx). Colonists identified
these people as "Bushmen."

9. Following an argument by John L. and Jean Comaroff, de Kock points out that
these rigid categories of difference contrast with the reality of interactions in the colony. The Comaroffs identify a "grammar of distinctions" (1997, 25) within colonial

discourse *"despite* the internal complexity of colonial society" (de Kock 2004, 13, his emphasis).

10. Even though Ross and Giliomee focused on the nonconflictual aspects of the frontier in their work, Newton-King nevertheless believes that both authors would freely admit to the continued presence of the conflictual aspects (1999, 39, 41).

11. Since his original explication of the seam theory, de Kock is "no longer certain that our current condition continues to be captured in the poetics of the seam" and believes that while this metaphor remains useful for the colonial and apartheid context, it may not apply as readily in the transnational, post-apartheid context (2005, 71, 81; see also de Kock 2008, 2009). I thus retain the use of the seam metaphor in the historical context of this chapter, but engage with de Kock's more recent ideas in Chapter 7.

12. For a well-known analysis of white people's writing in South Africa, see Coetzee (1988/2007).

13. These thoughts are, of course, also influenced by important debates in anthropology and also in ethnomusicology, which rely heavily on anthropological methodology. For example, the so-called crisis in the field questions the objectivity and validity of ethnographic narratives and argues instead for self-reflexive narrative strategies and the presence of multiple voices within a single text (Clifford 1986, 3).

14. Despite entries in early journals and diaries of contact with the Inqua people, they disappeared from the historical narratives in 1720 and by the 1760s were no longer in evidence. A raid during which colonial tradesmen stole 2,000 cattle and 2,500 sheep from the Inqua in 1702 is one possible reason for their demise, combined with the smallpox epidemic of 1713, which caused many Khoekhoe casualties (a contemporary estimate from the southwestern Cape states that only one in ten Khoekhoe people survived) (Elphick and Malherbe 1989, 21). This story of the Inqua mirrored the general pattern of the eastern Cape Khoekhoe because travelers initially reported independent groups with particular names, and by the 1750s, Carel Albregt Haupt stated that many of them no longer knew to which group they belonged (Newton-King 1999, 28, 36). Legassick mentions that groups of "Bastaards" owned land in the Graaff-Reinet area in the late eighteenth and early nineteenth centuries but moved either to the Kat Rivier mission settlement or across the Orange River to Griqualand by the 1820s (1980, 56). "Bastaard" refers to people of mixed European-Khoekhoe or European-slave parentage who were permitted to own land under colonial rule, especially if they were baptized (Legassick 1989, 370, 373).

15. Although Newton-King states that the term "San" will most likely be used for some time to come and is certainly better than the derogatory term, "Bushman," the many bewildering meanings of "San" lead me to follow her and other historians' example, namely, to use the term "hunter-gatherers" instead to refer to these communities (1999, 28).

16. This was especially true in the case of Khoekhoe language survival (Elphick 1985, 36).

17. Newton-King believes that a possible reason for the constant and vicious attacks on the colonists by the mountain peoples lies in understanding aspects of their cosmology and belief systems. Drawing on David Lewis-Williams's work, she suggests that "in the world-view of the southern San, land and culture, matter and spirit, nature and community, were aspects of a whole and could not be separated. For these people,

the loss of territory and the violation of hunting grounds entailed more than the loss of livelihood and exile from the places to which memory attached; it was an attack on the symbolic system through which they understood their world. As such, it was an attack on their very being" (1999, 97). This deeply felt colonial attack, she concludes, may be why the Karoo mountain people fought so desperately and for so long against the colonists.

18. Later on, however, Khoisan people became increasingly caught between the battles of colonists and Xhosa, which meant that Khoisan servants working for either side often became the first casualties of a raid or attack. Records from the Graaff-Reinet area indicated that a total of 107 herders were killed in mountain people–colonist attacks during 1786–88; this figure included seven slaves (Giliomee 1989, 431; Newton-King 1999, 106–7).

19. This tendency appears to be in contrast with the Khoekhoe people near Cape Town, who "brought back [Dutch East India] Company deserters as well as slaves in return for payment in tobacco and brandy" (Mostert 1992, 135).

20. The majority of Europeans in the area during the eighteenth century came from Germany and the Netherlands. Arriving as destitute (and, by some accounts, disease-ridden) people forced into being soldiers or sailors for the Dutch East India Company, these men found more lucrative occupations by taking leave of the company and finding their way into the interior. The early colonists, therefore, did not enjoy the luxury of powerful military and financial backing; the Dutch East India Company's interests rested primarily in the Cape Town region. After the British occupied the Cape (1795–1803) and again from 1806, many settlers of British origin arrived; the first large group of 4,000 people arrived in 1820. These literate and commercially oriented settlers became farmers and tradesmen (Schutte 1989, 292; Newton-King 1999, 14; Davenport and Saunders 2000, 44–45).

21. Trekboers in the eighteenth century often sent "Bastaard" or Khoisan servants to serve on commando raids in their stead (Legassick 1989, 373). The Xhosa people much appreciated the skills developed by these servants, and escapees often brought a weapon belonging to their former masters with them, thus adding to their new hosts' military power (Giliomee 1989, 437; Mostert 1992, 245).

22. The typical trekboer had acquired a loan farm from the government. The loan farm system originated in permits for grazing rights and allowed for a trekboer to claim a farm of 2,000 *morgen* (4,500 acres) indefinitely with an annual payment to the Dutch East India Company (Davenport and Saunders 2000, 30). Those living on the farm comprised the trekboer as dominant male, his extended family, one or two *bijwoners* (Europeans without their own land who assisted in managing the owner's farm in return for being able to graze their stock or plant crops on land allocated to them), Khoekhoe servants and their families, and one or two slaves. Khoekhoe people often insisted on bringing their families and livestock with them when they worked on colonial farms (Giliomee 1989, 424, 431).

23. In 1798, 8,635 "Hottentots" were recorded as working for colonists, compared to the official slave figure of 579 in 1796. This provides a clear idea of the numbers of Khoisan and captives the trekboers managed to subjugate in the decades after their arrival in the Graaff-Reinet area (Newton-King 1999, 118 n. 12).

24. "Landdrost" is the colonial term for mayor or magistrate (the word "landdros" meaning "magistrate" in Afrikaans is still in use). Andries Stockenström Sr. served as

Graaff-Reinet's Landdrost from 1804 to 1811, when he was murdered by a group of Xhosa people. His son became the Landdrost from 1815–27 (Smith 1976, 39; Minnaar 1987, 3). According to Ross, Stockenström Jr. was the grandson of a slave (1999, 173), but it is not clear whether this connection came from his mother's or his father's side of the family. This background may have influenced Stockenström Junior's views on those in servitude, however.

25. In its early years, the district of Graaff-Reinet had no northern border, as the San people in this area prevented further colonial expansion. A northern border was established in 1798 (Smith 1976, 16; Minnaar 1987, 5).

26. From the 1770s until at least the 1930s, *smousen* roamed the rural countryside with their goods. They traveled deep into colonial, Xhosa, Ndebele, and Tswana territory. A monument to their honor (the only known one of its kind) still stands in Graaff-Reinet today (Ross 1989, 267; Westby-Nunn 2004, 144).

27. C. G. Henning stated in the 1970s that "the origin of the Coloured race in Graaff-Reinet may have been commenced by the indiscretions of certain Boers" but quickly defended the trekboers by adding that, "the population was further augmented in the 1850s by the lower class of English and German immigrant tradesmen and labourers. It is maintained that the Coldstream Guard Regiment [British troops stationed at Graaff-Reinet during the Anglo-Boer War] added considerably to this problem between 1899–1901" (1975, 30–31). The association of miscegenation with coloured people is clear in this statement, as is the partial denial of trekboer-Khoisan relationships. As Ross states, "Especially in the eastern Cape, Khoikhoi and whites ate and drank together, slept together, prayed together, fought alongside each other, hunted together, and generally worked together in the farms and households of the colony" (Ross, Van Arkel, and Quispel 1993, 84).

28. "Drostdy" refers to the seat of local government (Oxford 2002b, 650). Graaff-Reinet's Drostdy building dates back to 1804 and has functioned as a hotel since 1876 (Westby-Nunn 2004, 66).

29. Magazine Hill is thus known because of a building erected on its summit in 1831 to house gunpowder at a safe distance from the town (Henning 1975, 191). A. de V. Minnaar states that many of the Sotho-speaking refugees (known locally as Mantatees) had moved farther north by 1890 in order to work on the mines (1987, 96). Although the majority of Xhosa-speaking residents arrived in Graaff-Reinet after the cattle killing, Ordinance 49 (1828) had already allowed Xhosa people into the colony as laborers for some time (Davenport and Saunders 2000, 19).

30. Former slaves served their masters as apprentices for a further four years (Davenport and Saunders 2000, 47).

31. Some organizations moved earlier, for example, the East Street Congregational Church and school moved in 1964 and became the first church and school to relocate to Kroonvale (Minnaar 1987, 96).

32. There may be one exception to this statement, as a relative of Sara Baartman informed the historians Clifton Crais and Pamela Scully that the cemetery near the old DRMC building in the town was flattened (2009, 179). I have since spoken to two Kroonvale residents who do not believe that a cemetery near this church building existed, and thus it is possible that the person interviewed was referring to another cemetery, perhaps one located in Umasizakhe (Bosch and Basson communication, February 2010). At present, an old cemetery for coloured DRMC and Congregational Church

members lies on the edge of the Sunday's River, and newer cemeteries are located near the entrance to Sunnyside, a Graaff-Reinet suburb next to Kroonvale.

33. The implication here is that the buildings facing these narrow streets housed the coloured people who originally lived at the back of the large white-owned properties.

34. Before the implementation of the Group Areas Act in Graaff-Reinet, the Congregational churches and DRMC each had their own school in the town, near the respective church buildings. In order to be employed at these institutions, teachers also had to be members of the particular church denomination. In 1975, the Parsonage Street School moved to Kroonvale, where it is known as the Ryneveld Primary School (Minnaar 1987, 112).

35. Henry Trotter's insightful analysis of people who suffered forced removals in Cape Town reveals a certain narrative strategy, which he terms "the commemoration narrative." He argues that these formulaic narratives construct the past, "the good old days," as much better than the present, especially since 1994 (2009, 56–58). Anecdotes told to me by community members certainly do suggest a nostalgia for the past, but this appears to be concentrated on childhood memories and relatives who are no longer alive. In order to test Trotter's analysis in the Kroonvale context, therefore, much additional work in the field of oral history is required. Reinet House embarked on an oral history project in March 2009, but this remains in the early stages of training fieldworkers in interview techniques (Kayster 2009).

36. Although Cape Town's Coon Carnival tradition only became formalized in the early twentieth century, the practice of New Year's parades in this city dates back to the 1830s (Martin 1999, 63; Bruinders 2005, 17).

37. There is an entire canon of local South African musical studies with titles such as "Music in Pietermaritzburg," "Music in Port Elizabeth," and so on, and many of these articles (often revised versions of dissertations) appear in the *South African Music Encyclopedia*, edited by J. P. Malan (see, for example, Henning 1986). This work is notorious for its exclusion of nonwhite South African musicians, yet these articles (despite their bias) can provide departure points for further study. I hope that my project, like that of Boudina Coetzer's work in Grahamstown, can add to the literature on local musical studies in a way that retrieves historical and musical circumstances of a particular place, but expands this discourse beyond contributions of white people only and includes more contemporary information based on ethnographic research.

38. To indicate the level of insult felt by the settlers at sharing the church with the Khoisan people, colonial rebels sent a demand to Graaff-Reinet officials on July 3 that the Khoisan be "refused access to the Graaff-Reinet church. Soon afterward, rebels added the requests that the seats and walls of the church be scrubbed clean, the churchyard fenced with a stone wall, and a black cloth be hung over the pulpit as a sign of mourning for the absence of a regular minister" (Elbourne 2002, 133). In 1857, the Dutch Reformed Church Synod meeting resolved to allow coloured people to attend their worship services; in Graaff-Reinet, they "occupied the rear pews" (Henning 1975, 104). This type of discrimination serves as an example of the tension between theological resolutions and the prejudices encountered in reality (De Gruchy 2005, 7).

39. The First Frontier War (between white settlers and Xhosa people of the eastern Cape) took place from 1779 to 1780 and the Second Frontier War took place in 1793.

40. The LMS was an interdenominational, Protestant society, which recruited missionaries of varying educational levels and backgrounds. This, together with the influence of Dutch evangelicalism in the society's early days, explains the presence of Dutch missionaries within its ranks. Van der Kemp offered his services to the LMS in 1797 and founded the Netherlands Missionary Society that same year, which would work with the LMS. J. J. Kicherer, another Dutch LMS missionary, would be recruited through this Netherlands society (Elbourne 2002, 62, 90, 91).

41. This constituted a severe insult to the colonists because their isolation from Cape Town meant that they could seldom find ministers to baptize their children. Soon thereafter, they complained bitterly that the Graaff-Reinet church had no minister while the Khoisan people in town had three (Elbourne 2002, 132).

42. For more information on Cupido Kakkerlak, see Malherbe (1979).

43. This building still stands today and is known as the Hester Rupert Art Museum. The Parsonage Street Church building in Parsonage Street is now the John Rupert Theatre (Minnaar 1987, 92).

44. These ministers included John Kicherer, Albert van der Lingen, G. A. Kolbe, Joseph Gill, and Thomas Merrington (Liebenberg n.d.). I am grateful to Virginia Christoffels for allowing me to access Liebenberg's unpublished manuscript.

45. At first, Klein Londen, a church also under the auspices of the London Missionary Society, comprised mainly Sotho-speaking congregation members. These people raised the money to build their own church on Middle Street in the 1870s, as they preferred sermons in Sotho and refused to join the Parsonage Street congregation. The Middle Street church lost many of its members due to the rise and labor demands of the mining industry in the late nineteenth century, and it joined the ESCC when it moved to Kroonvale in the 1960s (Minnaar 1987, 96).

CHAPTER 3

1. This statement indicates an unreflective correlation between the racial stereotype of coloured people and their music (see Chapter 1).

2. For a detailed review of Scott's work, see Gal (1995).

3. South African history reveals a complex relationship between religion and politics, which complicates the private/public dichotomy even further. The most obvious example is the political role played by the Dutch Reformed Church, the official church of the apartheid state (see Chapter 4).

4. At a conference presentation of this material, a colleague perceptively questioned whether the evidence of encounter in this music is best interpreted instead as cultural assimilation and acculturation over a long period of time (International Council for Traditional Music conference, Durban, South Africa, July 4, 2009). While the hints of disparate musical styles suggest the presence of a certain degree of assimilation, I believe that to accept this music merely as a result of acculturation ignores the specific cultural formation that is South African colouredness. By stating that this music is a specifically coloured people's tradition, I align my work with the social constructionist category of writing as advanced by Mohamed Adhikari (see Chapter 1). I am grateful to Brett Pyper for his comment in this regard.

5. Many African Christian converts used biblical text (particularly the Old Testament) to prove that they were more faithful to the Christian religious tradition than

their colonizers (Draper 2003, 5; see also Muller 1999, 162). Examples of this included the designation of Saturdays (and not Sundays) as the day of worship and obedience to the biblical prohibition on eating pork. As the Kroonvale churches where I conducted my fieldwork belonged within the mainline Protestant tradition, this strict adherence to Old Testament laws did not feature.

6. The Congregational Church tradition in South Africa stems mainly from British influence, in particular, the London Missionary Society, whereas the Uniting Reformed Church's very early origins are found in the transplantation of the Netherlands Dutch Reformed Church tradition in colonial South Africa. An additional important difference between the two denominations is that a congregational vote is permitted in the Congregational Church, whereas in the URC, all decisions come through the Synod, assembly, or church elders (Basson interview, August 11, 2004). Congregationalists thus believe firmly in "the autonomy of the local church," in contrast to the URC denominations that are required to follow instructions from the various organizational structures (de Gruchy 1997, 156). For additional information on the origins of the Reformed tradition in South Africa, see Gerstner (1997) and de Gruchy (1997).

7. In addition to being an important body in terms of major decisions affecting the church, the church council members assisted with collections and communion tasks where necessary. As URC ministers generally served a number of congregations and traveled to these in turn, lay preachers often took the service at the "home" church when the minister was away.

8. In this community, women are usually expected to join their husband's church denomination after marriage (A. Kayster communication, September 2006).

9. American revival melodies (such as those popularized by D. L. Moody, leading revivalist of the time and his music leader, Ira Sankey) became well known in South Africa and can be seen as part of the traffic in cultural artifacts across the "black Atlantic." Examples of these include "tracts, books, gramophone records, and choirs" (Gilroy 1993, 4).

10. According to a report submitted in 1942 to the Dutch Reformed Church Synod, Dutch Reformed Mission Church congregations were using the following hymnbooks: the Dutch Reformed Church official hymnbook, the Rhenish hymnbook, the Independent (Congregational) hymnbook, the Berlin hymnbook, and the *Nuwe Halleluja* (New Halleluja), the latter another Dutch Reformed Church publication. According to a survey at the time, most congregations used the *Nuwe Halleluja* ("Voorwoord," *Sionsgesange*, 1947; W. Strydom 1983, 120).

11. During my fieldwork, I also heard about a local Christian band, called "Forgiveness," which was affiliated to the ESCC. Community members deemed the lyrics of the music as the most important because of their religious content, so they had mixed feelings about this band's music due to the sometimes overpowering sound of the lead guitar, drum kit, and bass guitar accompaniment (Bezuidenhoudt interview, December 8, 2004).

12. When I returned briefly to Kroonvale in June 2010, I noted that both the PSCC and URC have acquired data projectors and large screens for the purposes of showing the hymn texts (see Figure 3.1). I observed, however, that quite a few congregation members (especially those of the older generation) still brought their hymnbooks and used them at services.

13. Gawie Basson informed me that slapping these books caused damage to them,

although the fact that they often had leather covers helped to solve this problem. Some congregation members also expressed disapproval of this practice, possibly due to its implied irreverence toward the "word of God" (Basson interview, August 4, 2004). I believe, however, that most of the congregation members who chose to provide percussive sounds during hymn and koortjie singing did not make a distinction between the use of Bibles, hymnbooks, and cushions. This tactile use of the Bible and hymnbooks does suggest an unconventional relationship with the written word, however, as the physical object of a literate tradition is used to add nonverbal, unwritten sounds to the oral tradition of congregational song performance style (see also Gates 1986, 130–31; Muller 2003, 100–101).

14. Scholars use a variety of symbols to refer to the various clicks in the Khoisan languages. Here, the forward slash symbol indicates a dental click produced "by a sucking motion with the tip of the tongue on the teeth" and a colon used in the middle of a word indicates vowel length (Barnard 1992, xix, xxiii).

15. A group of Khoekhoe people performed on reed flutes for the Portuguese explorer, Vasco da Gama, when he landed near the present Mossel Bay in 1497 (Kirby 1935/1953, 135).

16. See also Olivier (1997) and Grauer (2009).

17. The Griqua people, of mixed slave, Khoisan, and European ancestry, initially occupied the fringes of colonial territory; in the mid-nineteenth century the government sought to reincorporate them in the colony by granting them the areas known as Griqualand West and Griqualand East (Davenport and Saunders 2000, 32–33).

18. Wayne Dooling notes that although the majority of female slaves worked in the domestic household context, some also became stock herders. In addition to herding, "slaves were generally used for the more labour intensive work of soap- and butter-making and arable cultivation" (1989, 7).

19. These impediments included their diverse origins, languages, belief systems, and cultural traditions, which made misunderstandings across ethnic boundaries common. In addition, slaves living on remote farms often communicated more with Khoisan laborers or white farmers and therefore assimilated these cultural traditions as their own. Finally, the high proportion of slave men to women meant that few men could find female partners and this limited the development of a slave cultural identity through marriage and children. (Slave children could be sold apart from their mothers up until 1782, and marriage between slaves was only recognized by law in 1823 [Armstrong and Worden 1989, 146–48].) In the eastern Cape region, children born of a slave father and Khoisan mother were often indentured under the apprenticeship system and thus made indistinguishable from other laborers in the *inboekselingen* category (Newton-King 1999, 134).

20. Ward and Worden identify the formation of a specific Cape Malay identity and its accompanying construction of a more "authentic" past as a contributing factor toward the forgetting of slave origins in Cape Town (1998, 207–8).

21. Within a few months after establishing the refreshment station at the Cape in 1652, Jan van Riebeeck requested the Dutch East India Company to provide the assistance of slave labor. Thus, slavery at the Cape existed almost immediately from the company's initial involvement there (Armstrong and Worden 1989, 111).

22. Dooling reports that a group of slave escapees brought Islam to this area around 1809, but the Graaff-Reinet population included only fifty Muslim people by the 1840s (1989, 9).

23. Elbourne is careful to point out, however, that many colonists did not allow their servants to be present at these prayer meetings and that, even if present, they usually did not participate in these events. She believes that joint worship meetings only became standard "further into the nineteenth century" (2002, 418).

24. Ironically, before Andrew Murray's appointment as minister in 1822, the 1807 church records indicated that the church itself owned slaves. The necessity for their accommodation may have led to the building of the parsonage in approximately 1806. This building still exists today as the Reinet House Museum (Minnaar 1987, 85, 141).

25. A teameeting is a Saturday-night event held to commemorate an anniversary or other type of special occasion (see also Bonner 1990, 231; Jorritsma 2006, 166–67; Coplan 2007, 97). As the DRMC church records date from 1881, it is difficult to ascertain when the congregation began holding annual teameetings to commemorate the end of slavery. I assume it started some time after the emancipation of slaves on December 1, 1834, and was well entrenched by the 1880s. The religious context used here to celebrate the emancipation of the slaves contrasts with the evidence of secular, outdoor activities (such as picnics) to mark this occasion in Cape Town (Armstrong and Worden 1989, 111).

26. Ward and Warden also identify this era as the period when slavery origins became forgotten in Cape Town (1998, 207).

27. Denis-Constant Martin states that, at the Cape, slaves and Khoisan people soon developed a reputation for being highly musical and some reports of slave orchestras exist (1999, 58). With the advent of missionization, however, Elbourne reports that Khoisan people rejected the secular trappings of their lives prior to conversion and even went as far as destroying violins due to their association with dancing and secular (Khoisan) songs (2002, 187). It is possible that eastern Cape slaves followed the same patterns in their conversion experiences.

28. Gawie Basson owns a second edition of *De Kinderharp* that belonged to his father, also a long-established Graaff-Reinet resident (Basson communication, February 8, 2005). This work has a direct Graaff-Reinet connection because Charles Murray (1833–1904), son of Andrew Murray, and also the minister of the Dutch Reformed Church, worked on a new edition that he published in 1882. C. G. Henning believes that Murray's tour to Holland, Scotland, and America in 1876 had a strong influence on the subsequent publication of this work (1975, 104, 105).

29. Despite the ambivalent attitude many colonists held on the matter of their servants' participation in the Christian religion, through sheer proximity of these servants to their masters, the former could not avoid exposure to household religious meetings, Bible readings, and the accompanying singing. Willem van Warmelo mentions a certain tune of South African origin that is well known in the eastern Cape and that coloured people learned from farmers (1958, 29). This tune is known as "Mackensie" and appears in several South African hymnbooks, for example *Sing Hosanna!*, the *Nuwe Hallelujah*, and the *Companion Tune Book*. A secular example of this type of musical exchange is the exposure of Zulu farmworkers to the music making of white farmers in KwaZulu-Natal during the nineteenth and early twentieth centuries. This contributed to the formation of the Zulu migrant guitarist genre known as *maskanda* (Muller 2008, 113).

30. The Dutch Reformed Church introduced the *Evangelische gezangboek* in 1814 (at a service in Cape Town) to be used in conjunction with the older psalm book. This

hymnbook contains 192 hymn texts set to 31 older psalm melodies, 44 melodies of German origin and 15 contemporary Dutch melodies (Cillié 1964, 65).

31. The original Afrikaans version of this quotation follows: So het die liederwysies langsamerhand ontstaan: uit die geeksalteerde sang van 'n half-vergete psalmmelodie, van 'n volksliedjie wat bly voortleef het, 'n eie improvisasie, of ook uit die herinnering aan 'n melodie van hierdie neef of daardie buurman, wat dit weer van 'n ander neef of buurman gehoor het. Baie liederwysies is kontaminasie-produkte, saamgestel uit gemeenplase en onststaan in die fantasie van lotgenote, sodat die oorspronklike melodie soms nie terug-gevind kan word nie en dit moeilik is om na te gaan wat eers was en wat later onstaan het.

32. Of the forty-seven hymns I recorded at the URC, the congregation sang three to different melodies than those printed in the hymnbook, namely *Nuwe Sionsgesange* 22 ("Juig aarde, juig"), 218 ("Heer ek hoor van ryke seën" [Lord I Hear of Rich Bless-ing]), and 376 ("Bread of the World in Mercy Broken"). Of the ten hymns recorded at the PSCC, four had alternative melodies: *Sing Hosanna!* 166 ("Neem my lewe laat dit Heer" [Take My Life and Let It Be]), 304 ("Worstel mens as Gods genade" [Wrestle Sinner When God Calls You]), 332 ("My Jesus, ek min u" [My Jesus I Love Thee]), and 343 ("Verheug tesame jonk en oud" [Rejoice Together Young and Old]). The eleven unofficial hymn melodies used by the ESCC include *Sing Hosanna!* numbers 1, 46, 65, 157, 168, 177, 266, 267, 301, 304, and 332. Marlene Jasson, organist of the ESCC, mentioned to me that when she performed at evening church services, the congrega-tion usually sang hymns to the official tunes she played, with the exception of three hymns. She explained that without an organist present at the morning church services, the voorsingers chose the hymn melodies, hence the increased numbers of alternative melodies found in my recordings (communication, July 7, 2006). The reason for the difference in number of hymns recorded at the URC and the Congregational churches is that I attended a few additional services at the URC at the beginning of my field-work period. Also, the URC congregation seldom sang koortjies (choruses), whereas in both Congregational churches, the congregation sang an equal number of koortjies and other praise and worship songs, and official hymns.

33. Authors of the Afrikaans texts include J. D. du Toit (Totius) (Figures 3.3, 3.4, and 3.6) and E. Hartwig (Figure 3.5). The English translation of the text for Fig-ures 3.3, 3.4, and 3.6 reads: "Rejoice all who live, rejoice before the Lord, serve Him with joy, give Him honour, approach His countenance and praise Him with a hymn of thanksgiving." The translation for Figure 3.5 differs slightly from the Congregational Church examples as it is a DRMC/URC text: "Rejoice earth, rejoice before God the Lord, serve Him with joy, give Him honour, come with a joyful hymn of thanksgiving and be jubilant in His presence."

34. In this paragraph, "mediant" refers to the third step or degree of the scale, "tonic" to the first degree of the scale, "dominant" to the fifth scale degree, and "lead-ing note" to the seventh scale degree.

35. This tendency is referred to as a *liederwysformule*, by which many old lie-derwysies can be recognized. Two other possible origins for the melody in Figure 3.5 include sources from beyond Graaff-Reinet. I. D. du Plessis notated a Cape Malay *Ghomma-liedjie*, which has similar contours (1935, 129), and Frikkie Strydom record-ed a version of the hymn among the mixed-race self-named "Baster" community of Rehoboth, Namibia, which has some similar rhythmic and intervallic aspects (1983, notation example 30).

36. Additionally, the majority of congregation members would have received education in tonic sol-fa notation and not in staff notation. Thus, even if the hymnbooks had contained the melodies in staff notation there would still have been scope for variations on official melodies due to the congregation members' unfamiliarity with this notation type.

37. An example of an earlier koortjie mentioned by June Bosch is "Sins Shall Never Enter There, We Are Going Home," which also had an Afrikaans version, "Sondaars sal nie inkom nie, ons gaan hemel toe" (Sinners Will Not Enter There, We Are Going to Heaven). In a hymnbook Mrs. Bosch lent to me, there is a section containing English and Dutch choruses (interview, July 5, 2006; Huskisson 1902).

38. The English translation for *Jesus is so lief vir my* is: "Jesus loves me very much; He can do everything." Although not always enjoyed and participated in by older members of the congregation (see Chapter 5), I believe that one of the reasons for the gradual acceptance of koortjies in the URC (whose congregation did not sing koortjies as frequently as the Congregational Church members) is due to the amalgamation of the Dutch Reformed Church in Africa, the mission denomination for black people, and the Dutch Reformed Mission Church (the Dutch Reformed Church mission for coloured people) in 1994. The Cape Synod of the Dutch Reformed Church is a member, but other Dutch Reformed Church Synods have been slow to respond to the call for this combined denomination, known as the Uniting Reformed Church in Southern Africa. Although I believe that the intermingling of Xhosa and coloured religious singing styles took place well before 1994, the continuation of this trend is assured, due to the combined denomination.

39. Strydom narrates a similar occurrence of free harmonization within the Rehoboth Baster community of Namibia. One of the choir leaders in this community, a teacher by the name of Paulus de Vries, always had to admonish his choir members to sing according to the original sol-fa notation instead of harmonizing freely (1983, 104).

40. The first and second phrases of "Worstel mens" outline the opening of the United Kingdom's national anthem, "God Save the King/Queen," which also indicates the enduring presence of the British colonial legacy in this area. The translation of this hymn text is, "Wrestle sinner, when God calls you, to come to his mercy seat, cast the burden of your misdeeds at the loving Saviour's feet." Verse 2 reads, "Ere you enter God's great city, you must struggle, toil and strive, up the pathway, steep and narrow, if you want to be alive" (UCCSA 1988, hymn 304).

CHAPTER 4

1. Many Afrikaans-speaking churches in the Reformed tradition have a women's society, known as the vrouevereniging, and a youth organization. In the Eastern Cape, churches also have a men's society, known as the broederband. These societies gather during the week for prayer meetings, and they often organize fundraising events. The broederband was formed as a men's-only group to balance the women's-only group the Christelike Sustersbond (Christian Sisters Association), the earlier name for the current women's society. The broederband allowed women to be present at meetings, primarily to enhance the singing, but women were not permitted to make any leadership decisions. Church records until the 1980s refer to the men's society as the *broederbond*, after which it became known as the broederband. In South African politi-

cal history, the name Afrikaner Broederbond also refers to a secret society of male Afrikaner intellectuals, politicians, and religious leaders, originally formed to promote Afrikaans language and culture after World War One, but said to have a significant influence on apartheid policy during the 1960s. By using the terms *broederbond* and *broederband* in this church context, these groups have loosely incorporated the notion of a males-only society, but disrupted the idea of a whites-only membership as found in the original Broederbond. In 1992, the political society became known as the Afrikanerbond and expanded its membership to include those of all racial groups as well as women (A. Kayster communication, September 2006; Giliomee 2003, 420–22, 660; W. Kayster communication, July 4, 2006; PSCC Records, 1953–1960, 1980–1992, and 1999–2000).

2. Broederband opening service, February 17, 2005, ESCC; Kayster interview, February 18, 2005. In interviews with well-known South African musicians, "Senzeni na" is spoken about with great reverence. Duma Ndlovu states, "Somewhere along the lines, a thousand years from now, we will be forced to sit down and review our history. 'Senzeni na?' like 'We Shall Overcome,' will take her rightful place in society, because at one time a mass body of people related to that song and touched each other's hearts using that song" (Hirsch and Simpson 2002).

3. The English translation I provide here is a literal one, as this hymn is understood to be the Afrikaans equivalent of the well-known English hymn "All People that on Earth do Dwell."

4. Even after apartheid, the debate about whether *Nkosi Sikelel' iAfrika* is a prayer or a resistance song continues (see also S. Muller 2001; Coplan and Jules-Rosette 2005). In a workshop held at Unisa (University of South Africa) in March 2006, students discussed this question with some vigor. Another example of a religious song used for resistance purposes is the Xhosa missionary Ntsikana's *Great Hymn*. Added text indicates that the Xhosa people used this melody as a freedom song during the War of Mlanjeni against white settlers in 1850–53 (Dargie 1997, 322).

5. See Kloppers (2007a, 2007b), B. Smith (1988/1989, 1997), and C. M. Smith (2007) for information on white people's church music in South Africa.

6. Jackson observes that this institution is specifically associated with coloured identity formation, culture, and political debates and thus became an ideal site to observe lecturer and student reactions to these demographic changes (2005, 210, n. 3). She does not, however, mention white students in this context. For a perceptive study of white Afrikaans-speaking students' reactions to change at the University of Pretoria, see Jansen (2009).

7. Toyi-toyi originated in the height of the anti-apartheid struggle in the 1980s when many black South African youths escaped over the border into Zimbabwe to obtain training as guerrilla fighters (Hirsch and Simpson 2002). Since the end of apartheid, communities frequently utilize toyi-toyi in their protests regarding poor service delivery and worker rights, among other issues.

8. Another example of this implied difference is a rally attendee's t-shirt, worn in 1997 which proclaims "*liewer Khoi-Khoi as toyi-toyi*" (rather Khoi-Khoi than toyi-toyi). This is a rich example of how indigenous Khoekhoe identity is used to make the black/coloured distinction. However, the "Khoi-Khoi" reference also suggests notions of an "authentic" African indigenous heritage for coloured people that realigns this statement with Africanness and constitutes an inherent contradiction (Jackson 2005,

212–13). On the subject of claiming Khoisan rather than slavery origins, Kerry Ward and Nigel Worden explain that "in the 1990s as land claims on the basis of original ownership became a possibility, to claim descent from original inhabitants rather than imported slaves was a distinct advantage" (1998, 209).

9. There are similarities here with the "respectability" discourse surrounding coloured identity (see Chapter 5).

10. I believe that an additional example of the permeable boundaries between religious gatherings and political rallies (mentioned by Tutu) is the role of travel in spreading news, updates, and messages of encouragement in small Karoo towns and settlements during the apartheid years. Many people would travel all over the Eastern Cape to share church services with members of the same denomination (or other denominations within the Reformed church tradition). I believe that these constituted opportunities both to express a collective religious faith and solidarity and to share information not available in official state-controlled mass media. Ministers also traveled often, both to different churches as guest speakers for their *jaarfees* (anniversary) celebrations and also to the outlying stations at farms in the region (called *buitewyke*, "outside wards") where they would administer the sacraments, carry out the services of baptism and marriage, and very possibly, update the farmworkers on town events and political news simultaneously.

11. Of course, each individual minister could run the service according to his personal religious and political beliefs, and it would be a gross generalization to declare that every minister in this denomination conformed to the requirements of the state church. Two famous examples include the Dutch Reformed Church minister, Beyers Naudé (1915–2004), who broke away from the DRC to form the Christian Institute in 1963 and endured painful isolation and a government banning order that lasted for seven years (1977–84). The second example is Allan Boesak (b. 1945), president of the World Alliance of Reformed Churches, who successfully carried a motion to have apartheid declared a heresy by this organization in 1982 (Villa-Vicencio 1985, 10–12; Davenport and Saunders 2000, 495, 686).

12. This became known as the Congregational Union in 1883 and the United Congregational Church of Southern Africa in 1967 (de Gruchy 2005, 15–16; UCCSA 2010).

13. Despite the mixed congregations in some of these churches, de Gruchy notes that discrimination still existed in terms of the reluctance to elect black leaders and in the local life of many congregations that still worshipped separately according to racial groups (2005, 22, 38).

14. That the government kept a close watch on political activities in rural areas is also confirmed in the brutal murder of four activists from the Karoo town of Cradock in 1985. State police killed Matthew Goniwe, Fort Calata, Sicelo Mhlauli, and Sparrow Mkonto, known as the Cradock Four, when the men were on a journey from Cradock to Port Elizabeth (Davenport and Saunders 2000, 509).

15. Venda (a "homeland" for Venda-language speakers) constituted one of ten *bantustans* (one for each ethnic group) designated for black South Africans by the apartheid government. They were "self-governing," but this system effectively designated black people as foreigners in their own country and forced 80 percent of the country's population to live on 13 percent of the land (Beck 2000, 134–36).

16. Throughout this book, I work with the premise that sound and style serve as

important vehicles of expression in Kroonvale. This owes much to Blacking's insights described here, but his ideas on political consciousness are particularly applicable in this chapter.

17. The subtleties of black South African resistance through language use did not apply to this situation. Black South Africans had a distinct advantage due to their languages, which were for the most part incomprehensible to white people. First, they could sing most apartheid resistance songs openly (apart from the overly familiar ones like *Nkosi sikelel' iAfrika*). Second, they could change existing words of Christian hymns to incorporate protest lyrics. For example, freedom fighter S'busiso Nxumalo describes this process as follows: "Those songs [of the armed anti-apartheid struggle] started . . . beginning to take on those overtones [of war] . . . just changing a word here, changing a word there; putting an AK [47 rifle] there, taking out a bible there" (Hirsch and Simpson 2002). Guerrillas fighting against the white regime in Zimbabwe also used this technique to teach local people about their political parties. Many *Chimurenga* songs of protest originated as Christian hymn tunes set to new political and educational lyrics. Thus, people could add new lyrics or change existing words to suit the historical moment (Turino 2000, 203, 205). Third, they could utilize the African tradition of "poetic license," as coined by Hugh Tracey in his book on Chopi musicians and defined as the use of satirical poetry in certain performance contexts (including singing) in which no action would be taken against those people ridiculed in the text (Tracey 1948/1970, 68; Vail and White 1991, 41, 43, 45).

18. Due to sanctions imposed by various countries, South Africa became increasingly isolated from global trade and investments, as well as international sport and cultural events (Davenport and Saunders 2000, 535–40, 669–70).

19. It is necessary to state here, however, that the Dutch Reformed Church repertory is by no means a collection of hymns of purely South African origin. Melodies originally of Dutch, German, and even English origin are treated as a legitimate part of this denomination's religious music (Drury 1985, 41).

20. I regard these musical practices as being analogous to marginalia in Medieval manuscripts. Even though the marginalia in coloured people's church music are not physically inscribed on the hymnbook page, they nevertheless are "able to gloss, parody, modernize and problematize the text's authority while never totally undermining it" (Camille 1992, 10).

21. A small number of people also belonged to Independent African denominations such as the Zion Christian Church and "Ethiopian type churches" (Statistics South Africa 2001). The diverse denomination choices exhibited in Graaff-Reinet also suggest musical influences not only from Umasizakhe but also from within the Kroonvale community itself. Although I attended one service of the Old Apostolic Church denomination in the Kendrew region near Graaff-Reinet, time constraints during my fieldwork period made it difficult to attend services at other church denominations.

22. I note here, however, that although he does not describe the music, Andries Schutte conducted an ethnographic study of a Dutch Reformed Church in Africa congregation in Meadowlands, Johannesburg (1968).

23. The move toward Africanizing of church repertories contrasts with a perception in the 1960s that African indigenous musics were part of the apartheid propaganda machine to ensure "separate development" along "tribal" lines. For example, each indigenous language radio station broadcast a large percentage of traditional music,

in other words, Zulu traditional music for Zulu people, Xhosa music for Xhosa people, and so on (Muller 2008, 29, 37; see also Hamm 1995). In the context of the Independent African religious denominations I believe that their need to break away from white mission domination as well as the gradual acceptance of Black Consciousness philosophy contributed to the development of "Africanized" religious music traditions. David Coplan suggests something similar to this in the context of urban black performance genres such as African jazz; this secular genre transcended ethnic divisions and appealed to a collective black audience (2007, 197).

24. These taboos were so entrenched that some congregations, even more recently, have not responded well to a relaxation of these rules and an attempt to introduce a more African style of hymnody into services. For example, Dargie reports that "on two occasions, nearly two thousand kilometres apart in South Africa, church and choir members threatened to burn down their (Catholic) churches if the missionary introduced the drum" (1997, 323). Carol Muller reports that traditional mission church members ridiculed Isaiah Shembe's new denomination, and only more recently, proponents of an "African Renaissance" viewed it as an important exponent of this philosophy (2002, 414). (A great deal of ink was spilled in the twentieth century about an "African" church music style, as it became clear that the direct translation of Western hymn texts into African languages ignored the tonal nature of the latter [see Wemen 1960; Jones 1976; Dargie 1997].)

25. Blacking does, however, point out that no existing research provided reasons for why Zionism would be a more attractive option, but suggests that this is due to the Independent Church religious denominations' "common desire to build an independent black society, just as their new church music both transcended traditional ethnic music divisions and broke away from the mission music model" (1995, 202–3).

26. As Sarah Nuttall and Cheryl-Ann Michael point out in the context of South African cultural studies, the "inflation of resistance" and emphasis on segregation, among other factors, can ignore the possibility of discovering connections and commonalities between people (2000, 1). While acknowledging that resistance and its associations of difference remain important constituents of both apartheid and post-apartheid South Africa, there are also more subtle stories to tell, particularly those about entities previously thought to be disparate (Nuttall 2009, 19–20).

27. Muller interprets the existence of these two styles as a representation of "the cultural accommodation Isaiah sought in what were quite clearly the conflicting demands of mission Christianity and traditional culture" (1999, 72).

28. Dargie also mentions the debt owed by protest songs to their mission church origins, thus explaining how congregations inserted these melodies, with their newer associations, back into religious repertories (1997, 326).

CHAPTER 5

1. The members of this choir are drawn from the PSCC choir and the URC choir. They identified their group as the "Ladies' Choir" and attended Tuesday afternoon rehearsals in addition to their own church choir rehearsal and performance commitments. During 2005 no rehearsals took place due to various members' other church commitments, and by early 2006, the choir appeared to have disbanded entirely. In addition to their other engagements, those members who taught at local schools

explained that the increased administrative duties required by the Department of Education added severe demands on their time.

2. I borrow the phrase, "Queen's English" from June Bosch (communication, November 16, 2004). I am very grateful to Mrs. Bosch for her extraordinary kindness in sharing her musical knowledge with me and for many happy hours spent in conversation.

3. As a white English-speaking South African, my own background and profession constitute markers of middle-class status and thus inform the opinions expressed in this chapter. I am aware that many Kroonvale residents (both choir members and ordinary congregation members) might disagree with my definitions and interpretations, and choir members would not always identify themselves first and foremost as being from a middle-class group. While remaining sensitive to these aspects, I nevertheless believe that musical manifestations of class status exist in Kroonvale and that choir music in particular serves as a vehicle for these expressions.

4. One of the main causes of this crisis included the disruption of the notion that the Europeans had of their inalienable right to land and indigenous labor. Khoekhoe, San, and Xhosa rebellions as well as the closing of the frontier and subsequent shortage of land checked this assumption. In addition, the British government exercised a more visible control in comparison to the Dutch East India Company, and with this, "liberalism, utilitarianism, and humanitarianism . . . were experienced by the colonists as threatening and alien impositions" (Elphick and Giliomee 1989, 554).

5. Thomas Turino describes a similar situation in Zimbabwe (then Rhodesia): "In white Rhodesian constructions of blacks, *class* was a relatively minor issue; the general tendency was to lump all 'natives' into a single group. . . . Many settlers viewed 'natives' as only fit for labor" (2000, 121).

6. In nineteenth-century South Africa, Christianity became synonymous with education, as many African converts and their families attended schools established by missionaries. The Bantu Education Act (1953) stipulated the withdrawal of state financial assistance for mission schools unless they were handed over to the state. Many churches capitulated and thus "los[t] . . . control of some of the finest educational institutions in the country, and also their influence in black education" (de Gruchy 1997, 161).

7. The name "Fingoes" refers to people from various defeated chiefdoms, also called Mfengu. They occupied positions as servants to Xhosa chiefdoms, but later became more prosperous as soldiers, farmers, and traders (Davenport and Saunders 2000, 65).

8. For a discussion of the opposing views of the "civilizing project" in the context of mission hymnody, see Muller (2005, 35, 52).

9. In his discussion of the social structures in Providencia, a Caribbean island, Peter Wilson outlines a theory of "respectability" and "reputation." Respectability is linked to status and forms a marker of high class, whereas reputation is specifically connected to men's individual status as fathers of many children (1973, 99, 149–51). Wilson's idea of the church as the "very source of the rationale of respectability" is useful when compared with similar attitudes in Kroonvale (100). For example, "Monogamous marriage, . . . premarital chastity for girls, sober living for men, self-improvement for all" (100) are also measures of respectability that pertain to the Christian community of Kroonvale. However, the particular circumstances of South African coloured-

ness introduce political, racial, social, and economic issues that differ from Wilson's research context.

10. Shame is also associated with coloured people because of their mixed racial heritage. As Zoë Wicomb states, "Miscegenation, the origins of which lie within a discourse of 'race,' concupiscence, and degeneracy, continues to be bound up with shame, a pervasive shame exploited in apartheid's strategy of the naming of a Coloured race, and recurring in the current attempts by coloureds to establish brownness as a pure category, which is to say a denial of shame" (1998, 92). In a different context, Nazarite hymn number 153 uses the word "brown" to refer to the Zulu and other African members of the Nazarite church. Bongani Mthethwa explained that the word "black" carried negative connotations after the impact of the Black Consciousness movement in South Africa, hence the use of "brown" instead (Muller 1999, 272, n. 19).

11. "Mevrou" is the Afrikaans word for "missus" and a respectful term of address. All the choir members are native Afrikaans speakers, but they are also very competent English speakers. As many of the choir members knew that I am a native English speaker, they often spoke a mixture of Afrikaans and English in order to aid my comprehension of the discussion as well as to acknowledge my presence.

12. Institutions for coloured people included the Cape Town Technical College, the North Cape Technical College at Kimberley, the Natal Technical College in Durban, and the Witwatersrand Technical College together with the Newtown Coloured School in Johannesburg. Sheila Patterson states that in 1946–47, nine teachers' training institutions for coloured people existed in the country (1953, 99). When I discussed education institutions with certain choir members, they stated that many of the Kroonvale teachers attended Dower College in Uitenhage (it has since moved to Port Elizabeth), with some community members going further afield to places in Kimberley and Oudtshoorn. After attending school until the age of sixteen (the state education requirement for coloured and white people), many members then obtained their teaching qualifications. Only after this training did they obtain their high school (or senior certificate) diploma through the correspondence colleges such as Damelin. In order to earn a living and fund their own further study, teachers obtained their qualifications before their high school diplomas (conversation with "Ladies' Choir" members, July 19, 2005).

13. At this point in the conversation I suddenly remembered that my mother had attended the Graaff-Reinet Teacher's Training College. It is one of the tragedies of apartheid that these two people, born in the same area and of roughly the same age, did not have the same educational choices available to them.

14. The notation the choir sang from that evening was similar to that presented in "Zion, City of God" (see Figures 5.1a and 5.1b), namely, staff notation with corresponding tonic sol-fa notation included. I have been unable to ascertain the original source of "Holy, Holy, Holy" from which the choir sang that night and thus make use of the *Oxford Anthem* book for this purpose.

15. The first existing written records for this church are dated 1881. This is the same year that the congregation became part of the newly established Nederduitse Gereformeerde Sendingkerk (Dutch Reformed Mission Church) for coloured South Africans. Unfortunately there is no evidence thus far of the existence of a choir since the formation of the church in 1821, but it must have been formed sometime before 1893.

16. The original Dutch reads: "Het koor verzoekt dat de collecte niet onder het zingen van het tweede gesang. Maar daarna terwyl zy (het koor) een gesang zingt zal gehouden worden. Toegestaan" (The choir requested that the collection not be taken during the singing of the second hymn. But, it could be held afterward, while it [the choir] sang a hymn. Permission granted) (DRMC Records 2, September 2, 1910).

17. Besides Kimberley, this choir toured to Paarl, Keimoes, Port Elizabeth, and Uitenhage. I am grateful to Mrs. Marjorie Visagie for making this program available to me. In addition to providing an idea of the type of repertoire performed by these choirs, the inclusion of *Nkosi Sikelel' iAfrika* as part of the program perhaps suggests the type of nonverbal political sign I described in Chapter 4. Here the anthem of the ANC's liberation struggle is innocently framed in a choral context of semiclassical and religious pieces. Due to its origins in mission church composition style, it does not appear out of place in this program, yet audience members would understand its associations with the anti-apartheid movement.

18. The minister of the PSCC, Rev. Bezuidenhoudt, states that although these are the general places within the service for choir performance, he believes that there should be flexibility in determining these moments (interview, June 15, 2005).

19. June Bosch informed me that she led a similar choir before the establishment of the current "Ladies Choir," but the former group only rehearsed for specific performances and not once per week like the latter group (communication, July 5, 2006).

20. This mixture of the sacred and the secular found here is mainly because the choir was an interdenominational one and often performed for charity functions where light secular pieces would not have been out of place. The historical origin of this type of repertoire is quite clear, however, in that those influenced by the missionaries did not always make the distinction between sacred and secular, as both came from the same source and were inextricably mixed with the missionary wish to convert people to Christianity as well as to European ways. As Carol Muller states, "All 'civilized' singing, sacred and secular, was foreign at the outset. The same four-part harmony style was used in both sacred and secular songs: it was only the words that differed. . . . This relationship between mission work and the civilizing project is one of the themes that is central to an understanding of much South African performance in the twentieth century" (2004, 4).

21. In my archival reading at this museum, I noticed that white English-speaking townspeople donated much if not most of this sheet music. This indicates how the people who chose to donate objects to this archive constructed its nature. This also affects the reconstruction of the region's history.

22. Radio has a contested history in South Africa due to its use by the apartheid government for promotion of its "separate development" policy (Hamm 1991, 1995). More recent studies of South African radio suggest that despite these government attempts at control, the auditory nature of radio programs offered scope for listeners to interpret different meanings and messages (Gunner 2000).

23. Although Coplan outlines the Salvation Army influence on African brass bands in the urban areas from the 1890s (2007, 63), the Salvation Army's role in the Graaff-Reinet music scene is unclear. Historical records do, however, state that two amateur brass bands flourished in the town during the mid-nineteenth century. After its formation in 1857 as an attachment to the two local volunteer defense organizations, the first group disbanded in 1882. The following year, James Saunders, chief

constable of the municipal police, formed the Quadrille Band, which performed for a weekly dance held every Wednesday night as well as other dance occasions until 1890. Dance events held during the twentieth century were often attached to the Agricultural Show, country clubs, or school fundraising events (Henning 1975, 131, 195, 213; Minnaar 1987, 36, 105, 120). Bands mentioned in the local press include the Kendrew Jazz Five and the Graaff-Reinet Jazz Orchestra (active in the 1920s), Keith's Keynotes (based in Uitenhage), and the Rayonettes (active in Graaff-Reinet dance occasions during the 1960s) (*Graaff-Reinet Advertiser*, September 8, 1926, November 8, 1926, March 30, 1964, August 27, 1964). In the coloured community, two bands existed, both attached to churches. Mr. A. Bosch led the DRMC band, while Mr. Baine led the PSCC band. Villa Louther remembers these bands playing in the streets at Christmas time (interview, June 23, 2005).

24. The tension between sacred and secular values and their relationship to class issues is not limited to this community. As Guthrie Ramsey states, "Within African American music history there exists a long-standing tension between Western ideas of the secular and the sacred and between other cultural sensibilities in which the split is not as profound. The appropriateness of certain musical gestures for worship, the secular nature of a song's subject matter, dress, body language, and the proper venue of presentation have become lightning rods for controversy" (2003, 212). For example, "During the 1920s Negro Renaissance, the struggle over cultural authority occurred not only between the black literati and proponents of 'oral' culture but also among the practitioners of vernacular music, namely, between secular and religious factions" (24). See also Maultsby (1992, 19–33).

25. In general, missionaries in South Africa disapproved of indigenous peoples' singing and dancing cultures. According to Coplan, Christian converts were forbidden "to perform the dances and dance songs that had been indispensable to organized social interaction in the traditional community" (2007, 41). In KwaZulu-Natal, the Zulu prophet, Isaiah Shembe, introduced the sacred dances of *ukusina* and *umgido* for performance by the women followers in his Nazarite religion. Shembe's eclectic mix of Christian and traditional Zulu theology allowed space for these dances to be preserved and imbued with a sense of the sacred. His religion therefore contrasted with the overwhelming Euro-American missionary pressure to adopt Western ways (Muller 1999, 56; 2003, 102). This discourse of Western civilization also extended to a disapproval of participation by young African girls in *marabi* dance parties in the 1940s and 1950s (Ballantine 1993, 82).

26. It is usual in these church records and also during church services and related activities that members' names are prefaced with "brother" or "sister." The church council punished more young women than men for dancing, but accused mainly men of drunk and disorderly behavior. "Tickey draai" refers to a certain type of dance, derived from Cape square dancing where couples turn around in one spot. It also refers to the guitar music, popular between 1880 and 1930, which accompanied this dance (Coplan 2007, 443). The original Dutch version of this church record entry follows: "5 Februari 1896 [:] De jonge zuster Maria Hermans beschuldigd van dansen werd ernstig vermaand zich van zulke onchristelyke byeenkomsten te onthouden en beloofde beterschap. . . . 17 Augustus 1908 [:] Anna Meyer, Hendrina Jacobs en Aletta Jacobs, drie jonger zusters stouden beschuldigd van tickey draaien. De eerste kwam vry met eene vermaning omdat het de eerste keer is maar de twee anderen

waren reeds vroegen vermaand en werden om voor drie maanden onder censuur gesteldt."

27. The original Afrikaans version follows:

8. Lede wat hulle skuldig maak aan onsedelikheid sal afgesny word vir ten minste 12 maande.

9. Lede wat hulle skuldig maak aan dronkenskap sal afgesny word vir ten minste 6 maande.

10. Lede wat deel neem aan dans partye sal afgesit word vir ten minste 3 maande.

28. This emphasis on hymns and anthems suggests a type of musical patriarchy imposed on the consciousness of church members. This is to be expected, especially in the DRMC tradition, because of its affiliation to the Calvinist Dutch Reformed Church. John de Gruchy warns, however, that the Dutch Reformed Church itself is not as Calvinist as one of the denominations that broke away from it in 1859. This neo-Calvinist denomination, known as the Gereformeerde Kerk (Reformed Church), or "Dopper Kerk," only sang psalms, in other words, not hymns. It obtained a big following in Potchefstroom and Rustenburg, in what is now the North West Province (2005, 6–7).

29. Charles Carson and Cathy Chamblee, two of my former PhD student colleagues at the University of Pennsylvania, reported a similar tension between the traditional and the newer gospel-influenced repertoire as sung in Monumental Baptist Church of Philadelphia. These observations stemmed from fieldwork research in the fall of 2003 (Carson communication, August 23, 2005; Chamblee communication, August 24, 2005). I believe that part of this tension is due to nostalgia for past musical experiences, particularly during childhood. For example, Marjorie Visagie remembered first joining the PSCC choir at the age of thirteen (communication, February 22, 2005). The formative musical experiences of singing choral anthems and hymns, especially for older choir members, infuse this more distanced repertory with a sense of longing that is as yet absent in the newer church repertory of koortjies (Stewart 1984, 145).

30. Anziske Kayster pointed out to me that these musical abilities constitute a type of unspoken requirement for choir membership among the older generation of churchgoers and that this does not necessarily apply to the young people (communication, September 2006).

31. Fort Beaufort is a town in the Eastern Cape Province, approximately 240 km/150 miles east of Graaff-Reinet.

32. Despite its continued pervasive use in South Africa, this system contains certain faults. According to Coplan, "The tonic solfa system, which for half a century remained the basis of modern African composition, is not entirely suitable for notating African music. Its indications for tempo, modulation and complex rhythms are awkward and inconvenient, and its simple harmonic scheme makes it difficult to accurately represent African melody and polyphony" (2007, 140). Due to these shortcomings, it is also difficult to teach instrumental music using this system. Other sources on tonic sol-fa in South Africa include Curwen (1891), Jones (1976), and Wemen (1960).

33. Sol-fa education in South Africa, as well as in England, has its own class and racial inscriptions (see Olwage 2003, 59–77).

34. Similarly, local South African musicians in the popular music industry often imitate American accents in their performances, which implies that South Africa is still a "music colony" despite its independence. As Robert Boake explains, "The career of original music in South Africa is thus structured as a 'following career' which mimics American and British music" (1994, 163–64).

35. One way of connecting to British culture is for community members to follow the lives of British royalty. For example, a member of the Old Apostolic Church in Kendrew, Mrs. Joyce Grootboom, explained her religious belief that God created all people equal because they are created in his image, by talking to me about Princess Diana in very familiar terms. In our interview she stated, "It didn't matter how it ended but we were all happy with her. I was immensely proud of her. She was a beautiful lady. . . . She did so many good things for us. Even though I never got near her I prayed for her. . . . And, I always say to my children, "those two [Charles and Diana] didn't leave the palace and live in Kroonvale shacks—they live in the palace because they had worked for it" (interview, February 16, 2005). The original Afrikaans version follows: "Al het dit hoe geëindig maar ons was almal happy met haar. Ek was vreeslik trots op haar. Dit was 'n mooi vrou. . . . Sy't soveel baie goete gedoen vir ons. Al het ek nie naby haar gekom het nie maar ek het vir haar gebid. . . . En altyd sê ek vir my kinders, "hulle twee het nie die paleis verlaat en dan in Kroonvale daar in die blikhokke kom bly nie—hulle bly in die paleis en dis die plek waar hulle mos voor gewerk het." British colonial influence is not limited to the Graaff-Reinet area of South Africa. The KwaZulu-Natal Province, for example, is sometimes jokingly referred to as "the last outpost of the British empire." The persistent manifestation of British influence today is a remnant of the earlier colonial period when the imperial presence was often larger than life in the minds of many people. For example, Katie Makanya, a member of the African Choir that toured England in 1891, was utterly shocked at the small stature of Queen Victoria and disappointed that "she wore no crown, no purple robes. She had no page-boys or soldier-guards or even advisers proclaiming her power. She was just like any old widow-woman" (McCord 1995, 35). In addition, Erlmann reports the existence of Zulu *isicathamiya* song texts that refer to the visit of Queen Victoria to South Africa (1996, 222).

36. It is necessary to state, however, that Johannes Theodorus van der Kemp, the London Missionary Society's first missionary to the area, held services in Dutch. The tendency to use English only came later, when the PSCC became affiliated with the Congregational Church in Southern Africa (Enklaar 1988, 111).

37. Modisane summarizes the ambiguous position of the English-speaking black South African as follows: "The educated African is resented equally by the blacks because he speaks English, which is one of the symbols of white supremacy, he is resentfully called a Situation, something not belonging to either, but tactfully situated between white oppression and black rebellion. The English regard him as a curio, they listen to him with critical attention to detail as regard to accent, usage and syntax; when they have taken a decision they pronounce, with almost divine tolerance and Christian charity, that the African speaks English beautifully. . . . The Afrikaners are almost psychotic in their reaction to the English-speaking African, whom they accuse of talking back with insolence and aping the white man" (1990, 94).

38. Despite the prominence of English choir compositions in the repertoire of the "Ladies' Choir," the PSCC choir, and the URC choir, most choir members are not

averse to singing Afrikaans and thus Afrikaans pieces are also performed on occasion. Nonetheless, it is also the case that, during the 1970s, some choir members affiliated with the PSCC refused to sing Afrikaans works (Bosch interview, June 19, 2005).

39. Ulf Hannerz explains this tendency in the context of Sophiatown (a Johannesburg suburb destroyed by the government): "Accepting New York could be a way of rejecting Pretoria, to refuse the cultural entailments of any sort of 'separate development.' We are inclined to think of local cultural resistance as something that draws its symbolic resources from local roots, and undoubtedly, Sophiatowners could use such resources as well. As things stood, however, it seems to have been in the logic of the situation rather to reaffirm the links between Sophiatown and the world" (1997, 168).

CHAPTER 6

1. This koortjie is based on the story of the healing pool of Bethesda, John 5:1–9. Rev. Barendse, ESCC minister, explained the women's actions at this service as part of a special monetary collection for the building fund (boufondskollekte). Each member is expected to place a contribution in the plate at the front of the church and they move toward the plate while dancing (interview, October 27, 2005).

2. Information for this chapter is based on women's society meetings I attended, mostly at the ESCC. I also attended a meeting of the PSCC women's society, a combined interdenominational service for the Women's World Day of Prayer, two sametrekking meetings which are interdenominational prayer meetings, and the 2005 jaarfees, or anniversary celebrations, of the ESCC women's society.

3. The effects of the settler and African patriarchal systems on coloured women are not clear; in addition, the question of whether a separate patriarchal system for coloured women existed remains unanswered. For the purposes of this chapter, I assume that "everywhere [in South Africa] women were subordinate to men but there were important contrasts in the operation of gender between different social systems in the region" (Walker 1990, 1).

4. In contrast to the use of motherhood as an act of resistance, male Afrikaans nationalists after the Anglo-Boer War (1899–1902) promoted it as part of an ideology of social upliftment. The ideology of the volksmoeder (mother of the nation) not only kept women in the home but also "depicted [them] as the cornerstone of the household . . . [and] a central unifying force within Afrikanerdom" (Brink 1990, 273–74).

5. Muller's work forms part of a small but growing body of literature that focuses on issues of music and gender in South Africa (see also, for example, Ballantine 1993, 2000; Lucia 1995; Allen 1997, 2000; James 1999; Walton and Muller 2005). This is a positive indication that the "respectability of the study of women and gender" continues to grow (Walker 1995, 419).

6. This is the usual manner of closing a meeting in the ESCC women's society and also at the interdenominational meetings, known as sametrekkings, that I attended. Sometimes, instead of shaking hands, members hugged each other, as I observed at the PSCC women's society meeting. At this particular occasion, the women did not sing, which was an exception to farewell rituals at the other meetings I experienced. According to Sabina van Jaarsveld, then-chairman, the members of the URC women's society do not have this manner of closing a meeting (interview, November 10, 2005).

7. November 11, 2004, Kroonvale. As this was my first women's society experi-

ence, many of the women's names and the names of the koortjies only became familiar to me later on, hence their absence in this account.

8. Gaitskell explains a further reason for the choice of Thursday for prayer meetings: "The long-entrenched use of Thursday afternoons for *manyano* meetings may even have been related to the rhythm of the washing week: bundles were fetched on Monday [from white homes in the suburbs of the Witwatersrand/Johannesburg], washed on Tuesday and ironed on Wednesday, freeing women for group prayer on Thursday" (1990, 257). Sabina van Jaarsveld states that in the post-apartheid era, women sometimes arrange especially with their employers to have Thursday afternoons free (interview, November 10, 2005; Marre 2000; Hirsch and Simpson 2002).

9. Gawie Basson informed me that women's societies were known through the years by various names, for example, Christelike Sustersbond (Christian Sisters Union), Christelike Sustersvereniging (Christian Sisters Society), Vroueaksie (Women [in] Action), and Vrouediens (Women [in] Service) (communication, October 11, 2005). Thus although the present societies date from the early twentieth century, it is possible that their ages have been calculated from the year of a name change, and that in fact, under different names, these societies go much farther back in time.

10. The PSCC records actually date the origin of the women's society to three years earlier, in 1922 (Liebenberg n.d., 1).

11. This uniform has obviously spread beyond what is now the KwaZulu-Natal Province, as I observed women wearing black skirts with red tunics both in Graaff-Reinet and Johannesburg.

12. Although R15,000 is approximately equivalent to US$2,000, the conversion is not a meaningful comparison here when taking the cost of living in South Africa into account.

13. In general, the social and *pennieslaan* traditions are similar to the idea behind African American rent parties held in the United States. These parties benefited a different individual every time and gave them a small income. Of course, the events I observed were in the context of church gatherings and not individual households, but the fact that every church holds various anniversary celebrations means that every church benefits at least twice or three times per year from these fundraising events. The South African *stokvel*, a working-class women's credit association, which required a cash payment from its members each week, works on similar principles. Every week a lump sum comprising these payments is paid to a certain member who then holds a party, charges admission fees, and uses a bidding system for providing entertainment (Coplan 2007, 123). For a discussion of stokvel versus manyano traditions in the Johannesburg area, see Coplan (2007, 124–25).

14. A similar instance of church members bringing religious texts to meetings despite differing levels of literacy is to be found in the Nazarite religion of KwaZulu-Natal. Muller states that the hymnbook is carefully wrapped up and "faithfully carried to religious services by all Nazarite members—regardless of whether they are able to read or not" (1999, 98).

15. An example of inscribing actual hymn texts with a feminine spirituality can be observed in the context of the nineteenth-century Baptist hymn. Women hymnists used their writing ability to "create . . . texts that undermined patriarchal religion by centering power in the home rather than in the church, by locating God within themselves, by separating physical intimacy from sexual submission, and by emphasizing service rather than conquest" (Hobbs 1995, 122, 140).

16. My conversations with women's society members usually focused on the history and traditions of the women's societies and the factual information about the music such as titles of hymns, lyrics of koortjies, and so on. As so little written evidence exists on this tradition in Kroonvale, I felt obliged to ascertain this type of information first and I found generally that the women I spoke to seemed more comfortable talking about these aspects.

17. Two separate worship styles also exist in the Nazarite religion of KwaZulu-Natal, namely, *inkhonzo* (congregational worship) and *ukusina* (religious dance). The former takes place at weekly Saturday (Sabbath) church services and the latter on Sundays, Tuesdays, or Thursdays, depending on the preference of Shembe, the religious leader. The differences between these two styles are far more pronounced within the Nazarite religion than the characteristics I observed in Kroonvale (Muller 1999, 71, 72, 74).

18. This effortless flow of activities during a society meeting has a long history. A Methodist Society periodical mentioned in 1906 that "reading, prayer, singing, and conversation followed each other quite naturally" at these gatherings (Methodist Society, *Foreign Field* [February 1906], 240; quoted in Gaitskell 1995, 215).

19. Supporting a woman preacher through song is referred to as "lifting them up," that is, giving them the strength to speak or pray (van Jaarsveld interview, November 10, 2005).

20. Aaron Fox describes a similar use of music as a source of social cohesion in working-class Texan society. In this context, however, the constant presence of live music and jukebox music allows performers and listeners in country music bars a platform for both spoken and sung expression (2004, 288–89, 294, 299).

21. An additional example of the freedom of women's singing can be found in Muller's work on the sacred songs of the Nazarite religious followers. Muller discusses an early recording of this music by Hugh Tracey, which is later described by Percival Kirby. Kirby states that the women's parts are "embroideries" thereby implying that they are secondary to the "main" melody sung by the men in this recording. Muller instead interprets these embroideries as the embodiment of the musical "freedom" and special rhythm inherent in this music (1999, 105).

22. I am aware that if I had been a male researcher, I probably would not have been called into the kitchen that morning. The strictly gendered division of labor in this community aided my research on women's society music a great deal.

CHAPTER 7

1. Of course, many national roads in South Africa bypass small rural towns completely, and in many cases, travelers do not need to stop in towns but rather at various fuel and takeout service stations along the highways.

2. The rise of game farming in the area also resulted in hardship for livestock farmers. Jackals and red cats, the natural predators of the area, began to target domestic livestock as an easier alternative to hunting game. The resulting stock losses and economic consequences for farmers also affected their staff members.

3. During the past few years, Karoo music also reached a wider market with David Kramer's production known as *Karoo Kitaar Blues* (Karoo guitar blues). In 2002, Kramer, a well-known white South African guitar player and cabaret artist, collaborated

with coloured musicians from the Northern Cape Province Karoo area in order to produce this compact disc. These guest performers included Tokas Lodewyk, Hannes Coetzee, Siena and Jan Mouers, Jakob Jaers, Koos Lof, and Helena Nuwegeld. All played guitar except for Nuwegeld, who is a singer, Lof, who performed on accordion, and Jaers, who played the homemade violin. Kramer had first met these musicians on a research trip with a documentary film producer, Jan Horn. The resulting program on indigenous guitar music, *Stoksielalleen: Langpad (Episode 1)* (All alone: Long road), aired on the South African TV channel, kykNET in March 2002. In addition to the production of the compact disc and the documentary, Kramer and these musicians also performed live at the 2001 Klein Karoo Nasionale Kunstefees (Little Karoo National Arts Festival) in Oudtshoorn. The show won an award at the festival and then toured nationally to packed houses. A recent documentary, directed by Liza Key, follows the musicians from their rural origins to their performances at Cape Town's Baxter Theatre (2004). Reviewers heaped praises on *Karoo Kitaar Blues,* and in some circles, it is affectionately known as the "Beaufort West Social Club" (a town in the Western Cape Province), the South African equivalent of Ry Cooder's famous *Buena Vista Social Club* (1997). As Kramer holds sole copyright to the compact disc, however, questions have also been raised about the power implications behind this collaboration (Lee 2005).

4. Alex van Heerden died tragically in a car accident on January 7, 2009. Although I did not know him well personally, I feel an immense sense of loss for his talents as a musician and researcher of previously unacknowledged vernacular music traditions of the Karoo.

5. In addition to my own work and the literature I have already mentioned (see Chapter 1), I know of two other research projects currently in progress at the time of writing. Liza Key is conducting work on rural musicians in the Northern Cape, namely, violinists, guitarists, accordionists, ramkie players, and mouth organists. She is particularly interested in ascertaining how these musicians learned to make and play their instruments and the various tuning systems they use. Hilde Roos and colleagues at the University of Stellenbosch are compiling an oral history publication on those involved with the Eoan group, a cultural organization that actively performed opera and other Western classical art forms in and around Cape Town from the 1940s through to the 1970s.

6. While some interest in mass resistance and Black Consciousness philosophies may have waned (Kruger 2002, 35), the ongoing service delivery protests around the country reveal that the culture of expressing political dissent has survived in the post-apartheid context, albeit in slightly altered form.

7. The departure from the need to write about political resistance is also paralleled in the creation of post-apartheid musical genres, for example, the kwaito genre that is identified by its practitioners as expressly nonpolitical. Kwaito is a South African form of hip-hop (Stephens 2000, 263; see also Steingo 2008).

8. Contemporary South Africa is caught between the ongoing use of ethnic identifiers such as "black," "white," "Indian," and "coloured" and the nation-building rhetoric of the Mandela era, which attempts to view the entire South African population as a "rainbow nation," united in its diversity. This tension becomes especially apparent when most official forms still require citizens to indicate their specific racial group, using the same or similar designations as the official apartheid racial categories. In addition, depending on the speaker and the context in which it is used, African Renais-

sance philosophy can imply that the category "African" only applies to certain black South African groups. Thus, sadly, the legacy of apartheid racial classification continues to survive in the present, whether expressed explicitly or in disguised form.

9. De Kock points out, however, that this situation can have both positive and negative results. While freedom of choice abounds, the danger also exists of developing an attitude of apathy and indifference within this context (2005, 78, 81–82).

Glossary

Agterryers. Coloured servants of white soldiers during the Anglo-Boer War (1899–1902).

Biduur. Hour of prayer. Name used for weekly meetings of a church women's society as well as other organizations within the church, for example, men's society or church council.

Bijwoner/bywoner. White tenant farmer who worked for landowner in exchange for stock grazing and an area of ground to cultivate crops.

Bioscope. Cinema.

Black Consciousness. A philosophical movement spearheaded by Steve Biko (1946–77) who believed that all South African black people (regardless of particular ethnic background) needed to free themselves from their self-conception as servants or inferior to white people.

Broederband. The men's organization of the church. Also called the *mannebond*.

Buitewyke. Outside wards. Outlying rural church stations.

Commando. A term used in South African history to describe a group of white frontier farmers, often accompanied by Khoisan servants, which formed specifically to murder San and Khoekhoe people and to capture young children in order to force them into farm labor.

Dagga. Marijuana.

Diaken. Church deacon.

Dominee (abbreviation: Ds). A minister, especially in the Dutch Reformed Church denomination.

Dutch Reformed Mission Church (DRMC). Originally established in 1821 by the Graaff-Reinetsche Zendelings Genootschap. This church's congregation held its worship services in a building, known as the Oefeningshuis (practicing house) in the main street of the town. Thus, it disguised the fact that this building (literally across the street from the main Dutch Reformed Church building in the town) was used for church services. This avoided overt violation of a colonial law of the time, which stated that church buildings had to be at least a three-day horse ride apart. In 1881 it became part of the newly established Dutch Reformed Mission Church, a nationwide "daughter" organization of the white Afrikaner Dutch Reformed Church. In 1994, it became known as the Uniting Reformed Church or Verenigende Gereformeerde Kerk (URC or VGK, respectively).

East Street Congregational Church (ESCC). Formed in 1938, the members of this church broke away first from the Middle Street Basotho Mission Church and then the Parsonage Street Congregational Church. At first, the church members met for worship in Cypress Grove (a small suburb near Umasizakhe), but with the implementation of the Group Areas Act (1950), a new building was consecrated for the ESCC in the early 1960s. Rev. B. B. Botha, the minister at the time, specifically requested that one of the streets in the newly built residential area of Kroonvale be named "East Street" so that the church could retain its name.

Erven. Properties.

Gesange. Hymns.

Ghomma-liedjie. Cape Malay picnic song.

Graaff-Reinetsche Zendelings Genootschap. Graaff-Reinet Missionary Organization.

Griqua. People of mixed slave, Khoisan, and European ancestry, initially occupied the fringes of colonial territory; in the mid-nineteenth century the government sought to reincorporate them in the colony by granting them the areas known as Griqualand West and Griqualand East.

Groot Londen. "Big London." Name used for Parsonage Street Congregational Church.

Huisboorlingen. Children of farm servants who were apprenticed to work on the farm until coming of age.

Huurkamer. Rental room. Accommodation for coloured and black people living in the town of Graaff-Reinet until at least 1910.

Inboekselingen. Indentured laborers.

Jaarfees. Anniversary. Used for both the church and the societies within the congregation.

Jeug vereniging. Church youth organization.

Kerkraad. Church council.

Khoekhoe/Khoikhoi. Collective term for indigenous pastoral peoples of the Cape.

Khoisan. Collective term for indigenous pastoral and hunter-gatherer peoples.

Klein Londen. "Small London." Name used for the Middle Street Basotho Mission Church for Sotho refugees, under the auspices of the London Missionary Society.

Koortjie. A short chorus with religious lyrics, often sung in Afrikaans but occasionally with verses in Xhosa or English.

Krijgsgevangenen. War captives.

Kroonvale. The residential area built for coloured people by the apartheid government. Many coloured people (and their churches) were forced to move from Umasizakhe and Graaff-Reinet to Kroonvale during the 1960s.

Kwaito. A South African form of hip-hop.

Landdrost. Mayor.

Liederwysies. Substitute melodies for official hymn melodies. These could be printed melodies of other psalm or hymn tunes used instead of the official printed melody for that specific text, or melodies from oral sources.

Location/Township. A specifically South African term referring to a segregated area on the outskirts of a town or city set aside for black residents.

Manyano. Xhosa word for "union." Used to refer to African Christian women's organizations.

Moeders. Mothers. Often used by women's society members to refer to themselves and each other.

Muti. Traditional or indigenous medicine.

Nguni. Group of peoples sharing related languages, namely, Ndebele, Xhosa, Zulu, and Swati.

Parsonage Street Congregational Church (PSCC). Established by the London Missionary Society in the early nineteenth century, this church is the oldest coloured church in the Graaff-Reinet area and the first Congregational Church of South Africa.

Pennieslaan. Penny-slam. Church fundraising event where members throw coins onto a table in time to singing.

Ramkie. Long-necked lute of Portuguese origin, adopted by the Khoisan and Bantu-speaking peoples during the colonial era.

San. Collective term for indigenous hunter-gatherer peoples of the Cape.

Social. All-night event held on the Saturday evening of a jaarfees (anniversary) weekend.

Susters. Sisters. General term for women members of a Reformed Church congregation.

Teameeting. Saturday night event held to raise church funds. Often used to commemorate an anniversary or another special occasion.

Tickey Draai. A certain type of dance, derived from Cape square dancing, where couples turn around in one spot. It also refers to the guitar music, popular between 1880 and 1930, which accompanied this dance.

Toyi-toyi. A type of military-style dance used as a form of anti-apartheid protest.

Trekboers. Dutch-speaking farmers who moved into the interior of the country in search of grazing for their livestock.

Veeboer. Stock farmer. An alternative term for trekboer.

Vrouevereniging/Vrouediens. Church women's society.

Umasizakhe. The residential area for black people near Graaff-Reinet.

Uniting Reformed Church (URC). The name for the Dutch Reformed Mission Church since 1994.

Voorsinger. Lead singer. A person (male or female) with a strong voice who begins a cappella hymns and koortjies for the rest of the church congregation to follow.

References

Adhikari, Mohamed. 2005. *Not White Enough, Not Black Enough: Racial Identity in the South African Coloured Community*. Athens: Ohio University Press.

———, ed. 2009. *Burdened by Race: Coloured Identities in Southern Africa*. Cape Town: UCT Press.

Akrofi, Eric, Maria Smith, and Stig-Magnus Thorsén, eds. 2007. *Music and Identity: Transformation and Negotiation*. Stellenbosch: SUN Press.

Allen, Lara. 1997. Introduction: South African Women of Song, Their Lives and Times. In *A Common Hunger to Sing: A Tribute to South Africa's Black Women of Song 1950–1990*, ed. Z. B. Molefe and M. Mzileni. Cape Town: Kwela Books.

———. 2000. Representation, Gender and Women in Black South African Popular Music, 1948–1960. PhD diss., University of Cambridge.

Alvarez-Pereyre, Frank, and Simha Arom. 1993. Ethnomusicology and the Emic/Etic Issue. *World of Music* 35 (1): 7–33.

Andersson, Muff. 1981. *Music in the Mix: The Story of South African Popular Music*. Johannesburg: Ravan Press.

Archer, Sean. 2000. Technology and Ecology in the Karoo: A Century of Windmills, Wire and Changing Farming Practice. *Journal of Southern African Studies* 26 (4): 675–96.

Armstrong, James C., and Nigel Worden. 1989. The Slaves, 1652–1834. In *The Shaping of South African Society, 1652–1840*, ed. R. Elphick and H. Giliomee, 109–83. Middletown, CT: Wesleyan University Press.

Attlee, Mary. 1947. The Coloured People of South Africa. *African Affairs* 46 (184): 148–51.

Ballantine, Christopher. 1993. *Marabi Nights: Early South African Jazz and Vaudeville*. Johannesburg: Raven Press.

———. 2000. Gender, Migrancy, and South African Popular Music in the Late 1940s and 1950s. *Ethnomusicology* 44 (3): 376–407.

Bank, Andrew, ed. 1997. *The Proceedings of the Khoisan Identities and Cultural Heritage Conference*. Cape Town: Infosource.

——. 2006. *Bushmen in a Victorian World: The Remarkable Story of the Bleek-Lloyd Collection of Bushman Folklore*. Cape Town: Double Storey.

Barber, K., ed. 1997. *Readings in African Popular Culture*. Bloomington: International African Institute in association with Indiana University Press; Oxford: James Currey.

——. 2001. Cultural Reconstruction in the New South Africa. *African Studies Review* 44 (2): 177–85.

Barnard, Alan. 1992. *Hunters and Herders of Southern Africa: A Comparative Ethnography of the Khoisan Peoples*. Cambridge, New York, and Melbourne, et al.: Cambridge University Press.

Barnard, Marius, and A. Johnson. 1975. *Karoo*. Cape Town: Don Nelson.

Barrow, John. 1801. *An Account of the Travels into the Interior of Southern Africa in the Years 1797–1798*. London: Strahan.

Barz, G. F., and T. J. Cooley, eds. 1997. *Shadows in the Field: New Perspectives for Fieldwork in Ethnomusicology*. New York: Oxford University Press.

Bauman, Max Peter. 1993. Listening as an Emic/Etic Process in the Context of Observation and Inquiry. *World of Music* 35 (1): 34–61.

Bebey, Francis. 1975. *African Music: A People's Art*. Translated by Josephine Bennett. New York: Lawrence Hill.

Beck, Roger B. 2000. *The History of South Africa*. The Greenwood Histories of the Modern Nations. Edited by F. Thackeray and J. Findling. Westport, CT, and London: Greenwood Press.

Besten, Michael. 2009. "We Are the Original Inhabitants of This Land": Khoe-San Identity in Post-Apartheid South Africa. In *Burdened by Race: Coloured Identities in Southern Africa*, ed. M. Adhikari, 134–55. Cape Town: UCT Press.

Bezuidenhoudt, Jacobus. 1999. The Renewal of Reformed Worship Through Retrieving the Past and Ecumenical Openness. MA thesis, University of Cape Town.

Bhabha, Homi K. 1994. *The Location of Culture*. London and New York: Routledge.

Biesbrouck, K., S. Elders, and G. Rossel, eds. 1997. *Central African Hunter-Gatherers in a Multidisciplinary Perspective: Challenging Elusiveness*. Leiden: CNWS.

Blacking, John. 1995. *Music, Culture and Experience*. Edited by Reginald Byron. Chicago and London: University of Chicago Press.

Blumhofer, Edith L., and Mark A. Noll. 2004. *Singing the Lord's Song in a Strange Land: Hymnody in the History of North American Protestantism*. Tuscaloosa: University of Alabama Press.

Boake, Robert Ian. 1994. Working Music: An Investigation of Popular, Non-Sponsored, Original Music Performance as a Career. Master of Social Science thesis, University of Natal.

Bonner, Philip. 1990. "Desirable or Undesirable Basotho Women?": Liquor, Prostitution and the Migration of Basotho Women to the Rand, 1920–1945. In *Women and Gender in Southern Africa to 1945*, ed. C. Walker, 221–50. Cape Town: David Philip; London: James Currey.

——. 1994. New Nation, New History: The History Workshop in South Africa, 1977–1994. *Journal of American History* 81 (3): 977–85.

Boonzaier, Emile, et al. 1996. *The Cape Herders: A History of the Khoikhoi of Southern Africa*. Cape Town and Johannesburg: David Philip; Athens: Ohio University Press.

Bosch, Tanja. 2008. Kwaito on Community Radio: The Case of Bush Radio in Cape Town, South Africa. *World of Music* 50 (2): 75–89.

Bourdieu, Pierre. 1984. *Distinction: A Social Critique of the Judgement of Taste*. Translated by R. Nice. Cambridge, MA: Harvard University Press.

———. 1985. The Social Space and the Genesis of Groups. *Social Science Information* 42 (2): 195–220.

Bozzoli, Belinda. 1983. Marxism, Feminism and South African Studies. *Journal of Southern African Studies* 9 (2): 139–71.

———. 1990. Intellectuals, Audiences and Histories: South African Experiences, 1978–88. *Radical History Review* 46 (7): 237–63.

———. 1991. *Women of Phokeng: Consciousness, Life Strategy, and Migrancy in South Africa, 1900–1983*. Portsmouth, NH: Heinemann; London: James Currey.

Bozzoli, Belinda, and Peter Delius. 1990. Radical History and South African Society. *Radical History Review* 46 (7): 13–45.

Brandel-Syrier, Mia. 1962. *Black Woman in Search of God*. London: Lutterworth.

Bregin, Elana, and Belinda Kruiper. 2004. *Kalahari Rainsong*. Scottsville, South Africa: University of Kwa-Zulu Natal Press.

Brink, Elsabe. 1990. Man-made Women: Gender, Class and the Ideology of the *Volksmoeder*. In *Women and Gender in Southern Africa to 1945*, ed. C. Walker, 273–92. Cape Town: David Philip; London: James Currey.

Bruinders, Sylvia. 2005. Performance of Place: How Musical Practices in Cape Town Recreate a Displaced Community. In *Papers Presented at the Symposium on Ethnomusicology Number 18*, ed. Andrew Tracey, 17–20. Grahamstown: International Library of African Music.

———. 2006. Christmas Band Competitions in the Western Cape. Paper presented at the Southern African Music Research Conference, North-West University, September 14–16.

Bull, Michael, and Les Back, eds. 2003. *The Auditory Cultures Reader*. Oxford and New York: Berg.

Burchell, William J. 1822/1953. *Travels in the Interior of Southern Africa*. 2 vols. Repr. London: University Press Glasgow.

Burden, Matilda. 1991. Die Afrikaanse volkslied onder die bruinmense (The Afrikaans Folk Song Among the Coloured People). PhD diss., Stellenbosch University.

———. 1996. *Yzerfontein: Wonder of the West Coast*. Translated by Sandra Belligan. Yzerfontein: Yzerfontein Ratepayer's Association.

Burnham, John, ed. c. 1892. *Choral Anthems: A Choice Selection of Music for Choir and Congregational Use*. Volume 3. London: W. Nicholson and Sons.

Camille, Michael. 1992. *Image on the Edge: The Margins of Medieval Art*. London: Reaktion Books.

Campbell, John. 1815. *Travels in South Africa*. London: Black and Parry.

Casey, Edward S. 1996. How to Get from Space to Place in a Fairly Short Stretch of Time: Phenomenological Prolegomena. In *Senses of Place*, ed. S. Feld and K. H. Basso, 13–52. Sante Fe: School of American Research Press.

Chakrabarty, Dipesh. 2000. *Provincializing Europe: Postcolonial Thought and Historical Difference*. Princeton, NJ, and Oxford: Princeton University Press.

Chapman, Michael. 1996. *Southern African Literatures*. Longman Literatures in English Series. London and New York: Longman.

Chidester, D., J. Tobler, and Darrel Wratten. 1997. *Christianity in South Africa: An Annotated Bibliography*. Bibliographies and Indexes in Religious Studies, Number 43. Westport, CT, and London: Greenwood Press.

Chiener, Chou. 2002. Experience and Fieldwork: A Native Researcher's View. *Ethnomusicology* 46 (3): 456–86.

Cillié, Gawie. 1964. Die musiek van ons Afrikaanse Gesangboek – 1944 (The music of our Afrikaans hymnbook – 1944). In *Die Gereformeerde kerklied deur die eeue: Referate gelewer by die kongres oor die kerkmusiek gehou in Kaapstad op 9 en 10 Oktober 1962* (The Reformed church hymn through the ages: Reports given at the congress on church music held in Cape Town on 9 and 10 October 1962), 65–71. Cape Town: Tafelberg-Uitgewers.

———. 1983. Die kerklied in Suid-Afrika, 1652–1800. In *'n Geskiedenis van die Afrikaanse protestantse kerklied: inleidende bydraes,* ed. J. H. H. du Toit, 1–10. Pretoria: NG Kerkboekhandel.

———. 1993. *Afrikaanse Liederwysies: 'n Verdwynende kultuurskat.* Johannesburg: SAMRO.

Citron, Marcia J. 1993. *Gender and the Musical Canon.* Cambridge: Cambridge University Press.

Clifford, James. 1986. Introduction: Partial Truths. In *Writing Culture: The Poetics and Politics of Ethnography,* ed. J. Clifford and G. E. Marcus, 1–26. Berkeley, Los Angeles, and London: University of California Press.

Coetzee, J. M. 1988/2007. *White Writing: On the Culture of Letters in South Africa.* Johannesburg: Pentz.

Coetzer, Boudina. 2005a. Coysan—The *Langarm* Experience: An Analysis of a *Langarm* Exhibition at the Grahamstown National Arts Festival 2005. Paper presented at the Annual Congress of the Musicological Society of Southern Africa, University of Cape Town, August 25–27.

———. 2005b. Langarm in and around Grahamstown: The Dance, the Social History and the Music. *Journal of the Musical Arts in Africa* 2: 70–83.

———. 2005c. *Langarm* in Grahamstown: The Dance, the Social History and the Music. In *Papers Presented at the Symposium on Ethnomusicology Number 18,* ed. Andrew Tracey, 36–41. Grahamstown: International Library of African Music.

Comaroff, Jean. 1985. *Body of Power, Spirit of Resistance: The Culture and History of a South African People.* Chicago and London: University of Chicago Press.

Comaroff, Jean, and John L. Comaroff. 1991. *Of Revelation and Revolution: Christianity, Colonialism, and Consciousness in South Africa.* Chicago: University of Chicago Press.

———. 1997. *Of Revelation and Revolution: The Dialectics of Modernity on a South African Frontier.* Chicago: University of Chicago Press.

Comaroff, John L., and Jean Comaroff. 1992. *Ethnography and the Historical Imagination.* Boulder, CO, and Oxford: Westview Press.

Coombes, Annie E. 2003. *History after Apartheid: Visual Culture and Public Memory in a Democratic South Africa.* Durham, NC, and London: Duke University Press.

Cope, Trevor. 1978. Towards an Appreciation of Zulu Folktales as Literary Art. In *Social System and Tradition in Southern Africa: Essays in Honour of Eileen Krige,* ed. E. Preston-Whyte and J. Argyle, 183–205. Cape Town and New York: Oxford University Press.

Coplan, David B. 1985. *In Township Tonight!: South Africa's Black City Music and Theatre*. London and New York: Longman.

———. 1991. Fictions that Save: Migrants' Performance and Basotho National Culture. *Cultural Anthropology* 6 (2): 164–92.

———. 1994. *In the Time of Cannibals: The Word Music of South Africa's Basotho Migrants*. Chicago and London: University of Chicago Press.

———. 1995. Review of *African Stars: Studies in Black South African Performance*, by Veit Erlmann. *Journal of African History* 36 (1): 160–61.

———. 2007. *In Township Tonight!: Three Centuries of South African Black City Music and Theatre*. 2nd edition. Johannesburg: Jacana.

Coplan, David B., and B. Jules-Rosette. 2005. *Nkosi Sikelel' iAfrika* and the Liberation of the Spirit of South Africa. *African Studies* 64 (2): 285–308.

Cox, Renée. 1991. Recovering *Jouissance*: An Introduction to Feminist Musical Aesthetics. In *Women and Music: A History*, ed. Karin Pendle, 331–40. Bloomington and Indianapolis: Indiana University Press.

Crais, Clifton, and Pamela Scully. 2009. *Sara Baartman and the Hottentot Venus: A Ghost Story and a Biography*. Johannesburg: Wits University Press.

Curwen, John Spencer. 1891. *The Story of Tonic Sol-fa*. London: J. Curwen & Sons.

Dargie, David. 1987. *Xhosa Zionist Church Music*. Johannesburg: Hodder & Stoughton.

———. 1997. South African Christian Music: B. Christian Music among Africans. In *Christianity in South Africa: A Political, Social and Cultural History*, ed. R. Elphick and R. Davenport, 319–26. Oxford: James Currey; Cape Town: David Philip.

———. 2010. Xhosa Zionist Church Music: A Liturgical Expression beyond the Dreams of the Early Missionaries. *Missionalia* 38 (1): 32–53.

Dash, J. Michael. 1994. Textual Error and Cultural Crossing: A Caribbean Poetics of Creolization. *Research in African Literatures* 25 (2): 159–68.

Davenport, Rodney, and Christopher Saunders. 2000. *South Africa: A Modern History*. 5th edition. London: Macmillan.

Davids, Achmat. 1985. Music and Islam. In *Papers Presented at the 5th Symposium on Ethnomusicology*, ed. A. Tracey, 36–38. Grahamstown: International Library of African Music.

De Gruchy, John W. 1997. Grappling with a Colonial Heritage: The English-Speaking Churches under Imperialism and Apartheid. In *Christianity in South Africa: A Political, Social and Cultural History*, ed. R. Elphick and R. Davenport, 155–72. Oxford: James Currey; Cape Town: David Philip.

———, ed. 2000. *The London Missionary Society in Southern Africa, 1799–1999*. Athens: Ohio University Press.

De Gruchy, John W., and Steve de Gruchy. 2005. *The Church Struggle in South Africa*. 3rd edition. Minneapolis: Fortress Press.

De Jongh, Michael. 2002. Itinerant and Sedentary: Karretjie People and "Karoo Culture." *South African Journal of Ethnology* 23 (1): 1–13.

De Kock, Leon. 2001. South Africa in the Global Imaginery: An Introduction. *Poetics Today* 22 (2): 263–98.

———. 2004. South Africa in the Global Imaginary: An Introduction. In *South Africa in the Global Imaginary*, ed. L. de Kock, L. Bethlehem, and S. Laden, 1–31. Pretoria: University of South Africa Press.

———. 2005. Does South African Literature Still Exist? Or: South African Literature Is Dead, Long Live Literature in South Africa. *English in Africa* 32 (2): 69–83.

———. 2008. A History of Restlessness: And Now for the Rest. *English Studies in Africa* 51 (1): 111–24.

———. 2009. Judging New "South African" Fiction in the Transnational Moment. *Current Writing* 21 (1/2): 24–58.

Delegorgue, Adulphe. 1838/1990. *Travels in Southern Africa.* Translated by Fleur Webb. Durban: University of Natal Press.

Denis, Phillipe. 2003. Oral History in a Wounded Country. In *Orality, Literacy, and Colonialism in Southern Africa,* ed. J. Draper, 205–16. Atlanta: Society of Biblical Literature.

Derrida, Jacques. 1995. *Archive Fever: A Freudian Impression.* Chicago: University of Chicago Press.

Desai, Desmond. 1985. "Cape Malay" Music. In *Papers Presented at the 5th Symposium on Ethnomusicology,* ed. A. Tracey, 39–44. Grahamstown: International Library of African Music.

———. 1993. The *Ratiep* Art Form of South African Muslims. PhD diss., University of Natal.

Dooling, Wayne. 1989. Slaves, Slaveowners and Amelioration in Graaff-Reinet, 1823–1830. BA thesis, University of Cape Town. Text-fiche.

Draper, Jonathan A., ed. 2003. *Orality, Literacy, and Colonialism in Southern Africa.* Atlanta: Society of Biblical Literature.

Drewett, Michael, and Martin Cloonan, eds. 2006. *Popular Music Censorship in Africa.* Aldershot and Burlington, VT: Ashgate.

Drury, Jonathan D. 1985. Coloured South African Folk Songs? *Ars Nova* 17: 39–50.

Du Bois, W. E. B. 1999. *The Souls of Black Folk.* Critical edition. Edited by H. L. Gates Jr. and T. H. Oliver. New York and London: W. W. Norton.

Du Plessis, I. D. 1935. *Die Bydrae van die Kaapse Maleier tot die Afrikaanse Volkslied* (The contribution of the Cape Malay to the Afrikaans folk song). Cape Town: Nasionale Pers.

———. 1972. *The Cape Malays: History, Religion, Traditions, Folk Tales, and the Malay Quarter.* Cape Town: A. A. Balkema.

Du Plessis, L. T. 1986. *Afrikaans in beweging.* Bloemfontein: Patmos.

Dutch Reformed Mission Church. 1881–1984. Notuleboeke (Record Books). Uniting Reformed Church, Kroonvale, Graaff-Reinet. Unpublished record books.

Du Toit, J. H. H., ed. 1983. *'n Geskiedenis van die Afrikaanse protestantse kerklied: inleidende bydraes.* Pretoria: NG Kerkboekhandel.

Elbourne, Elizabeth. 2002. *Blood Ground: Colonialism, Missions, and the Contest for Christianity in the Cape Colony and Britain, 1799–1853.* Montreal, Kingston, et al.: McGill-Queen's University Press.

Elbourne, Elizabeth, and Robert Ross. 1997. Combating Spiritual and Social Bondage: Early Missions in the Cape Colony. In *Christianity in South Africa: A Political, Social and Cultural History,* ed. R. Elphick and R. Davenport, 31–50. Oxford: James Currey; Cape Town: David Philip.

Eldredge, Elizabeth A., and Fred Morton. 1994. *Slavery in South Africa: Captive Labor on the Dutch Frontier.* Boulder, CO, San Francisco, and Oxford: Westview Press; Pietermaritzburg: University of Natal Press.

Elphick, Richard. 1985. *Khoikhoi and the Founding of White South Africa.* Johannesburg: Raven Press.

Elphick, Richard, and R. Davenport, eds. 1997. *Christianity in South Africa: A Political, Social and Cultural History.* Oxford: James Currey; Cape Town: David Philip.

Elphick, Richard, and H. Giliomee, eds. 1989. *The Shaping of South African Society, 1652–1840.* Middletown, CT: Wesleyan University Press.

Elphick, Richard, and V. C. Malherbe. 1989. The Khoisan to 1828. In *The Shaping of South African Society, 1652–1840,* ed. R. Elphick and H. Giliomee, 3–65. Middletown, CT: Wesleyan University Press.

Elphick, Richard, and Robert Shell. 1989. Intergroup Relations, 1652–1795. In *The Shaping of South African Society, 1652–1840,* ed. R. Elphick and H. Giliomee, 184–239. Middletown, CT: Wesleyan University Press.

Enklaar, Ido H. 1988. *Life and Work of Dr. J. Th. Van der Kemp 1747–1811: Missionary Pioneer and Protagonist of Racial Equality in South Africa.* Cape Town and Rotterdam: A. A. Balkema.

Erasmus, Zimitri, ed. 2001. *Coloured by History, Shaped by Place: New Perspectives on Coloured Identities in Cape Town.* Colorado Springs: International Academic Publishers.

Erlmann, Veit. 1991. *African Stars: Studies in Black South African Performance.* Chicago and London: University of Chicago Press.

———. 1996. *Nightsong: Performance, Power, and Practice in South Africa.* Chicago and London: University of Chicago Press.

———. 1997. Africa Civilized, Africa Uncivilized: Local Culture, World System and South African Music. In *Readings in African Popular Culture,* ed. K. Barber, 170–77. Bloomington: International African Institute in association with Indiana University Press; Oxford: James Currey.

———. 1999. *Music, Modernity, and the Global Imagination: South Africa and the West.* New York and Oxford: Oxford University Press.

———, ed. 2004. *Hearing Cultures: Essays on Sound, Listening, and Modernity.* Oxford and New York: Berg.

February, Vernon A. 1981. *Mind Your Colour: The Coloured Stereotype in South African Literature.* London and Boston: Kegan Paul.

Feierman, Steven. 1993. African Histories and the Dissolution of World History. In *Africa and the Disciplines: The Contributions of Research in Africa to the Social Sciences and Humanities,* ed. R. H. Bates, V. Y. Mudimbe, and Jean O' Barr, 169–211. Chicago and London: University of Chicago Press.

Feld, Steven. 1982. *Sound and Sentiment: Birds, Weeping, Poetics, and Song in Kaluli Expression.* Philadelphia: University of Pennsylvania Press.

———. 2003. A Rainforest Acoustemology. In *The Auditory Culture Reader,* ed. Michael Bull and Les Back, 223–39. Oxford and New York: Berg.

Field, Sean. 2001. Fragile Identities: Memory, Emotion and Coloured Residents of Windermere. In *Coloured by History, Shaped by Place: New Perspectives on Coloured Identities in Cape Town,* ed. Z. Erasmus, 97–113. Colorado Springs: International Academic Publishers.

Fox, Aaron. 2004. *Real Country: Music and Language in Working-Class Culture.* Durham, NC: Duke University Press.

Fox, Richard G., ed. 1991. *Recapturing Anthropology: Working in the Present*. Santa Fe, NM: School of American Research Press.

Franco, Jean. 1985. Killing Priests, Nuns, Women, and Children. In *On Signs*, ed. Marshall Blonsky, 414–20. Baltimore, MD: Johns Hopkins University Press.

Gaitskell, Deborah. 1990. Devout Domesticity?: A Century of African Women's Christianity in South Africa. In *Women and Gender in Southern Africa to 1945*, ed. C. Walker, 251–72. Cape Town: David Philip; London: James Currey.

———. 1995. "Praying and Preaching": The Distinctive Spirituality of African Women's Organizations. In *Missions and Christianity in South African History*, ed. H. Bredekamp and R. Ross, 213–32. Johannesburg: Witwatersrand University Press.

Gal, Susan. 1995. Language and the Arts of Resistance. *Cultural Anthropology* 10 (3): 407–24.

Gates, Henry Louis, Jr. 1988. *The Signifying Monkey: A Theory of Afro-American Literary Criticism*. Oxford and New York: Oxford University Press.

Gerstner, Jonathan Neil. 1991. *The Thousand Generation Covenant: Dutch Reformed Covenant Theology and Group Identity in Colonial South Africa, 1652–1814*. Studies of the History of Christian Thought Volume XLIV. Leiden, New York, Cologne, et al.: E. J. Brill.

———. 1997. A Christian Monopoly: The Reformed Church and Colonial Society Under Dutch Rule. In *Christianity in South Africa: A Political, Social and Cultural History*, ed. R. Elphick and R. Davenport, 16–30. Oxford: James Currey; Cape Town: David Philip.

Giliomee, Hermann. 1981. Processes in Development of the Southern African Frontier. In *The Frontier in History: North American and Southern African Compared*, ed. H. Lamar and L. Thompson, 76–119. New Haven, CT, and London: Yale University Press.

———. 1989. The Eastern Frontier, 1770–1812. In *The Shaping of South African Society, 1652–1840*, ed. R. Elphick and H. Giliomee, 421–71. Middletown, CT: Wesleyan University Press.

———. 1995. The Non-Racial Franchise and Afrikaner and Coloured Identities, 1910–1994. *African Affairs* 94: 199–225.

———. 2003. *The Afrikaners: Biography of a People*. Charlottesville: University of Virginia Press.

Gilroy, Paul. 1993. *The Black Atlantic: Modernity and Double Consciousness*. Cambridge, MA: Harvard University Press.

Glissant, Edouard. 1989. *Caribbean Discourse: Selected Essays*. Translated by J. Michael Dash. Charlottesville: University Press of Virginia.

Goldin, Ian. 1987. *Making Race: The Politics and Economics of Coloured Identity in South Africa*. London: Maskew Miller Longman.

Goodall, Sallyann. 1993. The Role of Devotional Music in the Homogenisation of South African Hinduism. *SAMUS* 13: 1–6.

Grauer, Victor A. 2009. Concept, Style, and Structure in the Music of the African Pygmies and Bushmen: A Study in Cross-Cultural Analysis. *Ethnomusicology* 53 (3): 396–424.

Gunner, Liz. 1995. Remaking the Warrior?: The Role of Orality in the Liberation Struggle and in Post-Apartheid South Africa. *Current Writing* 7 (2): 19–30.

———. 2000. Zulu Radio Drama. In *Senses of Culture: South African Culture Studies*, ed. S. Nuttall and C. Michael, 216–30. New York and Oxford: Oxford University Press.

Halstead, Normala. 2001. Ethnographic Encounters: Positionings Within and Outside the Insider Frame. *Social Anthropology* 9 (3): 307–21.

Hamm, Charles. 1991. "The Constant Companion of Man": Separate Development, Radio Bantu, and Music. *Popular Music* 10: 147–73.

———. 1995. *Putting Popular Music in Its Place.* Cambridge: Cambridge University Press.

Hannerz, Ulf. 1996. *Transnational Connections: Culture, People, Places.* London and New York: Routledge. 160–71.

———. 1997. Sophiatown: The View from Afar. In *Readings in African Popular Culture,* ed. K. Barber, 164–70. Bloomington: International African Institute in association with Indiana University Press; Oxford: James Currey.

Hansen, Deidre. 1996. Bushman Music: Still an Unknown. In *Miscast: Negotiating the Presence of the Bushmen,* ed. Pippa Skotnes, 297–306. Cape Town: University of Cape Town Press.

Haring, Lee. 2003. Techniques of Creolization. *Journal of American Folklore* 116 (459): 19–35.

Harlow, Barbara, and David Attwell. 2000. Introduction. *Modern Fiction Studies* 46 (1): 1–9.

Heilbut, Anthony. 1985. *The Gospel Sound: Good News and Bad Times.* Revised and updated edition. New York: Limelight Editions.

Hendrickson, Hildi, ed. 1996. *Clothing and Difference: Embodied Identities in Colonial and Post-Colonial Africa.* Durham, NC: Duke University Press.

Henning, Cosmo Grenville. 1975. *Graaff-Reinet: A Cultural History, 1786–1886.* Cape Town: T.V. Bulpin.

———. 1979–1986. Graaff-Reinet, Music In (1786–1960). *South African Music Encyclopedia,* ed. J. P. Malan, 2:103–17. Cape Town and Oxford: Oxford University Press.

Herndon, Marcia. 1993. Insiders, Outsiders: Knowing Our Limits, Limiting Our Knowing. *World of Music* 35 (1): 63–80.

Hobbs, Catherine, ed. 1995. *Nineteenth-Century Women Learn to Write.* Charlottesville and London: University Press of Virginia.

Hofmeyr, Isabel. 2004. Popular Literature in Africa: Post-Resistance Perspectives. *Social Dynamics* 30 (2): 128–40.

Hollandsche Gereformeerde Kerk. 1895. *De Evangelische Gezangen.* Cape Town: Jacques Dusseau.

Huskisson, Frank. 1902. *Hymns for Life and Service: A Collection of Hymns for Evangelistic Meetings, Meetings for the Deepening of Spiritual Life, Convention Gatherings, Children's Services, Missionary Meetings, and the Home Circle.* Cape Town and Johannesburg: South Africa General Mission Christian Literature Department.

Hutchinson, Y., and E. Breitinger, eds. 2000. *History and Theatre in Africa.* Bayreuth African Studies 50. Bayreuth, Germany: E. Breitinger; Stellenbosch: University of Stellenbosch.

Impey, Angela. 2001. Re-fashioning Identity in Post-Apartheid South African Music: A Case for Isicathamiya Choral Music in KwaZulu-Natal. In *Culture in the New South Africa: After Apartheid,* vol. 2, ed. R. Kriger and A. Zegeye, 229–36. Cape Town: Kwela Books.

Jackson, Melveen. 1989. Tiger Dance, *terukuttu,* Tango, and Tchaikovsky: A Politico-Cultural View of Indian South African Music before 1948. *World of Music* 31 (1): 59–76.
———. 1991. Popular Indian South African Music: Division in Diversity. *Popular Music* 10 (2): 175–88.
Jackson, Shannon. 2005. "Coloureds don't Toyi-toyi": Gesture, Constraint and Identity in Cape Town. In *Limits to Liberation after Apartheid: Citizenship, Governance and Culture,* ed. S. L. Robins, 206–24. Oxford: James Currey; Cape Town: David Philip.
Jacobs, Sean, and Herman Wasserman. 2003. Introduction. In *Shifting Selves: Post-apartheid Essays on Mass Media, Culture, and Identity,* 15–28. Cape Town: Kwela Books.
James, Deborah. 1990. Musical Form and Social History: Research Perspectives on Black South African Music. *Radical History Review* 46 (7): 309–19.
———. 1997. "Music of Origin": Class, Social Category and the Performers and Audience of "Kiba," a South African Migrant Genre. *Africa* 67 (3): 454–75.
———. 1999. *Songs of the Women Migrants: Performance and Identity in South Africa.* Edinburgh: Edinburgh University Press for the International African Institute.
James, W. G., and M. Simons, eds. 1992. *Class, Caste and Color: A Social and Economic History of the South African Western Cape.* New Brunswick, NJ: Transaction Publishers.
James, Wilmot, Daria Caliguire, and K. Cullinan, eds. 1996. *Now that We Are Free: Coloured Communities in a Democratic South Africa.* Boulder, CO, and London: Lynne Rienner.
Jansen, Jonathan D. 2009. *Knowledge in the Blood: Confronting Race and the Apartheid Past.* Stanford: Stanford University Press; Cape Town: UCT Press.
Jeppie, Shamil M. 1990a. Aspects of Popular Culture and Class Expression in Inner Cape Town, Circa 1939–1959. MA thesis, University of Cape Town. Microfiche.
———. 1990b. Popular Culture and Carnival in Cape Town: The 1940s and 1950s. In *The Struggle for District Six: Past and Present,* ed. S. Jeppie and C. Soudien, 67–87. Cape Town: Buchu Books.
———. 1996a. Commemoration and Identities: The 1994 Tercentenary of Islam in South Africa. In *Islam and the Question of Minorities,* ed. Tamara Sonn, 73–91. Atlanta: Scholars Press.
———. 1996b. Leadership and Loyalties: The Imams of Nineteenth Century Colonial Cape Town, South Africa. *Journal of Religion in Africa* XXVI (2): 139–62.
———. 2001. Reclassifications: Coloured, Malay, Muslim. In *Coloured by History, Shaped by Place: New Perspectives on Coloured Identities in Cape Town,* ed. Z. Erasmus, 80–96. Colorado Springs: International Academic Publishers.
Jewkes, R., L. Penn-Kekana, J. Levin, M. Ratsaka, and M. Schreiber. 1999. *He Must Give Me Money, He Mustn't Beat Me: Violence Against Women in Three South African Provinces.* Pretoria: CERSA (Women's Health) Medical Research Council.
Jones, A. M. 1976. *African Hymnody in Christian Worship: A Contribution to the History of its Development.* Gwelo, Rhodesia: Mambo Press.
Jorritsma, M. R. 2006. Sonic Spaces: Inscribing "Coloured" Voices in the Karoo, South Africa. PhD diss., University of Pennsylvania.
———. 2008a. The Hidden Transcripts of Sacred Song in a South African Coloured Community. *African Music* 8 (2): 56–75.

———. 2008b. Mothers of the Church: Coloured Women's Society Music and South African Gender Issues. *SAMUS* 28: 73–92.

Kiernan, J. P. 1974. Where Zionists Draw the Line: A Study of Religious Exclusiveness in an African Township. *African Studies* 33 (2): 79–90.

———. 1977. Poor and Puritan: An Attempt to View Zionism as a Collective Response to Urban Poverty. *African Studies* 36 (1): 31–41.

———. 1990. The Canticles of Zion: Song as Word and Action in Zulu Zionist Discourse. *Journal of Religion in Africa* XX (2): 188–204.

Kirby, Percival R. 1934/1953. *The Musical Instruments of the Native Races of South Africa*. Repr. London: Oxford University Press.

———. 1986. The Musics of the Black Races of South Africa. In *South African Music Encyclopedia*, ed. J. P. Malan, 2:267–94. Cape Town and Oxford: Oxford University Press.

Kirshenblatt-Gimblett, Barbara. 1998. *Destination Culture: Tourism, Museums, and Heritage*. Berkeley: University of California Press.

Kloppers, Elsabé. 2007a. The Hymnic Identities of the Afrikaner. In *Music and Identity: Transformation and Negotiation*, ed. E. Akrofi, M. Smith, and S. Thorsén, 181–98. Stellenbosch: SUN Press.

———. 2007b. Singing Hymns Under the Southern Cross: The *Liedboek van die Kerk*, a New Afrikaans Hymnal. *Fontes Artis Musicae* 54 (3): 291–307.

Krog, Antjie. 2004. *Die sterre sê "tsau."* Cape Town: Kwela Books.

Kruger, Loren. 2002. "Black Atlantics," "White Indians" and "Jews": Locations, Locutions, and Syncretic Identities in the Fiction of Achmat Dangor and Others. *Scrutiny2: Issues in English Studies in Southern Africa* 7 (2): 34–50.

Kubik, Gerhard. 1988. Nsenga/Shona Harmonic Patterns and the San Heritage in Southern Africa. *Ethnomusicology* 32 (2): 39–76.

———. 1989. The Southern African Periphery: Banjo Traditions in Zambia and Malawi. *The World of Music* XXXI (1): 3–29.

Kuper, Leo. 1965. *An African Bourgeoisie: Race, Class, and Politics in South Africa*. New Haven, CT, and London: Yale University Press.

Labaree, Robert V. 2002. The Risk of "Going Observationalist": Negotiating the Hidden Dilemmas of Being an Insider Participant Observer. *Qualitative Research* 2 (1): 97–122.

Labuschagne, Pieter. 1999. *Ghostriders of the Anglo-Boer War (1899–1902): The Role and Contribution of the* Agterryers. Pretoria: University of South Africa.

Layne, Valmont. 1995. A History of Dance and Jazz Band Performance in the Western Cape in the Post-1945 Era. MA thesis, University of Cape Town.

Lee, C. 2009. "A Generous Dream, But Difficult to Realize": The Making of the Anglo-African Community of Nyasaland, 1929–1940. In *Burdened by Race: Coloured Identities in Southern Africa*, ed. M. Adhikari, 208–32. Cape Town: UCT Press.

Lee, Christopher J. 2005. Review of *Karoo Kitaar Blues*. *African Studies Review* 48 (3): 155–56.

Legassick, Martin. 1980. The Frontier Tradition in South African Historiography. In *Economy and Society in Pre-Industrial South Africa*, ed. S. Marks, and A. Atmore, 44–79. London and New York: Longman.

———. 1989. The Northern Frontier to c. 1840: The Rise and Decline of the Griqua

People. In *The Shaping of South African Society, 1652–1840,* ed. R. Elphick and H. Giliomee, 358–420. Middletown, CT: Wesleyan University Press.

Levine, Laurie. 2005. *The Drumcafé's Traditional Music of South Africa.* Johannesburg: Jacana.

Lewis, Desiree. 2001. Writing Hybrid Selves: Richard Rive and Zoë Wicomb. In *Coloured by History, Shaped by Place: New Perspectives on Coloured Identities in Cape Town,* ed. Z. Erasmus, 131–58. Colorado Springs: International Academic Publishers.

Lewis, Jon. 1990. South African Labor History: A Historiographical Assessment. *Radical History Review* 46 (7): 213–35.

Liebenberg, Herbert Daniel. n.d. Pastoriestraat Hoogtepunte 1801–1981 (Parsonage Street High Points, 1801–1981). Unpublished manuscript. PSCC records, Graaff-Reinet, South Africa.

Lucia, Christine. 1995. Songs of War and Peace: The Lives of Five KwaZulu-Natal Women Reflected in Their "Songprints." In *Women, the Arts and South Africa: 26–28 January 1995: Conference Proceedings,* by the Gender Studies Programme, I:154–63. Pietermaritzburg: University of Natal.

———, ed. 2005. *The World of South African Music: A Reader.* Cambridge: Cambridge Scholars Press.

MacCrone, I. D. 1937. *Race Attitudes in South Africa: Historical, Experimental and Psychological Studies.* London: Oxford University Press.

Malan, Jacques Pierre, ed. 1979–1986. *South African Music Encyclopedia.* 4 vols. Cape Town and Oxford: Oxford University Press.

Malherbe, V. C. 1979. The Life and Times of Cupido Kakkerlak. *Journal of African History* 20 (3): 365–78.

Manuel, Peter. 1993. *Cassette Culture: Popular Music and Technology in North India.* Chicago and London: University of Chicago Press.

Marais, J. S. 1957. *The Cape Coloured People 1652–1937.* Johannesburg: Witwatersrand University Press.

Martin, Annie. 1890. *Home Life on an Ostrich Farm.* London: George Philip.

Martin, Denis-Constant. 1999. *Coon Carnival: New Year in Cape Town Past and Present.* Cape Town: David Philip.

Maultsby, Portia K. 1992. The Impact of Gospel Music on the Secular Music Industry. In *We'll Understand It Better By and By: Pioneering African American Gospel Composers,* ed. Bernice Johnson Reagon, 19–33. Washington and London: Smithsonian Institution Press.

McCord, Margaret. 1995. *The Calling of Katie Makanya.* Johannesburg and Cape Town: David Philip.

McNaughton, Andrew. 2000. *When Ants Get Angry!: The Importance of Graaff-Reinet in the Anglo-Boer War.* Graaff-Reinet.

Messner, Gerald Florian. 1993. Ethnomusicological Research, Another "Performance" in the International Year of Indigenous Peoples? *World of Music* 35 (1): 81–95.

Mesthrie, R., ed. 1995. *Language and Social History: Studies in South African Sociolinguistics.* Cape Town: David Philip.

Middleton, Richard. 2000. Musical Belongings: Western Music and Its Low-Other. In *Western Music and Its Others: Difference, Representation, and Appropriation in Music,* ed. G. Born and D. Hesmondhalgh, 59–85. Berkeley and Los Angeles: University of California Press.

Minnaar, A. de V. 1987. *Graaff-Reinet: 1786–1986*. Pretoria: Human Sciences Research Council.

Modisane, Bloke. 1990. *Blame Me on History*. New York: Simon and Schuster/Touchstone.

Mostert, Noël. 1992. *Frontiers: The Epic of South Africa's Creation and the Tragedy of the Xhosa People*. London: Jonathan Cape.

Mugglestone, Erica M. H. 1984. "Colored" Musicians in Cape Town: The Effect of Changes in Labels on Musical Content. *Current Musicology* 37/38: 153–58.

Muller, Carol Ann. 1996. Sathima Bea Benjamin, Exile and the "Southern Touch" in Jazz Creation and Performance. *African Languages and Cultures* 9 (2): 127–43.

———. 1999. *Rituals of Fertility and the Sacrifice of Desire: Nazarite Women's Performance in South Africa*. Chicago and London: University of Chicago Press.

———. 2001. Capturing the "Spirit of Africa" in the Jazz Singing of South African-Born Sathima Bea Benjamin. *Research in African Literatures* 32 (2): 133–52.

———. 2002. Archiving Africanness in Sacred Song. *Ethnomusicology* 46 (3): 409–31.

———. 2003. Making the Book, Performing the Words of *Izihlabelelo zamaNazaretha*. In *Orality, Literacy, and Colonialism in Southern Africa*, ed. J. Draper, 91–110. Atlanta: Society of Biblical Literature.

———. 2004. *South African Music: A Century of Traditions in Transformation*. World Music Series. Santa Barbara, CA: ABC-CLIO.

———. 2005. "Reading" the Book, Performing the Words of *Izihlabelelo zamaNazaretha*. *World of Music* 47 (1): 31–64.

———. 2008. *Focus: Music of South Africa*. 2nd edition. New York and London: Routledge.

Muller, Carol, and Janet Topp Fargion. 1999. Gumboots, Bhaca Migrants, and Fred Astaire: South African Worker Dance and Musical Style. *African Music* 7 (4): 88–109.

Muller, Carol A., with Sathima Bea Benjamin. *Musical Echoes*. Forthcoming.

Muller, Stephanus. 2001. Exploring the Aesthetics of Reconciliation: Rugby and the South African National Anthem. *SAMUS* 21: 19–37.

———. 2007. [Review of] *The World of South African Music: A Reader*. Edited by Christine Lucia. *Fontes Artis Musicae* 54 (3): 374–79.

Murray, C. 1894. *De Kinderharp: Verzameling van liederen voor huis en school*. New edition. Cape Town and Johannesburg: Juta.

Nederlandse Gereformeerde Sendingkerk. 1947. *Sionsgesange*. Cape Town: Ned. Geref. Sendingkerk in S.A.

Nettl, B., C. Capwell, P. Bohlman, et al., eds. 1992. *Excursions in World Music*. 2nd edition. Upper Saddle River, NJ: Prentice-Hall.

Newton-King, Susan. 1999. *Masters and Servants on the Cape Eastern Frontier 1760–1803*. Cambridge: Cambridge University Press.

NG Kerk-Uitgewers. 2001. *Liedboek van die kerk*. Wellington: NG Kerk Uitgewers.

Nixon, Rob. 1999/2001. *Dreambirds: The Strange History of the Ostrich in Fashion, Food, and Fortune*. Repr. New York: Picador USA.

Nketia, J. H. Kwabena. 1974. *The Music of Africa*. New York: W. W. Norton.

Nuttall, Sarah. 2009. *Entanglement: Literary and Cultural Reflections on Post-Apartheid*. Johannesburg: Wits University Press.

Nuttall, Sarah, and Cheryl-Ann Michael, eds. 2000. *Senses of Culture: South African*

Culture Studies. New York and Oxford: Oxford University Press.

Olivier, Bert. 2004. Urban Space in 21st Century South Africa. *Leading Architecture and Design* (May/June): 63–66.

Olivier, E., and S. Fürniss. 1997. Pygmy Music/Bushman Music: New Elements of Comparison. In *Central African Hunter-Gatherers in a Multidisciplinary Perspective: Challenging Elusiveness,* ed. K. Biesbrouck, S. Elders, and G. Rossel, 105–20. Leiden: CNWS.

Olivier, Emmanuelle. 1997. The Art of Metamorphosis—Or the Ju|'hoan Conception of Plurivocality. In *The Proceedings of the Khoisan Identities and Cultural Heritage Conference,* ed. A. Bank, 263–68. Cape Town: Infosource.

Olwage, Grant. 2002. Scriptions of the Choral: The Historiography of Black South African Choralism. *SAMUS* 22: 29–45.

———. 2003. Music and (Post)Colonialism: The Dialectics of Choral Culture on a South African Frontier. PhD diss., Rhodes University.

———. 2004. The Class and Colour of Tone: An Essay on the Social History of Vocal Timbre. *Ethnomusicology Forum* 13 (2): 203–26.

———. 2005. Discipline and Choralism: The Birth of Musical Colonialism. In *Music, Power, and Politics,* ed. Annie J. Randall, 25–46. New York and London: Routledge.

Opland, Jeff. 1995. The Image of the Book in Xhosa Oral Poetry. *Current Writing* 7 (2): 31–47.

Ortner, Sherry B. 1998. Identities: The Hidden Life of Class. *Journal of Anthropological Research* 54 (1): 1–17.

———. 2003. *New Jersey Dreaming: Capital, Culture, and the Class of '58.* Durham, NC, and London: Duke University Press.

Oxford University Press. 2002a. *The New Oxford Easy Anthem Book: A Collection of 63 Anthems for the Church's Year.* Oxford: Oxford University Press.

———. 2002b. *South African Concise Oxford Dictionary.* Edited by the Dictionary Unit for South African English. Oxford: Oxford University Press.

Parsonage Street Congregational Church. 1953–1960, 1980–1992, and 1999–2000. Notuleboeke (Record Books). Parsonage Street Congregational Church, Kroonvale, Graaff-Reinet. Unpublished record books.

Parsons, Neil. 2009. *Clicko: The Wild Dancing Bushman.* Johannesburg: Jacana.

Patterson, Sheila. 1953. *Colour and Culture in South Africa.* London: Routledge and Paul.

Pickel, Birgit. 1997. *Coloured Ethnicity and Identity: A Case Study in the Former Coloured Areas in the Western Cape/South Africa.* Demokratie und Entwicklung 28. Hamburg: LIT.

Pogrund, Benjamin. 1997. *How Can Man Die Better: The Life of Robert Sobukwe.* Johannesburg: Jonathan Ball.

Preston-Whyte, E., and J. Argyle, eds. 1978. *Social System and Tradition in Southern Africa: Essays in Honour of Eileen Krige.* Cape Town and New York: Oxford University Press.

Puri, Shalini. 2004. *The Caribbean Postcolonial: Social Equality, Post-Nationalism, and Cultural Hybridity.* New York: Palgrave Macmillan.

Ramsey, Guthrie P. 2003. *Race Music: Black Cultures from Bebop to Hip-Hop.* Berkeley: University of California Press.

Reardon, William Sr. 2001. The African American Congregational Song Tradition. In

If You Don't Go, Don't Hinder Me: The African American Sacred Song Tradition, 42–67. Lincoln and London: University of Nebraska Press.

Reddy, Thiven. 2001. The Politics of Naming: The Constitution of Coloured Subjects in South Africa. In *Coloured by History, Shaped by Place: New Perspectives on Coloured Identities in Cape Town*, ed. Z. Erasmus, 64–79. Colorado Springs: International Academic Publishers.

Rennie, Gillian. 1999. Built to Last. *Condé Nast House and Garden* (September): 138–41.

Robins, S. L., ed. 2005. *Limits to Liberation after Apartheid: Citizenship, Governance and Culture*. Oxford: James Currey; Cape Town: David Philip.

Rommen, Timothy. 2002. "Watch Out My Children": Gospel Music and the Ethics of Style in Trinidad and Tobago. PhD diss., University of Chicago.

———. 2007. *"Mek some noise": Gospel Music and the Ethics of Style in Trinidad*. Berkeley: University of California Press; Columbia University Center for Black Music Research.

Rörich, Mary. 1989. *Shebeens*, Slumyards and Sophiatown: Black Women, Music and Cultural Change in Urban South Africa c 1920–1960. *World of Music* 31 (1): 78–103.

Ross, Robert. 1989. The Cape of Good Hope and the World Economy, 1652–1835. In *The Shaping of South African Society, 1652–1840*, ed. R. Elphick and H. Giliomee, 243–80. Middletown, CT: Wesleyan University Press.

———. 1999. *Status and Respectability in the Cape Colony, 1750–1870: A Tragedy of Manners*. Cambridge: Cambridge University Press.

Ross, Robert, D. van Arkel, and G. C. Quispel. 1993. Going Beyond the Pale: On the Roots of White Supremacy in South Africa. In *Beyond the Pale: Essays on the History of Colonial South Africa*, by R. Ross, 69–110. Hanover and London: Wesleyan University Press.

Routley, Erik. 1983. *Christian Hymns Observed*. London and Oxford: Mowbray.

Rycroft, David K. 1977. Evidence of Stylistic Continuity in Zulu "Town" Music. In *Essays for a Humanist: An Offering to Klaus Wachsmann*, 216–60. New York: Town House Press.

Sales, Jane. 1972. The Mission Station as an Agency of "Civilization": The Development of a Christian Coloured Community in the Eastern Cape, 1800–1859. PhD diss., University of Chicago.

Sales, R. W., A. E. Barry Smith, Reino Otterman, et al. 1972. Hymns and Other Sacred Songs. In *Standard Encyclopaedia of Southern Africa*, 6:11–17. Cape Town: Nasou.

Salo, Elaine. 2004. Respectable Mothers, Tough Men and Good Daughters: Producing Persons in Manenberg Township. PhD diss., Emory University.

———. 2005. Negotiating Gender and Personhood in the New South Africa: Adolescent Women and Gangsters in Manenberg Township on the Cape Flats. In *Limits to Liberation after Apartheid: Citizenship, Governance and Culture*, ed. S. L. Robins, 173–89. Oxford: James Currey; Cape Town: David Philip.

———. 2007. "Mans is maar soe": Ganging Practices in Manenberg, South Africa, and the Ideologies of Masculinity, Gender, and Generational Relations. In *States of Violence: Politics, Youth, and Memory in Contemporary Africa*, ed. E. Bay and D. Donham, 148–75. Charlottesville: University of Virginia Press.

Sanders, Cheryl J. 1996. *Saints in Exile: The Holiness-Pentecostal Experience in African*

American Religion and Culture. New York and Oxford: Oxford University Press.

Sanders, Mark. 2002. *Complicities: The Intellectual and Apartheid*. Durham, NC, and London: Duke University Press.

Sankey, Ira D. n.d. *Sacred Songs and Solos: Twelve Hundred Hymns*. London: Harper-Collins.

Scanlon, Helen. 2007. *Representation and Reality: Portraits of Women's Lives in the Western Cape 1948–1976*. Cape Town: HSRC Press.

Schapera, Isaac. 1930. *The Khoisan Peoples of South Africa: Bushmen and Hottentots*. London: Routledge and Kegan Paul.

Schutte, Andries Gerhardus. 1968. 'n Gereformeerde Bantoegemeente: 'n etnografiese beskrywing van 'n stedelike gemeente; spesiale verwysing na religieuse verskynsels daarbinne. MA thesis, Potchefstroom University for Christian Higher Education.

Schutte, Gerrit. 1989. Company and Colonists at the Cape, 1652–1795. In *The Shaping of South African Society, 1652–1840*, ed. R. Elphick and H. Giliomee, 283–323. Middletown, CT: Wesleyan University Press.

Scott, James C. 1990. *Domination and the Arts of Resistance: Hidden Transcripts*. New Haven, CT, and London: Yale University Press.

Shell, Robert. 1994. *Children of Bondage: A Social History of the Slave Society at the Cape of Good Hope 1652–1838*. Hanover and London: University Press of New England.

Skotnes, Pippa, ed. 1996. *Miscast: Negotiating the Presence of the Bushmen*. Cape Town: University of Cape Town Press.

Smith, Barry. 1988/1989. The Royal School of Church Music and the Church in South Africa. *SAMUS* 8/9: 49–51.

———. 1997. South African Christian Music: A. Christian Music in the Western Tradition. In *Christianity in South Africa: A Political, Social and Cultural History*, ed. R. Elphick and R. Davenport, 316–19. Oxford: James Currey; Cape Town: David Philip.

Smith, Christy M. 2007. Reidentifying an Auditory Community: Worship in an Independent South African Church. In *Music and Identity: Transformation and Negotiation*, ed. E. Akrofi, M. Smith, and S. Thorsén, 277–96. Stellenbosch: SUN Press.

Smith, Kenneth Wyndham. 1976. *From Frontier to Midlands: A History of the Graaff-Reinet District, 1786–1910*. Grahamstown: Rhodes University.

Smith, Raymond T. 1984. Anthropology and the Concept of Social Class. *Annual Review of Anthropology* 13: 467–94.

Stamelman, Richard. 1993. The Strangeness of the Other and the Otherness of the Stranger: Edmond Jabès. *Yale French Studies* 82: 118–34.

Statutes of the Union of South Africa. 1950. Parow: Government Printer.

Steingo, Gavin. 2008. Preface. *World of Music* 50 (2): 5–14.

Stephens, Simon. 2000. Kwaito. In *Senses of Culture: South African Culture Studies*, ed. S. Nuttall and C. Michael, 256–73. New York and Oxford: Oxford University Press.

Stewart, Susan. 1984. *On Longing: Narratives of the Miniature, the Gigantic, the Souvenir, the Collection*. Baltimore, MD, and London: Johns Hopkins University Press.

Steyn, Melissa. 1998. A New Agenda: Restructuring Feminism in South Africa. *Women's Studies International Forum* 21 (1): 41–52.

Stockenström, Andries. 1887. *The Autobiography of the Late Sir Andries Stockenström*,

Bart. 2 vols. Edited by C. W. Hutton. Cape Town: Juta.

Strauss, Helene. 2009. ". . . [C]onfused About Being Coloured": Creolisation and Coloured Identity in Chris van Wyk's *Shirley, Goodness and Mercy.* In *Burdened by Race: Coloured Identities in Southern Africa,* ed. M. Adhikari, 23–48. Cape Town: UCT Press.

Strydom, Frederik Jacobus. 1982. The Music of the Rehoboth Basters. In *Papers Presented at the Second Symposium on Ethnomusicology, 24–26 September 1981,* 80–83. Grahamstown: ILAM.

———. 1983. Die musiek van die Rehoboth Basters van Suidwes-Afrika (The music of the Rehoboth Basters of Southwest Africa). PhD diss., University of Stellenbosch.

Strydom, W. M. L. 1983. Die Sionsgesange (The *Sionsgesange*). In *'n Geskiedenis van die Afrikaanse protestantse kerklied: inleidende bydraes,* ed. J. H. H. du Toit, 118–30. Pretoria: NG Kerkboekhandel.

Suid-Afrikaanse Bybelvereniging. 1932. *Die nuwe halleluja: Psalms, gesange en ander liedere vir huis, dag-en Sondagskool en jongeliedeverenigings.* 3rd edition. Cape Town: Suid-Afrikaanse Bybelvereniging.

Sundkler, B. G. M. 1961. *Bantu Prophets in South Africa.* 2nd edition. Oxford: Oxford University Press.

Swart, Sandra. 2003. Mythic Bushmen in Afrikaans Literature: The *Dwaalstories* of Eugène N. Marais. *Current Writing* 15 (1): 91–108.

Theal, George M. 1905. *Records of the Cape Colony.* Volume XXVIII. London: William Clowes.

Thom, H. B. 1965. *Die lewe van Gert Maritz.* Cape Town and Johannesburg: Nasou Beperk.

Thompson, George. 1827/1962. *Travels and Adventures in Southern Africa.* Repr. Cape Town: Africana Connoisseurs Press.

Titlestad, Michael. 2004. *Making the Changes: Jazz in South African Literature and Reportage.* Pretoria: Unisa Press and Leiden: Brill.

Tracey, Hugh. 1948/1970. *Chopi Musicians: Their Music, Poetry, and Instruments.* Repr. London: Oxford University Press for the International African Institute.

Trotter, Henry. 2009. Trauma and Memory: The Impact of Apartheid-Era Forced Removals on Coloured Identity in Cape Town. In *Burdened by Race: Coloured Identities in Southern Africa,* ed. M. Adhikari, 49–78. Cape Town: UCT Press.

Tsampiras, Carla. 1999. ". . . It's Many Attendant Evils . . .": Women, Violence and Slavery in Graaff Reinet 1830–1834. MA thesis, School of Oriental and African Studies, London.

Turino, Thomas. 2000. *Nationalists, Cosmopolitans, and Popular Music in Zimbabwe.* Chicago and London: University of Chicago Press.

UCCSA. 1988. *Sing Hosanna!* Johannesburg: UCCSA.

———. 2000. *Sing Hosanna! Old Notation.* Compiled by G. Owen Lloyd. Revised version. Gaborone, Botswana: Pula Press.

Vail, L., and L. White. 1991. *Power and the Praise Poem: Southern African Voices in History.* Charlottesville: University Press of Virginia; London: James Currey.

Van Warmelo, Willem. 1958. *Liederwysies van vanslewe* (Liederwysies of long ago). Amsterdam and Cape Town: Balkema.

Verenigende Gereformeerde Kerk in Suider-Afrika. 1978. *Nuwe Sionsgesange.* 4th edition. Cape Town: Lux Verbi and Lus Uitgewers.

————. 2003. *Nuwe Sionsgesange: Koraalboek.* Second revised edition. Cape Town: Lux Verbi and Lus Uitgewers.

Villa-Vicencio, Charles. 1996. *The Spirit of Freedom: South African Leaders on Religion and Politics.* Berkeley, Los Angeles, and London: University of California Press.

Villa-Vicencio, Charles, and John W. de Gruchy, eds. 1985. *Resistance and Hope: South African Essays in Honour of Beyers Naudé.* Cape Town and Johannesburg: David Philip; Grand Rapids, MI: William B. Eerdmans.

Walker, Cherryl. 1982. *Women and Resistance in South Africa.* London: Onyx Press.

————, ed. 1990. *Women and Gender in Southern Africa to 1945.* Cape Town: David Philip; London: James Currey.

————. 1995. Conceptualising Motherhood in Twentieth-Century South Africa. *Journal of Southern African Studies* 21 (3): 417–37.

Walshe, Peter. 1983. *Church Versus State in South Africa: The Case of the Christian Institute.* London: C. Hurst; Maryknoll, NY: Orbis Books.

Walton, Chris, and Stephanus Muller, eds. 2005. *Gender and Sexuality in South African Music.* Stellenbosch: SUN Press.

Ward, Kerry, and Nigel Worden. 1998. Commemorating, Suppressing, and Invoking Cape Slavery. In *Negotiating the Past: The Making of Memory in South Africa,* ed. S. Nuttall and C. Coetzee, 201–17. Cape Town: Oxford University Press.

Wells, Julia. 1982. Passes and Bypasses: Freedom of Movement for African Women Under the Urban Areas Act of South Africa. In *African Women and the Law: Historical Perspectives,* ed. M. J. Hay and M. Wright, 125–50. Boston: Boston University African Studies Center.

————. 1991. The Rise and Fall of Motherism as a Force in Black Women's Resistance Movements. In *Conference on Women and Gender in Southern Africa,* University of Natal, Durban, January 30–February 2, 1–31.

Wemen, Henry. 1960. *African Music and the Church in Africa.* Translated by E. J. Sharpe. Studia Missionalia Upsaliensia 3. Uppsala: Svenska Institute för Missionsforskning.

West, Norman X. 1964. Oosstraat-kerk was eers in wolstoor gehuisves (East Street Church initially housed in wool shed). *Graaff-Reinet Advertiser,* November 5.

Westby-Nunn, Tony. 2004. *Graaff-Reinet: An Illustrated Historical Guide to the Town; Including Aberdeen and Nieu-Bethesda.* Capricorn Square, South Africa: Elephant Head Publications.

Whitlock, E. S. 1991. *Graaff-Reinet: National Monuments and Places of Interest.* Graaff-Reinet, South Africa: Graaff-Reinet Publicity Association.

————. n.d. *An Album of Old Photographs: Graaff-Reinet.* Graaff-Reinet: Historic Homes of S.A. Ltd.

Wicomb, Zoë. 1998. Shame and Identity: The Case of the Coloured in South Africa. In *Writing South Africa: Literature, Apartheid, and Democracy, 1970–1995,* ed. D. Attridge and R. Jolly, 91–107. Cambridge: Cambridge University Press.

Wilson, Peter J. 1973. *Crab Antics: The Social Anthropology of English-Speaking Negro Societies of the Caribbean.* New Haven, CT, and London: Yale University Press.

Worden, Nigel. 1985. *Slavery in Dutch South Africa.* Cambridge: Cambridge University Press.

INTERVIEWS WITH AUTHOR

Barendse, Leon. November 11, 2004, October 27, 2005, and July 6, 2006. Kroonvale, South Africa.
Basson, Gawie. July 14, 2004, August 4, 2004, August 11, 2004, and November 17, 2004. Graaff-Reinet, South Africa.
Bezuidenhoudt, Jacobus. November 26, 2004, December 8, 2004, June 15, 2005, and July 6, 2006. Kroonvale, South Africa.
Bosch, June. August 19, 2004. Kroonvale, South Africa.
Christoffels, Virginia. October 28, 2005 and July 7, 2006. Kroonvale, South Africa.
Esterhuysen, Johan. October 5, 2005. Graaff-Reinet, South Africa.
Grootboom, Joyce. February 16, 2005. Kendrew region, Graaff-Reinet, South Africa.
Jasson, Marlene. November 3, 2005. Kroonvale, South Africa.
Kayster, Willem. August 18, 2004, February 18, 2005, and July 4, 2006, Graaff-Reinet, South Africa.
Louther, Villa. June 23, 2005. Graaff-Reinet, South Africa.
Van Jaarsveld, Sabina. November 10, 2005 and July 5, 2006. Kroonvale, South Africa.
Visagie, Marjorie. March 8, 2005. Kroonvale, South Africa.
Whitlock, Teddy. August 5, 2004. Graaff-Reinet, South Africa.
Informal conversations with Gawie Basson, June Bosch, Desmond Desai, Patrick Hector, Marlene Jasson, Suster Kalse, Anziske Kayster, Gerrit Olivier, and various members from the Uniting Reformed, Parsonage Street Congregational, and East Street Congregational churches, respectively.

DISCOGRAPHY

Cooder, Ry. 1997. *Buena Vista Social Club*. World Circuit/Nonesuch 79478–2, compact disc.
Hirsch, Lee, and Sherry Simpson. 2003. *Amandla!: A Revolution in Four-Part Harmony*. ATO Records 9, compact disc.
Kramer, David. 2002. *Karoo Kitaar Blues*. Blik Music 07, compact disc.

VISUAL SOURCES

Hirsch, Lee, and Sherry Simpson. 2002. *Amandla!: A Revolution in Four-Part Harmony*. Santa Monica, CA: Artisan Home Entertainment, DVD.
Key, Liza. 2004. *Karoo Kitaar Blues*. Produced by Philip Key. 90 min. Key Films and Blik Music Productions, DVD.
Marre, Jeremy. 2000. *Rhythm of Resistance: Black South African Music*. Directed by Chris Austin and Jeremy Marre. 60 min. Shanachie, DVD.
Marshall, John. 1973. *Curing Ceremony*. 8 min. Documentary Educational Resources, Videocassette.
———. 1988. *!Kung San: Resettlement*. Compiled by Sue Marshall Cabezas and Judith Nierenberg. 28 min. Documentary Educational Resources, Videocassette.
———. 1991. *Bitter Melons*. 32 min. Documentary Educational Resources, Videocassette.
Marshall, John, and Lawrence K. Marshall. 1974. *N/um tchai: The Ceremonial Dance of*

the !Kung Bushmen. Produced by John Marshall. 20 min. Bushman Film Studios, Videocassette.

Marshall, John, and Sue Marshall Cabezas. 1980. *N!ai: The Story of a !Kung Woman.* Directed by Adrienne Miesmer and John Marshall. 58 min. Documentary Educational Resources and Public Broadcasting Associates, Videocassette.

South African Broadcasting Corporation. 2005. *Vetkat Regopstaan Longlife Kruiper.* 48 min. Directed by Johan van Jaarsveld, DVD.

WEBSITES

Anonymous. n.d. Graaff-Reinet: The gem of the Karoo. [Online] (Accessed August 11, 2009). Available from http://www.karoopark.co.za/facts.html.

Anonymous. n.d. Graaff-Reinet: History. [Online] (Accessed August 11, 2009). Available from http://www.no6guesthouse.co.za/graaffreinet.htm.

Brett, Judith. 2010. Australia. [Online] *The Oxford Companion to the Politics of the World.* 2nd edition. Edited by Joel Krieger. Oxford Reference Online. (Accessed January 26, 2010). Available from http://0www.oxfordreference.com.oasis.unisa.ac.za/views/ENTRY.html? subview=Main&entry=t121.e0050.

DOMUS. 2010. Eoan Group Documents in Care of DOMUS. [Online] (Accessed February 11, 2010). Available from http://www.domus.ac.za/content/view/39/.

Encyclopaedia Britannica. 2010. Central-place theory. Encyclopædia Britannica Online. (Accessed January 26, 2010). Available from http://0–www.search.eb.com .oasis.unisa.ac.za/eb/article-9022085.

———. 2010. Democratic alliance. Encyclopædia Britannica Online. (Accessed January 26, 2010). Available from http://0–www.search.eb.com.oasis.unisa.ac.za/eb/article-9474478.

———. 2010. Great Karoo. Encyclopædia Britannica Online. (Accessed January 24, 2010). Available from http://0–www.search.eb.com.oasis.unisa.ac.za/eb/article-9037861.

———. 2010. Karoo. Encyclopædia Britannica Online. (Accessed January 24, 2010). Available from http://0–www.search.eb.com.oasis.unisa.ac.za/eb/article-9044767.

———. 2010. National Party. Encyclopædia Britannica Online. (Accessed January 26, 2010). Available from http://0–www.search.eb.com.oasis.unisa.ac.za/eb/article-9055001.

Iafrica News. 2008. Rhino horns go walking (April 19). [Online] (Accessed January 19, 2010). Available from http://news.iafrica.com/crime/684265.htm.

Jacobs, Sean H. 2002. Review of Nuttall, Sarah; Michael, Cheryl-Ann, eds., *Senses of Culture: South African Culture Studies* (September). [Online] (Accessed October 18, 2009). H-SAfrica, H-Net Reviews. Available from http://www.h-net.org/reviews/showrev.php?\.

Kayster, Anziske. 2009. Annual Report of the Chairman of the Board, Graaff-Reinet Museum. (Accessed October 22, 2009). Available from www.graaffreinetmuseums.co.za.

———. 2008. Annual Report of the Chairman of the Board, Graaff-Reinet Museum. (Accessed October 22, 2009). Available from www.graaffreinetmuseums.co.za.

Nuttall, Sarah. 2002. Jacobs on Nuttall, *Senses of Culture* Review: Reply (November). [Online] (Accessed October 18, 2009). H-SAfrica, H-Net Reviews. Available from http://www.h-net.org/reviews/showrev.php.

Solms Delta. 2010. Music van de Caab. [Online] (Accessed February 22, 2010). Available from http://www.solms-delta.co.za/heritage/music-van-de-caab/.

Statistics South Africa. 2001. Census 2001. [Online] (Accessed February 11, 2010). Available from http://www.statssa.gov.za/census01.

UCCSA. 2010. United Congregational Church of Southern Africa: History. [Online] (Accessed February 12, 2010). Available from http://www.uccsa.org.za/history/.

Weaver, Tony, Jeremy Michaels, and Nazma Dreyer. Van Schalkwyk's reign crashes to an end. n.d. [Online] (Accessed November 14, 2009). Available from http://www.iol.co.za/index.php?sf=2902&art_id=vn20040416015422313C418664&click_id=2902&set_id=1.

Willis, Rose. n.d. The Central Karoo. [Online] (Accessed November 14, 2009). Available from www.centralkaroo.co.za.

Zuma, Jacob. 2010. State of the Nation address by his excellency JG Zuma, president of the Republic of South Africa, at the Joint Sitting of Parliament, Cape Town, February 11, 2010. [Online] (Accessed July 10, 2010). Available from http://www.info.gov.za/speeches/2010/10021119051001.htm.

Index

Illustrations are indicated by italicized page numbers. Page numbers containing "n" indicate footnotes. Page numbers ending in "f" indicate figures.

About the Author

Marie Jorritsma is Senior Lecturer at the University of the Witwatersrand, South Africa.